SOUL
ARCHAEOLOGY

SOUL ARCHAEOLOGY

A (TOTALLY DOABLE) APPROACH
TO CREATING A SELF-LOVING
AND LIBERATED LIFE

—◆—

SARAH SAPORA

balance

NEW YORK BOSTON

Balance
Hachette Book Group
1290 Avenue of the Americas
New York, NY 10104
GCP-Balance.com
Twitter.com/GCPBalance
Instagram.com/GCPBalance

First Edition: August 2023

Balance is an imprint of Grand Central Publishing. The Balance name and logo are trademarks of Hachette Book Group, Inc.

The publisher is not responsible for websites (or their content) that are not owned by the publisher.

The Hachette Speakers Bureau provides a wide range of authors for speaking events. To find out more, go to hachettespeakersbureau.com or email HachetteSpeakers@hbgusa.com.

Balance books may be purchased in bulk for business, educational, or promotional use. For information, please contact your local bookseller or the Hachette Book Group Special Markets Department at special.markets@hbgusa.com.

Library of Congress Cataloging-in-Publication Data has been applied for.

ISBNs: 978-1-5387-2574-0 (trade paperback); 978-1-5387-2575-7 (ebook)

Printed in the United States of America

LSC-C

Printing 1, 2023

For every chubby child convinced they could never be enough.

For those who were underestimated, by others and by themselves.

For everyone who has ever felt invisible.

For my mother, who never gave herself the love she deserved . . .

Let's learn it now, together.

For my dad, and how we've grown. I love you.

CONTENTS

III

SELF-LOVE OUT IN THE WORLD

The Importance of Owning Your Shit, Seeing Your Story, and Loving into It When the Rubber Hits the Road

IV

LET GO TO LET LOVE

Saying Goodbye to Expectations, Other People's Shit, and Your Own Damn Shame

INTRODUCTION

This is not a book about "fat" self-love. This is a book about self-love (there is a difference). This is, to be precise, a book about self-love from the perspective of a woman who has been varying degrees of plus size (fat) her entire adult life.

A "fat self-love book" would center my identity and the context of this book around my weight and ask you to do the same with your weight—I do not do this. At the same time, I would be lying to you if I told you that my weight did not impact my life, my growth, and my unfurling in general... It has. And, if you are one of those people who have had a challenging relationship with their weight, I would be doing you an injustice if I told you there was no connection between your body and your Soul Archaeology journey... There is.

This book talks *very little* about weight loss and fatness. This book has no agenda other than to empower you to think critically about what has held you back in your own life and to figure out what the most aligned version of your Ultimate You is—mind, body, and soul (more on that in chapter 3). Regardless, if you want to lose weight, I support that. If you don't, I support that too. When it comes to body stuff, what I care about is that you are honest with yourself when you think about the role that your weight plays in finding body liberation—because body liberation is an essential part of your liberation in general.

When it comes to the relationship I have with my body, there are a few things I have learned in the more recent years of my life. I have learned, for example, that being physically fit does not mean you are mentally fit. You can look the best you've ever looked on the outside but, at the same time, be betraying your self-worth on the daily. You can fool people into thinking things are great, get the accolades and all the attention your little codependent heart desires by performing the perfect life for anyone and everyone, and all the while you can be taking an ice pick and chipping away at your self-esteem all day long, every day. What I mean is that all of the stuff you can do to the outside layers of your life does not necessarily mean evolution on your core inside. And yet it is only inside the heart of who you are that you can do the work that really needs to be done in order to liberate yourself from the expectations of others and from yourself. I am invested in my health—both mental and physical.

I have lost weight dozens of times, trying to love myself more. I have moved cross-country and back (several times) in an attempt to outrun what hurt me. I have dyed my hair. Bought new clothes. Slept with new men. Gotten new jobs. Not one of these things broke me free from the shame of my perceived mistakes, the shame that I had no idea was coloring my life in such intense and pernicious ways. Not one of these things opened the door for me to look at the stuff that was really hurting me. It took me until I turned forty to see that while I could not ignore the impact my body had on my life (and that I would have to address my health and my mobility), "fixing my weight," as I had been taught to do since I was a child, was not the answer to the nagging, painful questions that crept into my brain in the darkness of night, alone in bed. *Why can't I find anyone to love me? What's wrong with me that everyone else seems happy and I'm just not? Am I so hard to love? I feel like everyone is alive and I'm just watching from the sidelines—is this all my life is going to be?*

You will not liberate your own life and take control of your own happiness by denying that your body has an impact on how you feel and how you exist within the world around you. Just the same, you will not achieve this liberation and control by making your body the only thing you focus on, your catchall, and your reason. The only way to do this is through deep, transformative soul work.

In light of this, we must address some things right at the beginning of this book so we can get them out of the way to focus on the process of Soul Archaeology instead. If I don't address these elephants in the room, they will linger over the entire book, so let's address them up front.

First, this book understands that many people seek a magical happiness they believe they can find only at a specific (lower) weight. It also understands that many of us have spent a lifetime dieting, and some of us may have even hit that number but found nothing had changed. This book understands that dieting fucking sucks, that you've probably tried to lose weight a bunch of times in your life, and that your weight may be impacting your quality of life. Most importantly, this book understands that you deserve to love yourself and feel empowered, EXACTLY AS YOU ARE RIGHT NOW. This book understands that the process of self-acceptance, and just feeling happy in the present, is complicated for everyone and can't be packaged into neat little boxes for fast consumption.

This book exists because I have yet to come across anything written by a fat person that fosters self-improvement and that is not dominated by a body agenda of some kind. Lots of books scream, "Weight loss is awesome!" or "Weight loss is terrible!" and offer either statement as a solution to living a happier life. Honestly, it's more nuanced; this book allows for that.

Second, if you are wondering, *Why is a fat person writing a self-help book? And why should I bother to read it? I mean, what can she be doing right in her life if she weighs that much?*, we need to talk, because people of every size deserve to have hope and take action to improve their quality of life in whatever way works for them. If we don't see people that look like us engaging in the process of personal growth, we subconsciously receive the message that we don't deserve to improve. Everyone deserves the right to feel greater and happier in their life. This is not "glorifying obesity" but creating a bridge to meet (many) people where they are at so they can be empowered to create change in their lives and on their terms.

We frequently get the message that wellness belongs only to youthful, thin, "pretty" people. It doesn't; it belongs to everyone. You don't age out of personal growth. Self-improvement does not have a dress size. At the heart of both these things is the process of removing yourself from pain. *That is what this book is about.* This book is not about chasing perfection or performing what it looks like to find a greater state of wellness in your life. It is about being messy, beautiful, and empowered in ways that are relevant for you.

Third, larger fat people have different life experiences than smaller fat people. This is important because what you think of when you think of the word "fat" may not be what someone else thinks of when they define "fatness." This is because fatness is a range, not a specific size. In light of this, the experiences fat people can have in life may vary dramatically based on their size as, in our current society, size equals accessibility.

We could debate just how accommodating the world should be to larger bodies, but I'm not here to do that. I'm here to help a group of people who feel left out of the conversation of self-improvement get a seat at the table, to help them know that they, too, deserve to find what is greater for them. I have known in my heart for years that living life as a fat person got more difficult the larger I was. However, the majority of research and work we see about the fat experience (whether it's regarding mental health, dieting, weight loss, or health in general) fails to differentiate between people who are only slightly heavy and those who are very heavy.

Though fat people make up a large percentage of the US population, they are nearly invisible in media and underrepresented in most aspects of society. The fatter someone is, the less represented they are, and that can result in feelings of social alienation and isolation. This, in itself, can lead to an increase in depression, a decrease in feelings of agency, and a reduced ability to create pathway thinking.[1]

Let me repeat that. Studies actually show that the larger a person is, the less agency they feel over their own life and the harder it becomes for them to see a path to achieving their goals and believing they can do the things necessary in order to accomplish those goals.[2] To put it bluntly, the larger a person is, the less likely they are to have a sense of hope for their life and the less empowered they feel to create change. This book seeks to undo all of that.

Last, I talk a great deal about my Soul Archaeology in the context of romantic relationships. This may not be the same for you, and that's totally okay—when it works, apply what I share to *your* life. This is because, besides the relationship with my father, my romantic relationships have been the biggest playing field for my Soul Archaeology in my recent years of focusing on my self-esteem and self-worth. My relationships have been huge containers for me to learn about myself.

Romantic relationships may not be your battleground. Maybe you will draw your examples from relationships with your parents or family, your friends, or your work. I encourage you to find what you can relate to in my personal narrative and make it apply in your own life. I feel confident you can, and I will work hard to show you what the "nuggets" of each of my life lessons are so that you can translate them for yourself.

Before we move on, two (more) quick things: You will note that the perspective of this book is decidedly feminine: I use "she" and "her" all the time, as these are my pronouns and how I identify. If you identify differently, please know this work is also for you. You are welcome in this space. As I teach from my personal perspective, my writing is also slanted from the feminine perspective. Second, and importantly, I am not a medical doctor nor a licensed mental health professional. I encourage you to use this book alongside any therapists, counselors, or professionals who are part of your support and care team! I hope there are things in this book that interest you, and that you will feel safe enough to explore what we talk about more deeply as you best see fit.

DIG SITE: THE O-WORD

There are many in the fat advocacy community who believe the word "obesity" is a harmful slur. They refer to it as "ob*sity." The general argument against its use is that it is both medically and ethically wrong to use it, given that the BMI on which the term is defined is such a flawed ideology and the social connotation of the word is so stigmatizing.[3] I do not censor the word in this book. I also regularly use the word "fat" because, to me, the word is just a descriptor, like "short" or "blond." All of this being said, if you find the various terms I use are not your preferred terms, I ask you to give me some grace; what bothers one person may not bother another, and I wrote this book according to my personal feelings.

THE MAIN ATTRACTION

There's stuff in here that may rub you the wrong way. That's okay. Some of it rubs me in uncomfortable ways too! If you don't like what you read

here, don't take it personally. It's not about you. You can love some of
what I say and not like some of it too. You might also find yourself judging me for things I've done or felt. *There are many things I have done while
trying to feel loved in my lifetime, my friend . . .*

At the end of the day, don't we all want to feel loved and totally
accepted for who we are in all our weird, unique glory? To know that we
are good enough just as we are? To be able to show up in our relationships
and our lives without armor, just pure embodiment of self in all its wacky
beauty? I have spent my life hiding away my wacky pieces. For example, interpretive dance is a language of love for me—so is a good random
dance break, regardless of location or situation. I snort when I laugh. I burp
like a velociraptor. I make boob jokes, and dick jokes, all the while sing-
ing opera. These are all things I used to feel made me hard to love, things
I used to hide—now I truly embrace that these are things that make me
who I am. I let them shine.

Life is lived to the fullest when we accept and fully embrace all of our
quirks and preferences. When we can detach ourselves from the idea of
who we believe we have to be in order to receive love—from others, and
to be worthy of our own love for ourselves. It is only when we find this
sense of liberation that these quirks, preferences, and silly things are what
make us who we are; they make our lives great and truthful and authentic.

If we cannot fully know ourselves, we cannot fully accept ourselves.
And if we cannot fully accept ourselves, we cannot fully show ourselves
to others. Without showing ourselves fully to others, we cannot be seen fully
for who we are and accepted fully for who we are. And yet that acceptance
of who we fully are is what so many of us crave. We crave our own deep
self-acceptance, and we crave the acceptance of others. The key with growth
is not to shape ourselves into something we believe others will find lovable;
it is uncovering what is truly real and lovable in ourselves. To unfurl fully so
that we can accept ourselves fully, so we can craft a life around the fullness
of who we are and not the pieces of what others need us to be for their
story. This is liberation, and liberation is what Soul Archaeology is about.

I

THE FOUNDATION FOR
A SELF-LOVING LIFE

The Magical Intersection Where Hope,
Action, and Self-Compassion Collide

Chapter 1

YOUR IMPERFECT, IN-PROCESS SELF

Welcome to the Messy-Beautiful

Dear **beautiful human,** I will now share with you the incredible secret to living a great life. Are you ready for this? This is what you were looking for when you spent your hard-earned money on this book. Here we go.

drumroll

Wait for it. Wait . . . for it . . .

Self-love is everything.

Yes. Everything.

Right now, you may be thinking, *What the fuck, Sarah? I didn't buy this book for that. Where's the secret formula? Where are the Oprah-esque words of wisdom and the coupon code to buy the $399 crystal healing wand handmade by virgins in the rain forest?*

Sorry, buddy, there will be none of that.

This process is about growth. There's no easy solution for getting to self-love. It is about an unfurling. Like the sail of a big, beautiful boat about to fully open and catch the wind, gliding over a glassy blue sea.

The ideas in this book are messy but tangible, like mushy, beautifully colored Play-Doh ready to be sculpted. Some of them don't fit neatly into prescribed little boxes. But what you need to know is that these ideas are for YOU.

You...who are tired. Worried. Feeling like the "best" years of life are in the rearview mirror.

You...who don't fit the mold, or wear the sample size, or even any size you can regularly walk into a store and buy off the shelf.

You...who stopped waging the war with gravity on your body parts.

You, who accepted getting older but, for heaven's sake *loud exhale*, just want to feel alive again.

You, with boob sweat.

You, who have laundry piled up on the chair in your bedroom. And a vibrator in the drawer you may or may not even use.

You, with frazzled hair.

You, who think that everyone else knows something special about life that makes them perfect while you stand on the sidelines going, *What am I missing here?*

You may be an average human *without* a zillion social media followers, a million dollars in the bank, or VIP access, but you are working to balance everything and trying to be happy all at the same time.

You? Yes. This book is for you. Do you know why?

Because your mess is beautiful. And, contrary to what most people believe, I think "happiness" and "messy" are a perfect match.

Everywhere, every day, we are sold a lie. From the time we're little, we are inundated with the message that in order to be great, we must be flawless. We must have our proverbial shit together at all times. Our weight must be at the right number; we must wear the right bra size, have our hair the right color and length, and always be wearing something trendy and figure flattering. We must be fit but not overly muscled. We must never have stomach rolls, unless they are the cute kind that get shown off on Instagram with girl-power word art.

We must never cry, certainly never, ever cry big Claire Danes–style tears, with snot bubbles and red eyes. We must be in a relationship that is well-documented on social media and be a boss babe, even if we stopped referring to ourselves as "babe" thirty years ago. We must be Beyoncé and Kate Middleton at the same time. We must strike the perfect pose;

oh, God, we must do this so well, in the right mirror, taking the right selfie every...single...day...in a different outfit. We must never question ourselves. We must always make the RIGHT choice. We can never be scared. Or get angry. Or emotionally eat a bag of Oreos. Or screw someone just because it feels good and we're lonely.

We can do none of this or *be* any of this if we expect to be loved.

If we hope to be valuable.

If we want to be happy.

Except, none of this is true.

I believe that the greatest version of ourselves might just be the messiest one. The one that questions herself. The one that cries. The one that feels. The one that makes a home in her body because it is HERS and not because it needs to look a specific way. The one who knows she is a creature of value, not because she fits some magic equation, but because she breathes and is alive and that is the only currency life requires of her.

But this woman? This messy, beautiful woman? She does a few things. Hugely important, life-changing things.

First, *she allows herself the hope that she can live the greater life she wants*; she has not given up or walked away from herself. And, if she has in the past, she knows that every day is a chance for her to come back to the one person most important in her life—herself.

Second, *she gets out of her own way and is willing to take action*. She is agile and self-compassionate when handling sticky, uncomfortable chapters, because sticky, uncomfortable chapters are a part of life.

Third, *she holds herself accountable and asks herself the tough questions*. Not because she wants to punish herself, but because she wants to *pour into* herself.

Fourth, *she answers her questions with beautiful, brutal honesty*. Because the only one that suffers when she paints the red flags green is her. She is the one who stunts the blooming.

But mostly? *She knows that she is deserving of her own love and acceptance*, all the while challenging herself to be greater. At the exact same time. Because she is fierce and graceful and knows that the two can very easily walk hand in hand into the sunset. This woman has self-love—but not the kind of self-love they sell you in a store. Rather, she lives a Self-Loving Life. She is committed to this path and to all of the above that helps her to grow into a greater version of herself.

What if the greatest version of you is imperfect? This version, your Ultimate You, is not a finished product, because there is no such thing as being "finished" in life. From the day you are born until the day you let out your last breath, the one thing that life guarantees is change—so why do we fight so hard to grab onto a constantly moving target? Why do we feel we must grasp on tightly to a mark whose rules are continually, persistently, incessantly changing?

I believe it is because we are told that the most valuable thing we can be in life is the version we'd present in the perfect After photo. Because our Before—before we are fixed and healed and primped and pulled—could never be good enough. *At least, that is what we are told to believe . . .*

So, let's shatter this idea, shall we? We can never be, and will never be, a perfect After. Let's change the rules of the game, the game that someone else created for us, and make the rules for ourselves.

New rule: You are in constant evolution, and that is all you must be. Because the only other choice is to stay stagnant, without stretching. Without falling down, brushing off, and getting back up.

Your Ultimate You is not designed to have it all, be it all, and be perfect.

No, my beautiful human. The greatest version of you is about the ride. Your sweet spot is that moment on a roller coaster when you've arrived at the top of the peak and the entire amusement park lies below you and time stops and, for a brief second, you are flying and weightless. Only power and possibility are coursing through your veins (except maybe the fear that you'll fart because you're so scared) but you know you'll be safe, so you just let go and let the wind rush through you and your hair whip around your face, your flushed cheeks, your body shaking from the motion, screaming, with one hand clinging to the rail and the other straight up to the sky.

Stop chasing perfect. Start creating YOU.

This is what this book is about. It is not about the After. It is not about the "magic solution." It is about the messy, beautiful, imperfect journey of living a Self-Loving Life. What this means. How it feels. And how we can shift what we focus on, what we tell ourselves, and what we do every day, in order to develop into the most badass version of ourselves, the one we were created to be.

SELF-LOVE IS THE FOUNDATION FOR EVERYTHING

I'm forty-two and my partner is fifty; neither of us has ever had boundaries in prior relationships (we are walking examples of what it means to learn about oneself later in life). Now that we are living together, we do a check-in every Sunday that we call "the Speaking Snapple," which serves as a dedicated time for us to address what went well and what was a challenge each week. We take turns holding a bottle of Diet Peach Snapple and share a totally open dialogue, telling each other what we need in order to be better teammates for each other. It's the first healthy relationship either of us has ever had.

You know all those things people do in their past when they're just trying to feel loved? The stuff we look back on with some shame and a whole lot of self-judgment? I've done a lot of those things, and some of them were pretty icky, but none of them weigh me down anymore. There isn't a single thing from my past that I feel shame for today; I've given myself the forgiveness I deserve, and my perception of myself is now totally shaped by my present.

When I was thirty-seven, I sat in the bath, naked and wet, and cried out loud because, for the first time ever, I saw that the crappy boyfriend I'd had when I was eighteen wasn't just a crappy guy but someone who had been emotionally and physically harmful to me. This led to my being angry, actually truly angry, for the first time ever because my whole life I'd never been allowed to feel anger or express anger, in any way, shape, or form, for fear of being abandoned, disliked, or rejected, and that scared me more than anything.

The year I turned forty, I learned what self-worth was for the first time. I learned that I'd spent my entire life more concerned with what every other person or entity I'd come into contact with thought of me than what I thought of myself. I learned I didn't even know what I thought of myself but that I was ready to find out. I learned I liked to bake challah bread and crochet. I told my father he scarred my self-worth when I was child, and my mother that the vegetable soup diet, the Optifast, the Weight Watchers I was put on when I was nine years old, and her general fixation on weight made me spend a lifetime trying to fix myself when I never, ever needed to be fixed in the first place.

I did all of these things, and more, because of self-love. Self-love has been the driving force of almost every single choice I have made since 2016 as I have skipped, and gloriously stumbled, along a journey of personal growth to learn how to become a truly happier person from the inside out.

The practice of self-love has allowed me to do some awesome things. It has allowed me to work through gritty, nasty feelings and emerge stronger and kinder than I ever imagined I could be and less concerned with what others think of me. I am more concerned with investing MY energy into me. I know that there is truly nothing that can have a greater impact on my life than self-love, so I'm just going to come out and say it: People have self-love all wrong (I know I did).

Bath bombs. Smelly candles. An extra splurge on payday. A sexy selfie on social media. This is how many people interpret self-love. In my twenties, I thought that self-love meant buying things that helped me fit in—like pistachio-green Christian Louboutins for hundreds of dollars on the $28,000 salary of an entry-level PR gal. I thought it meant being accepted by the right people and being able to text and juggle a bunch of guys all at once who all wanted to sleep with me. What I didn't realize at the time was that self-love had nothing to do with other people, and everything to do with me.

Today, I believe that self-love means something entirely different. Self-love isn't having a sincere fondness for ourselves (though it can include those thoughts) or self-adoration to the extreme. It also isn't saying, "I LOVE myself!" and then believing everything is perfect and rad.

I define "self-love" as an action. A process. It's a verb, bringing you closer to your Ultimate You.

DIG SITE: SARAH'S DEFINITION OF "SELF-LOVE"

Self-love is any thought you think or any physical thing you do that helps you connect to that greater version of you that you know exists, your Ultimate You.

The Ultimate You is the most authentic and empowered version of ourselves that we have inside us. It's a version of us that feels fear but isn't held back by it. Fear (of what we are not, of who we are, etc.) is not something we are born with, but as we go through life negative experiences can color us, and the words and actions of hurtful people and situations can leave imprints on our self-perception. Seventeenth-century English philosopher John Locke theorized that we are born into the world with tabula rasa—untainted by backstory and, therefore, without limiting beliefs about who we are programmed into our brains. With each instance of hurt, therefore, we are pulled further and further away from our natural, loving state. Outside forces shape us and mold us, until who we are is no longer representative of our truest self, but a reflection of those around us and the things that have happened to us. Which means in order to become our Ultimate You, we oftentimes have to "un-become" other things. We have to un-become the version of ourselves that is based on what other people have told us about who we are and what we are worth, so that we can create a version of ourselves based on the things we know are true.

I'm not a spiritual teacher. I'm a nonpracticing Jew who flunked out of Hebrew school and had allergic reactions to the concept of faith until her late thirties. I prefer to think about it *this* way: We are all born with qualities embedded in our DNA—and life experiences can either nurture the great we are born with so we can embody it and express it, or lead us to keep it locked away. We can't remove the things that have happened to us, but we can shift our perspective on them and our relationship to them, so that they weigh less and color us less, so what is left to shine through in life is more of who we naturally, authentically are.

Self-love is what will help us do this. Through actions and thoughts that connect us to this dialed-in version of ourselves, we can consciously create our narrative and define our own sense of self and then DO things that bring us life in full, vivid color.

Diets, new haircuts, shakes and cleanses, makeovers, new jobs, and new geographic locations won't do this for us, though we've probably all done one or two of those things in the hope that they would. (Lord knows I have. I've moved back and forth across the country three times, dieted, and had every hair color under the sun in the hopes that that would be the thing to make me happy . . . It didn't.)

If you picked up this book, you are seeking answers of some kind. You're probably wondering what you need to be doing, right now, in order to find your own solutions. You want it all and you want it right away.

I see you. We'll get there. This whole book will help you guide yourself into seeing what things in life *are not working* for you, so that you can create the things in life that do work for you.

For now, let's keep working toward getting on the same page about the power of self-love and what it actually means in simple, mystical-free language. This will be the basis of everything that we talk about.

Some Important Shit About Self-Love

We've defined "self-love." But now there are things we need to clarify— because it will help to have a full picture before we dive into the deep end.

1. *It's natural for us to compare ourselves to other people—unhealthy, but natural. Because of this, you need to know that self-love is going to mean different things to different people.* Humans are different. We have different hopes and dreams, and different shitty backstories. Because of this, what serves your Ultimate You may not serve your best friends', right? For example...

- If gluten turns your stomach into an act from Cirque du Soleil, avoiding eating bagels (aka the food of the gods) is an act of self-love. Where, for someone else, toasting a perfect bagel, smearing it with cream cheese, and enjoying it while slowly drinking a cold brew may be a self-loving expression of intentional and mindful eating that liberates them from food fear.

- If someone, in their deepest soul, knows they are meant to have kids, staying in a relationship with someone who doesn't want them just because the sex is great may not be so self-loving.

- If your partner is interested in exploring nonmonogamy and the idea makes your skin crawl and cringe, doing it to please them isn't self-love, even if you think exploring it will somehow make things better. Whereas for another person, exploring nonmonogamy may be a true expression of their sexual desires.

One example of how my personal self-love journey serves a different Ultimate You than someone else's would begins with my awareness and decision to pursue weight loss in my late thirties. In retrospect, I can see that much of my process was a little dysfunctional: I was hyperfocused on my physical limitations, such as the inability to cross a street without stopping in pain, or to step off a sidewalk without fear of my knees buckling out from under me—not on figuring out what life would actually look like aligned with my core values. But what I was doing was in service of my Ultimate You as I understood it, because, at the time, I desired nothing more than to live in a body that wasn't screaming and miserable from carrying the excess weight it did. While many saw me as an ambassador for body positivity, I knew that my life was getting smaller and shrinking by the day to match the ever-increasing limits of my body. At that time, my desire to experience weight loss was in service of my Ultimate You and an act of self-love—I wanted to DO more and stop living with a body that was keeping me from experiencing things in life. My Ultimate You dreamed of action, adventure, hiking, dancing—all things that were getting harder and harder that I knew weight loss would positively impact. For someone else—for example, someone with a history of restrictive eating disorder—weight loss could be the exact opposite of self-love. Their act of self-love would be avoiding any food restrictions. For them, the Ultimate You would have the ability to eat freely.

We are all different. We have the opportunity to be empathetic and aware of this when we catch ourselves judging others for what their priorities are.

2. *Because sometimes there are illusions that need to be shattered, understand that self-love isn't always easy.* Sometimes the most self-loving things we can do are the hardest things. (If I could put this on a bumper sticker, I would.) They are no fun; they scare the shit out of us and may even have no immediate payout. But, in the long run, they are going to be thoughts or actions that are deeply valuable to our growth. They are going to be the things that truly help us to be greater. For example...

- Quitting a six-figure job working for someone who belittles you and negatively impacts your mental and emotional well-being—the money is great, as are the privileges it brings, but you leave the office every day feeling insignificant and broken down.
- Leaving a relationship with a partner who gives you the most intense orgasms known to humankind but won't be seen with you in public, because you really, really want to date them traditionally.
- Getting a mammogram when you know your family has a documented genetic predisposition to breast cancer, even though you've been avoiding it because the idea of what could happen terrifies you.

- Cutting out your daily Starbucks run because it adds up to $223 a month that you don't have, and you're already behind on your cable, power, and credit card bills. (*Cough* *Me. Truth.*)

The hardest, most self-loving thing I ever did in my life was to emotionally untangle myself from a partner who made me cuckoo for Cocoa Puffs—a man who challenged me intellectually, sexually, and every way in between (let's call him George, because he's going to come up a few times in this book). My feelings for him also left me crawling on the floor of my closet and falling asleep next to a bottle of tequila one night. Rationalizing, every single day. Telling myself I didn't want things from him that in my heart I was desperately screaming for. The process of walking away from our relationship moved me to pray to God for the first time as I begged for help, but was also the greatest thing I ever did for myself. It helped me learn how to be true to myself. Helped me work through my greatest core wounds (more on that later) and empowered me in ways I couldn't imagine. But it hurt like hell. It sucked. Because, sometimes, self-love is absolutely brutal and brings you to your knees.

3. *Because a lot of us hate the idea of change, we need to accept that self-love will change as we change.* How you interpret self-love will evolve as you evolve. What serves you at twenty-one will probably be different from what serves you at forty-one, which will be different from what serves you again at sixty-one. The key to self-love is not to think about it as a one-time "wham and bam done" but to do it again and again, and regularly reevaluate what you need at any given moment in your current chapter. In short, be aware that self-love grows right alongside you.

I get that you like to wrap your hands around things. Once you have an "Aha!" you want it done, neatly and cleanly, yes? This is not self-love. Self-love is more like living a game of catch and release. Once you learn what self-love means for you in the current moment, you live with it and allow it to run its course and then you release to make room for what's next to flow in its place.

At the start of my journey, some of the most loving things I did for myself were physically forceful and aggressive—like pushing my body at the gym multiple times a week. The container of a sweaty workout was like therapy for me—I found clarity in the gym. I found a connection to myself I had never experienced before. And the changes in my body literally gave my quality of life back to me. Two years later, I'd find myself in exactly the opposite of places—I had to strip things away to find my thoughts. My body screamed for peace and rest while my mind went deep into places I'd never explored. Movement didn't feel safe—stillness did. It took great compassion to allow for this change. Less time at the gym meant my body would change, and it did. It got softer. Heavier. But in the back of my mind, I knew I was serving myself with what I needed in that exact moment.

If you trust in the process of self-love, if you hone your ability to listen and take action, you can learn to trust that you will always be on the "right" track—your own unique and beautiful path.

4. *Because a lot of us are addicted to productivity, we get to learn that self-love doesn't necessarily mean ACTION.* I think we can all agree that society is addicted to the Hustle. This is the idea that we are worthy only when we are kicking ass and taking names and (most probably) burning the candle at both ends, sleep deprived, and walking around like zombie food. It's bullshit. Yes, it is great to respect discipline and value productivity, but doing so to the detriment of your mental health gets old real fast, or whenever it is you realize enough is *enough*. Sometimes, the action that serves us the most is *inaction*— the stripping away, the removing, and the stillness.

I learned this in 2019 during a particularly difficult season in life when I found myself utterly and entirely burned out. For nine months straight I hustled my ass off to write a draft of a memoir and plan my largest live event, all while working through my biggest and most painful breakup; I was fried and had nothing left to give. The idea of posting on social media made me want to shut off. For me, the most self-loving thing I could do in that exact moment... was to peel it all away and strip it down. Remove pressure. Pull back from social media, from my purpose-driven work, and just... breathe for a few months. Inaction. Comfort in the discomfort of empty space. To the outside, this looked like failure. On the inside, I knew this was love for myself from myself.

If you are starting to think that self-love actually sounds like it sucks, I don't blame you. We are conditioned to want things to be easy; we're trained to avoid pain. But nobody said that growth was easy. And, if you want to experience something different in your life from what you've felt up to now, you have to be willing to do something different.

What's more important to you... Making a familiar and strangely comforting home in the dysfunction you are living in now? Or avoiding the possibility that your life will look exactly the same in five years or ten years (or even twenty years) as it does right now? Which of those ideas scares you more? Is that fear of what could happen (or not happen) in the future enough to fuel you in the present? You probably have pain, and you probably hate that pain. But, in many ways, that pain is comforting to you right now—it's reliable and you know it. So, it feeds your patterns and puts you in boxes and runs the risk of making you a foregone conclusion to your own life.

Do you want to know what's going to happen the rest of your life before you even get a chance to live it?

If not, it's up to you to make sure that doesn't happen. Because nobody is coming to change your life but you.

SO, WHAT HAPPENS NOW?

If you haven't figured it out yet, this is not your everyday self-help book. I'm not a therapist of any kind—I'm just a woman who was ready to roll up her sleeves and do the work. Because of this, things are going to get personal around here. My hope is that this gives you some room to breathe. By witnessing my totally imperfect, messy-beautiful journey to unfurling my Ultimate You, I want you to exhale and open yourself to the idea that you, too, can do the same.

This book also doesn't have any dramatic end, because YOU don't have an end.

There is evolution, but no neat little bow smacked onto the final chapter.

There is no happily-ever-after promised to me, and so I am not promising you one either. What there is, what there can be, is a shift into your bright, sparkling, effervescent self. *Whatever she looks like.*

There can be an expansion into your ability to create a meaningful life in a way that rocks your socks off.

Because this is available to us all, in some way or another. We never age out of hope. We never size out of recognizing the "more" for us that is just beyond our fingertips.

It is never too late for us to take action.

Sure, the older we get, the harder it can be because we juggle more shit at forty, fifty, sixty, and seventy than we did at twenty-five. But it's possible.

Every breath is a chance to think something new. *To inhale possibility and to exhale doubt.* Every moment is the perfect time to allow yourself a shift.

So let's shift. Let's explore. Let's create self-love...together.

SURVEYING THE SITE: WHAT WE DUG UP IN THIS CHAPTER

Each chapter will conclude with a quick summary of what we just discussed. In these reviews, I'll help you to understand how the information you've learned can assist in your path of Soul Archaeology, and how it can help you to live a self-loving and liberated life.

In this first chapter, we covered some essential basics of self-love. We started with my personal definition of what self-love is—I describe self-love as being any thought you think or action you do that helps you connect to your Ultimate You. We also talked about how each person's Ultimate You is not actually perfect, but messy and beautiful at the same time. We then covered a few important things to understand about self-love. First, that self-love and "the Hustle" are not always the same thing, and that sometimes the most self-loving action is *inaction*. Next, that self-love evolves as we evolve, both emotionally and physically. We also acknowledged that self-love means different things to different people. And the big one? That self-love is not always easy.

We talked about what it means to live a Self-Loving Life. That a person living a Self-Loving Life allows herself to have hope that she can live a greater life. This person also is willing to take action to get out of her own way. They hold themselves accountable and ask themselves the tough questions, answering them as honestly as they can at any given time. Last, this person understands that they are deserving of love and acceptance exactly as they are. To do all this and to prioritize these attributes is what paves the way for a truly Self-Loving Life.

Remember... Stop chasing "perfect" and start creating you! Let's keep going.

Chapter 2

UNCOVERING YOUR ULTIMATE YOU

The Path of Soul Archaeology

You are about to begin an excavation of the soul, and I am your guide. When we excavate ourselves, we are digging things up and uncovering them, like they do at archaeological sites you see in the movies. (Hello, *Jurassic Park* and *Indiana Jones*!) Except, instead of old bones or relics, we will uncover valuable pieces of you. As I guide you along the path, it might help if you think of me like Lara Croft in *Tomb Raider*. I speak in an English accent and am wearing short shorts (with no chub rub to speak of), my perky breasts are untouched by gravity, and I'm wearing a fedora...like Angelina Jolie in the movie, except I'm fat. Imagine me perched atop an old ruin, perhaps in Bali. I am glistening and perfectly moist, but not sweaty, and definitely no under-boob sweat. And then I speak...

When you make a conscious effort to change things in your life, you may want everything to happen RIGHT NOW and RIGHT AWAY. Unfortunately, every piece of your personal growth journey happens in the order it "needs" to happen. The process and its elements reveal themselves in a way that makes sense. We cannot start at zero and expect to dive to the bottom of an Olympic-depth pool. Instead, we must start in the shallow end and explore our way into the deep, guided by self-love and by asking ourselves key questions like *What is hurting me right now?* and *What do I observe and what can I love into?* As we answer these questions, we'll go deeper and uncover one layer of ourselves at a time—hopefully without wanting to emotionally eat an entire bag of dark chocolate chips with a spoon. I refer to this order, this divine timing of our own exploration, as Soul Archaeology.

Archaeology involves digging things up. Excavating, right? (*Remember, I'm Angelina Jolie right now, okay?*) So, let's just say you collect priceless ancient ruins and, one day, someone gives you a tip that there's a valuable fertility statue buried somewhere in the Peruvian rain forest. In order to obtain said statue, you have to trek to Peru and fight your way through the jungle with nothing more than a machete and a roll of duct tape. Once you get to the site of this insanely valuable relic, you know you have to get it out of the ground before you can either donate it to a museum or sell it to antiquities traders for millions of dollars on the black market.

You start at the top layer of dirt. You brush it off. You see what you see. Then you do it again. And again. And, suddenly, you see what looks like a nipple poking out of the dirt. A nipple? Yes! This is a fertility statue we're in search of, so nipples are par for the course! What do you do next? You brush off more dirt around the nipple to reveal the whole boob. And then you look at the boob, and you get a feel for the boob, and you observe the boob. Is it large? Small? Round? Based on what you observe, you then dig around the boob again till you see a torso. And again, and again. Each time you reveal another body part by removing a layer of dirt, you reassess where to dig next. Eventually, you reveal the whole statue. A glorious ancient fertility statue. And then you schlep it out of the forest and decide to be a good person and donate it to a museum for the sake of history because, frankly, you don't need the millions you'd get from selling it on the black market and humanity will be much better off with the naked fertility statue safely ensconced in a museum than in the hands of smugglers who might hollow out the inside and load missiles inside it. (What? I saw *True Lies* one too many times.)

That's what personal growth is like. When you get the idea that there's something in you that you want to dig up (maybe it's an ancient relic... maybe it's "Daddy Issues"), you first have to get to the site, or to the place in your life where you are ready to focus. Then you stand in this spot and look at what you can see right from the beginning, right on the surface. You start with what you see. You stand on the surface of that dirt and go, "Fuck, look at all this dirt; let's check it out," and you observe and see as much of the dirt as you can. You look at the soil. You look at the clumps that are in it. You get used to it and you study it. In our Soul Archaeology, it's not actual dirt that we are clearing, but our own feelings and thoughts and memories and experiences and learned behaviors. You know, our "shit." We start our journey by simply allowing ourselves to see what we are standing on. We ask ourselves, *What is my life like? What am I feeling? What do I observe?* This stuff on the top is the surface-level dirt. You spot the pieces of gravel and the choices you've made that you can see right away. You see them, you get comfortable with them, and you accept that these things exist and that they are real, because you can't brush aside what you cannot acknowledge. Then you go one layer at a time, until your patterns and habits and choices all start to come together to form the stories and the experiences that shape you into who you are.

Several years ago, there was no way you could have told me one day I'd be sitting on a couch with the boyfriend I was living with, holding a Diet Peach Snapple, expressing my need for personal space and my desire for more sexual intimacy clearly and without any reservation. And that this would be a good thing. And, even more, that I would be having the conversation with a partner who actually listened to my requests and would actually act on them to the best of his abilities. Frankly, until I started to dig into my Soul Archaeology, I thought I'd done pretty good at speaking up for myself in life . . . Boy, was I wrong!

If I'd been able to see the vertical cross section of this part of my Soul Archaeology—this slice of terrain from the surface top level to the deepest bottom level—I'd have been able to see I had a long history of being with men who blatantly ignored my needs. Almost to the point that I'd stop requesting things in general—you get disregarded enough that one day you just learn that your voice doesn't matter, so you stop using it entirely. But when I was standing on the surface, looking at the first level—this recognition that I was really unhappy in my personal life—I couldn't see all the deep stuff I know now. I had to learn things about myself in order, with each discovery and each bit of truth paving the way for the next one. For me, the process of learning and uncovering looked like this:

SOUL ARCHAEOLOGY OF THE SPEAKING SNAPPLE

**Sarah acknowledges that she always feels invisible
in romantic relationships.**

Sarah sees that she uses casual relationships as a form of coping
so she can feel less alone.

Sarah sees that men don't want something serious from her, but
she doesn't TELL them she wants something serious. She leads
with the casual; it makes her feel in control.

Sarah sees that seeking control has been a huge thing for
her in relationships with dudes.

Sarah sees that she was emotionally abused in a relationship when she
was young where her answers of "No" were ignored.

Sarah sees how a deep desire to have a "home" with her male partners
has caused her to chronically self-abandon to keep them happy.

Sarah learns that she has never allowed herself to express anger
in general—not toward her father or toward anyone else, especially
romantic male partners she longed to feel safe and seen with.

Sarah comes to understand that it's important for her to start recognizing
feelings when she has them in order to heal her core wounds.

Sarah accepts that she must express her feelings and
that she deserves boundaries.

Sarah understands that self-love means to express her feelings and
boundaries; to live a Self-Loving Life, she must be in relationships that
allow her to do this safely so she feels seen and heard.

**Sarah practices boundaries and expresses her feelings safely
within the context of a healthful relationship.**

I had to do this all one step at a time. It took years. Each step prepared me for the next. Each step armed me with the skills and subconscious know-how to handle one thing more than I did before.

And somewhere down the road, I began to understand what the whole self-love puzzle looked like for me. You can do the same.

SHATTERING THE MYTH OF BEFORE AND AFTER

I need to remind you that you were never broken. Because as you start to dig, armed with a stockpile of self-love, you will start to *feel* more. The more you feel, the more broken you might think you are.

You might even think that in order for you to be a greater you at some point in the future, you must first be terrible in the present.

That is a lie.

Your shame is not required.

The belief that your previous choices have made you broken is not the food your growth should be feeding on.

You do not have to hate yourself first in order to love yourself next.

It's true that once you commit to the process, what you start to dig up as you begin may make you feel like you are shattered beyond repair, because finally looking at the things that have hurt you, things that have gone unseen for so long, can be so overwhelming and raw. This makes it even easier to fall for the lie that the only way to exist in life is on either side of the dichotomy: Broken or fixed. Not worthy or worthy. Slouching and miserable "Before" or a glowing and deserving "After."

We should never be ashamed of where we have been in our lives. But we must also never wait to be perfectly "healed." What we really are, what we should find comfort in becoming, is a stack of squiggles. Each layer is the ending of one thing blended into the start of something new, seamlessly transitioning and overlapping, messy and beautiful both at the exact same time. But the more we see our own mess, the more we may want to hate ourselves...and we may want to use that hate as fuel.

Self-love is the antithesis of contempt; the two cannot exist in the same vacuum together. In order to fully accept ourselves, we have to fight the urge to vilify our past and how it brought us to where we are now. We get to decide: Do we want to make this version of us the "bad guy"? Or do we want to decide, in spite of all the hard stuff, that our past self is just as worthy as our future self? Both versions are in us and are part of what makes us "us." And we have never been broken.

In Japan, there's a tradition of taking fractured pottery and mending the pieces together with lacquer dusted or combined with gold. In doing this, the item becomes more valuable, having been beautifully mended into something new built upon fissures and cracks. This type of repair highlights the history of these objects, rather than disguising the damage. They call this art form kintsukuroi, or "golden repair."

No matter how we feel tempted to paint our past so that we can be the self-righteous hero of our own story in the future, remember that we have never been, and will never be, a Before and an After. We are a gold kintsukuroi bowl. In that is great beauty.

DIG SITE: LIVING A SELF-LOVING LIFE

To live a Self-Loving Life means that you consciously choose to prioritize the self-love that connects you to your Ultimate You. It means you value a commitment to your own growth, and you let this commitment to growth be your guide. It is about asking oneself, *What do I need now to help me grow and unfurl into who I am meant to be?* In order to live a Self-Loving Life, you must do the following:

- Allow yourself to have hope that you can live a greater life than the one you are currently experiencing.
- Be willing to take action to create change.
- Hold yourself accountable by asking yourself the tough questions.
- Answer your questions with as much honesty as you're capable of.
- Know, regardless of all this, that you deserve love and acceptance exactly as you are.

THE STRATEGY (AND REWARD) OF
LIVING A SELF-LOVING LIFE

If we know that living a "Before and After" life sets us up to flail aimlessly in a quest of unattainable perfection, what is the alternative? There needs to be one, right? A way to approach life that is more kind, yet more rooted in our ability to expand ourselves than it is obsessed with erasing all our so-called flaws? Enter the Self-Loving Life.

When you live a Self-Loving Life, you make a conscious decision to let self-love direct your actions and thoughts, and this becomes your guiding light. You live in service of prioritizing your Ultimate You and doing what it takes to bring that person to life. You value vulnerability, self-compassion, accountability, and self-awareness—the qualities we must embody in order to unfurl with Soul Archaeology as our guide.

To live a Self-Loving Life means that we embrace that we are ever changing—there is no "fixed" version of us. Our greatest job is to simply evaluate where we are right now and determine our needs the best that we can. *Living a Self-Loving Life is a complete lifestyle choice.* It's a shift from asking, *What do I want in the moment?* to asking, *What do I need to grow and evolve into who I know I'm meant to be?* Because sometimes, many times, the answers to those questions can be entirely different.

For most of my adult life, I did not live a Self-Loving Life—I subconsciously sought escape time and time again, I avoided things that were hard, and I was mostly unwilling to be truthful with myself (and incapable of doing so). I was committed to making my life as awesome as possible in the present moment. I wasn't committed to myself or to my growth. Hell, I didn't even know that I *could* grow.

I hit a breaking point in 2016 when I realized I had to save my whole life, physically and emotionally. I experienced an overwhelming sadness from watching everyone else grow and get married, start families, and go on vacations, while I felt stuck in the mud, spinning my wheels and going nowhere. The pain was palpable; I felt like I was on the outside of my own life, looking in. And my body wasn't helping me to feel any better. Just a week before I'd been at choir practice walking—literally, just walking—and I'd fallen down in front of everyone, my knees giving out from under me. I'd screamed, "Hunger Games, Hunger Games! Keep walking!" to make a joke that would hide how humiliated I was and, even more than that, how fucking defeated I felt that my thirty-six-year-old body felt like it was starting to break down and betray me. Did I mention that I also had two parents with a history of heart disease, and that I'd spent the summer in New York City with my mom in one hospital room and my father in a different hospital at the exact same time? So, on top of everything else, the idea of my mortality was looming over my head and threatening to rain like that annoying pish-rain that spits out enough condensation to make the sidewalk slippery and dangerous, but not enough to make you stay indoors. In this moment, at this time, the idea of self-love suddenly had meaning to me. At that time, I decided that self-love meant doing everything I could to stop my heart from emotionally hurting, get my body into better physical shape so I no longer felt trapped in it, and do whatever I could to prevent a medical future that looked a lot like my parents'.

I had no answers then. I couldn't even envision what a life would look like where guys wanted to spend the night and actually talk to me, or one where I had enough strength and stamina to hike a (small) mountain or walk from the parking lot and through the grocery store without having to lean on the cart, or what it would mean for me to be emotionally "healthy," but I needed to figure it out. I was tired of saying no to things because I couldn't do them. I was unwilling to keep going on the path I was on, and so I called on self-love to be my guide. I had nothing to direct me other than a willingness to do something different because of the crippling fear of staying where I was.

Self-love became following the path of my own pain to see where it would lead. I knew if I had the courage to ask myself, *What's hurting me right now?* and if I actually stopped to listen to what I felt in my body and my mind, I could use the answer to be my guide. I knew, if I did something differently, I would experience something different in my life. And different was exactly what I needed.

Since then, I have referred to this process of *asking* + *answering* + *action* as "living a Self-Loving Life." This guiding philosophy requires regular self-evaluation to see what area of one's life needs pouring into—what in life needs attention and care, observation, and action. And when I come up with that answer, I adjust accordingly so that I may serve my needs exactly as they exist right at that moment. I see myself without judgment; I observe and uncover stones. It is as if I say, "Oh, this might be a thing— let's explore this a little bit, shall we?"

My commitment to living a Self-Loving Life has taken me through places I did not even know were crying out to be explored. Some of my journey has made sense to other people, and some of it has not—but that doesn't matter, because ALL of it has made sense to me. And, at the end of the day, isn't that one of the greatest gifts in life? Finding out what is meaningful to you without worrying what others think?

Living a Self-Loving Life guided me from barely being able to walk a single city block without stopping in pain, to climbing six flights of stairs while holding fifty pounds of weight in under a minute and being able to leg press over seven hundred pounds, which made me feel very strong and very sexy. (At the same time, my commitment to living a Self-Loving Life also allowed me to see that, during this same time, I was the most codependent I'd ever been, fixated with how I was seen on social media, insistent I'd be taken seriously by "the industry," and completely, utterly blind with passion for my romantic partner, who consumed most of the thoughts I was having when I wasn't obsessed with proving my value to people who didn't know me.) It helped me make peace with pulling away from fitness and "dieting" and the resulting weight gain, and then helped guide me again, years later, into a place of healing when it came to my relationship with food, and action when it came to prioritizing my health and fitness again—just in a different way.

Living a Self-Loving Life opened my eyes to finally seeing the level of cognitive distortion I experienced on a daily basis (that's a fancy way of saying I had a deeply ingrained habit of speaking and thinking negatively about myself that stemmed from my own prior lived experiences). It opened the door for me to finally tell my father how much it hurt me that I'd never had a bedroom in any of his houses after my parents divorced. It uncovered my deepest core wounds and then showed me that my sexy, magnetic partner—whom I was crazy about, literally crazy about—with his deep, growling laugh and the voice that went straight to my lady parts, was a walking representation of every one of the unhealed pieces of me rolled into a single package wearing snug jeans and cowboy boots. That I'd have to walk away from him and learn how to stand on my own.

Living a Self-Loving Life revealed to me my shocking lack of self-worth. It showed me how little I knew about myself when, in fact, I was left alone with nothing but ME to love into. At forty, quite literally, I was a woman who had never really truly accepted herself AS SHE WAS.

Living a Self-Loving Life taught me how to listen to myself. It taught me how to want things for myself and not because those things made other people like me more and having them like me made me happy. It opened the door for me to make peace with myself. And, at the same time, to become my most passionate cheerleader for change and growth. Showing me how to build myself from the ground up, one self-loving action at a time.

Here are some things I want you to understand about living a Self-Loving Life:

- At any given time, you are either living a Self-Loving Life or you aren't. Many things are nuanced—this is not.
- You can vacillate back and forth between the two based on your priorities; there may be a time when don't feel connected to the work of self-love, and other times when you are deeply passionate about it.
- Living a Self-Loving Life means a willingness to regularly reevaluate yourself. We are not "one and done" creatures, so self-love is not stagnant; self-love ebbs and flows right along with us.
- Because of this, what it means to actually live your Self-Loving Life will change alongside you.

THE UNEXPECTED GREATNESS OF
YOUR ULTIMATE YOU

What exactly is the greatest version of us? Is it the unattainable? The flawless? The envied? No. Not in the least. Spiritual teachers call it your highest self. Gary Zukav refers to it as Authentic Power. I prefer to call it something even more simple—your Ultimate You.

We all have an Ultimate You. Whether or not we embrace them is up to us, but they are there.

But contrary to the idea that most media, influencers, and boss babe business coaches want to sell us, your Ultimate You is not dependent on being the skinniest, most in shape, prettiest, youngest, richest, or most successful you there is. It is not about your weight, your income, your breasts, your "slay all day" attitude, or your followers on social media. I believe that your Ultimate You is the version of you that does two things—she SEES and she takes ACTION. This version of you:

1. **Is as real and honest with herself as she can be at any given time about who she is and what she feels.** She can observe herself like an alert outsider looking in, with clarity and objectivity.

2. **Is driven to take self-loving action that serves the observations.** You don't just think; you *act* in order to make yourself live greater, as defined by your own values and desire. It doesn't mean you don't feel fear—quite the opposite. You feel fear; you just choose to focus on the action to move forward rather than the things that can hold you back.

Notice I didn't say that your Ultimate You fits into the same jeans you wore in high school or has a Pinterest-worthy house, with two and a half kids, a dog, and a swoon-worthy partner. Your Ultimate You doesn't care that you make six figures a month, or whether or not you show off your body for social media.

Your Ultimate You has not only compassion and space for you, exactly as you are right now, but also an awareness and appetite to stretch and grow into even MORE. Your Ultimate You can be accomplishing a half-marathon for the first time, getting a huge promotion, or lying on the couch in sweatpants and a sloppy bun looking like a hot mess and working through a tremendously painful breakup. It can be you in any state of activity as long as that state is mindful, intentional, and in service of you. So, let's clarify a few important things:

- Your Ultimate You is attainable at ANY and EVERY phase in your life, in a way that is relative to you.
- Your Ultimate You is not a specific age or weight.
- Your Ultimate You will not be the same as someone else's Ultimate You.
- Your Ultimate You does not exist in a bubble. Therefore, it is NOT about "positive thinking" your way out of crappy and oppressive systems, denying that your chronic pain impacts your life, or pretending things are great when they hurt like hell.
- Your Ultimate You is your skill and willingness to see yourself with clarity and compassion and your personal commitment to take self-loving action.

And to get even more clear, let's look at this helpful chart:

Your Ultimate You is not...	Because it is...
Perfect.	Human, and is therefore innately flawed and not bothered, or at war, with the idea of being naturally imperfect.
Determined by what someone else says or thinks about you.	Shaped by how YOU decide you want to be seen.
Guided by other people's value systems.	Guided by your values, mindfully shaped to reflect what you believe.
Existing for the approval of other people.	Existing for your own confidence and esteem.
A dress size, a bra size, a hair color, a skin color, or the size of your ass or your bank account.	About the depth and strength of the relationship you have with yourself and the world around you.

Your Ultimate You is not...	Because it is...
Privilege.	Rising to meet oneself, not society's standards.
The "Dream Job."	About personal fulfillment.
Someone "showing off" but crumbling on the inside.	About making mistakes and showing up messy, but showing up REAL and happy.
Hiding true physical desires while remaining unhappy in a relationship.	Expressing true desire for sexual connection and a willingness to explore and grow as feels true.
Wanting to be fifty pounds thinner than you are right now because it's the magic fix.	Looking at why you are really unhappy and addressing that instead.

DIG SITE: YOUR ULTIMATE YOU

Your Ultimate You is the greatest version of you. It is the most powerful and the truest version of you that exists. Your Ultimate You is not perfect—it is the state of self in which you are fully connected and listening to yourself. This is a version of you that *feels* fear but is not ruled by it. A you that is imperfect but authentic. Your Ultimate You sees herself with clarity and compassion and is committed to taking action to grow in the ways that serve her.

THE IMAGE VS. THE REALITY

Red dress. Tan. Long blond hair. I have this picture of me where I look sexy and strong—these are words I rarely use to describe the way I look, but, almighty, I look all of those things here. I am glowing. I am buzzing and alive. My thighs are thick and well-muscled, my waist definition strong. Off to the side of the camera, out of view, is a six-foot-tall man wearing a well-fitting three-piece suit with a red tie he picked out to match my red dress. He has the power to make me orgasm just from touching. He is waiting for me; he kisses me in front of other people. Earlier in that day I went scuba diving—there was salt in my hair and on my skin; I smelled like Coppertone. I feel lucky. I feel beautiful. From the outside looking in, I am my Ultimate You.

The reality of this exact moment was very different. Oh no, this was absolutely not my Ultimate You. Earlier that day I'd walked away from this same man, feeling defeated to my core, because he still insisted on calling us "friends" even though we both very well knew we were far from that. It was the same heated conversation we'd had a dozen times because I hated the expression—it made me feel disposable and insignificant—but he wouldn't budge. We were friends. Just friends. Only friends... *Yeah, right. Fuck.* But when I had my arm linked through the crook of his, I felt in those few minutes like I belonged somewhere, so if "friends" was what it was, then I guess I could handle it. I ignored the hurt and I tucked it away for another time.

Except I couldn't get it out of my head that he had stopped to buy women's perfume for another "friend," to thank her for helping him with something. He remembered what kind of perfume she wore; you don't remember what kind of perfume someone wears unless you're used to smelling it and seeing it. "Do you know what kind of perfume I wear?" I asked. He didn't know. "Michael. Michael Kors," I said, but I knew he'd never remember. I felt like I'd never be enough. I wondered if this friend was the same person I saw him texting when we were on the plane a few days before, when I opened my eyes after falling asleep with my head on his shoulder... *Fuck.*

That was not my Ultimate You. As beautiful as I looked, as great as the picture was that I posted to social media, which was, soon after, flooded with likes and comments telling me how awesome I was, that was not it.

You cannot be your Ultimate You when you are abandoning yourself.

You cannot be your Ultimate You when you tell yourself your feelings do not matter.

You cannot be your Ultimate You when you trade away pieces of yourself in order to turn someone on or keep them by your side.

You cannot be your most vibrant self, your most connected self, when your insides are screaming, *Something is wrong*, and you decide that nothing is wrong because *it can't be wrong.*

Fast-forward to a few years later, when it appears as if everything in my life is fucked but I am more my Ultimate You than I have ever been before. Parts of my business are crumbling, and I am questioning my next steps. I sit on the couch in sweatpants and a T-shirt, with my two-day dirty hair tangled in a bun. I'm twenty pounds heavier than I was that day in the red dress, and far less tan. The man I'd craved has not spoken to me in months, and though at first I thought I'd never make it without him, I am crying less and less every day and, to be honest, feeling pretty strong on my own. Even though things feel like they are falling apart, I am safe, and I know it.

That day sitting on the couch I wasn't coping. I was listening to myself. I was making changes. I was reevaluating the hard stuff, which my eyes were finally open to—I had walked away from a relationship that didn't serve me, had turned down work gigs that didn't feel like ME, and was sitting in the emptiness without freaking out. And when my best friend came over, she sat on my couch, drinking a latte, and said, "I know you're kind of a hot mess right now, but I gotta tell you I'm not worried about you one bit. You're taking care of you. For you. You're raw but you've got this."

And she was right.

In that time, I was more my Ultimate You than I had ever been before. Because I was aligned. My eyes and heart were open. And I was serving *myself.*

Your Ultimate You is not performing. She certainly doesn't exist to impress others. She is not an unreachable expectation you have of yourself that you can (probably) never be, at least not for more than a fleeting moment in time.

Your Ultimate You is messy-beautiful. Because that's what self-love is. And she is full of it.

DIG DEEPER:
Figuring Out Who Your Ultimate You Is

Right now, you may be asking yourself, *How do I know who my Ultimate You is?* This is a natural question. My bet is that it's also a really hard one to answer. You may know bits and pieces of who this version of you is, but a fuller picture may allude you. Don't worry—you'll uncover her! This whole book is devoted to helping you meet her. One step at a time, through the process of Soul Archaeology, you'll come face-to-face with your Ultimate You. We will get there.

You may not know who your Ultimate You is, but you probably know who she is *not*. Right now, let's focus on that. This may sound silly and counterintuitive—why pay attention to the past and not focus on the future instead?

Here's the thing . . . You want to honor and love the crap out of both who you have been in life and also who you are in the moment. Who you have been will always be within you. You want to see that version of you with clarity and without judgment. (You cannot hate yourself into loving growth.) But, right now, let's just see who you are *in this moment*.

In a journal, answer the following questions:

1. Who do I think I have to be in order to be loved by others?
2. What have I been believing the "best" version of me is?
3. Who is the "Before Me" that I'm worried I am now?
4. Who is the "After Me" that I feel I have to chase in order to be worthy of happiness?

Answering these questions will help you to see yourself as you are, honor your messy-beautiful, and uncover the initial layers of your Soul Archaeology.

SURVEYING THE SITE:
WHAT WE DUG UP IN THIS CHAPTER

Personal growth is like an archaeological dig where you excavate pieces of yourself one layer at a time—this is why I've called this process Soul Archaeology. When it comes to self-reflection, you are capable of seeing only what you are capable of seeing at any given time. We may want to dive into the big stuff right away—breathe. You aren't in a rush—at least, you don't need to be. You can exhale into this process. To start the journey, we only need to look at where we are right now. Have faith! As long as you are always honest with yourself and willing to see, you will keep growing.

My hope for you is that you live a Self-Loving Life. This means shaping your life so that self-love directs your thoughts and actions, and your strategy in life is to prioritize your Ultimate You. When you do this, you have permission to assess and determine, at any time, if you are on the most aligned path for you. You can adjust and bob and weave as you need to! What it means for you to live a Self-Loving Life will evolve as you evolve.

Last, a big thing. Big…huge thing. We are never a "Before" and "After" picture. We are constantly in flux and growing; think of your life more as a beautiful, messy squiggle than a straight timeline. Along this line, don't aspire to be perfect. Instead, aim to unfurl into your Ultimate You. This is the most powerful and true version of you that exists. Your Ultimate You is not perfect. Instead, this is the you that you are fully connected to—when you are able to listen to yourself and take action based on what you observe. Your Ultimate You sees who you are and where you have been with both clarity and compassion. Your Ultimate You is messy and beautiful at the same time. She is human.

Chapter 3

THE SELF-LOVE OF BODY LIBERATION

Your Body, Your Weight, and Your Ultimate You

I think you are like me.

You were born in the '70s or '80s (maybe even the late '60s).

You graduated high school before the internet really took off. (If you did have an email or AIM screen name, it was probably a garbled mix of letters or some random phrase you never want to admit out loud again.) I graduated in 1996. This was the year that mad cow disease hit the UK. Suspected "Unabomber" Ted Kaczynski was arrested. Tiger Woods made his professional debut, Bill Clinton won a second term in office, and Los Del Rio's "Macarena" and the Spice Girls' "Wannabe" were the biggest hit singles on the radio.

Before Google. Before Facebook.

You never saw plus-size people in a positive light in the media—it was always some exposé about a celebrity getting fat and letting themselves go, or a huge diet reveal.

We got Kirstie Alley. Rosie O'Donnell. Roseanne. Camryn Manheim. Wendy, the Snapple Lady. Carnie Wilson (who they totally screwed over with that stupid blazer on the beach) and Oprah, wheeling her cart of fat onto the stage to demonstrate her miraculous weight loss. Ricki Lake and Queen Latifah were our goddesses.

If you had to buy plus-size clothing, you shopped in the dark basement corners of a department store next to luggage, or at a specialty chain store called (can't make this up) the Forgotten Woman,[1] or Lane Bryant if you were lucky enough to have one in your city. Or you wore men's clothes.

Your mother dieted and you watched her. Or she put you on a diet.

Maybe you were a large child, or maybe you weren't—it doesn't actually matter. But, if you were anything like me, you did any one of the following diets, all of which I experienced, in some way, shape, or form, by the time I graduated high school:

- Weight Watchers (several times)
- Optifast
- The grapefruit diet
- The vegetable soup diet
- The cabbage soup diet
- The Zone Diet
- SlimFast
- Jenny Craig
- The Sadkhin Therapy Method
- Nutrisystem
- Hypnotism for weight loss
- Richard Simmons's diet plan and workout video *Sweatin' to the Oldies*
- Weight loss camp the summers before I turned thirteen, fourteen, sixteen, and seventeen

I did teenage aerobics classes with weekly weigh-ins. I told a hypnotherapist that I had a vision of my father coming down from a cloud holding Entenmann's chocolate-glazed donuts just to shut her up as she attempted to "cure" me. I went to a Russian doctor who spoke with a heavy accent and used medical tape to secure metal balls to pressure points behind my ears. Every time I felt hungry, I was supposed to rub the balls, and—*POOF!*—hungry no more. My grandmother told my mother that someone she knew from art class had a friend who knew someone who had lost twenty pounds in one month just from rubbing her balls a few times a day. (*Word travels fast among Jews in Brooklyn . . .*)

I've colored circles in that represented milk, bread, and fat.

I've eaten prepackaged frozen low-cal desserts with a baby spoon because it made the eating last longer.

I've had the SnackWell's.

I've spent summers at camps, eating "diet" food and exercising multiple times a day, so I could stand on a scale each week and watch the numbers go down, so I could show off to my parents, buy a new wardrobe, and go back to school in the fall, where everyone would fall in love with the new and more awesome, more popular, more "thin" me.

It is safe to say that I spent my entire childhood aware that my weight needed fixing. Which, in my child-brain, I translated into the idea that I, myself, needed fixing.

Did you do any of that? Did you feel any of that?

UNDER THE INFLUENCE—RECLAIMING YOUR OWN THOUGHTS ABOUT YOUR OWN BODY

As an adult you've heard about body positivity, and it sounds *AWE-SOME*. You want to believe you are lovable, exactly as you are, because that's the message you've always struggled with—the one you've always been denied—and this new generation of body-inclusive visibility and empowerment is exciting. There are more clothes online to shop for than you ever imagined as a girl. More models that look like you. More celebrities... You see Lizzo perform and you practically cry, thinking of what young you would have felt like if she had been able to see what you see. You marvel at what it must be like today growing up. How inclusive. How much easier it must be... You follow plus-size influencers and body positive accounts; you love seeing it all, but you still have this feeling you can't quite shake... *You're not sure how you feel about being fat.*

It's not that you want to be skinny or small—but you may want to be "less heavy" than you are right now.

You feel guilty and conflicted about this. You're worried that thinking this makes you a bad person because everything you read online tells you that dieting is bad, that weight loss is impossible, and that you should be happy with your body as it is. You've dieted and chased the prize of being thin so many times in your life, and it never worked—it usually made things worse.

But, truthfully, how you feel right now isn't about vanity. You just want your life to be *easier*. Being heavier feels different now than it did when you were younger; physically, it truly *feels* different. You want to spend less time doing endless calculations in your head. *How long will I have to walk? Am I wearing the right shoes? Will there be stairs? Chairs? How much more time do I need? Will I be able to shop there or do I need to go somewhere else?*

You want to experience your life freely in the present and not always be distracted by the things your body can and cannot do. You know your value as a human has nothing to do with your weight, but you feel weight stigma from others all the time—and, if you are being honest, you feel it from yourself too. You want to be taken seriously by doctors when you talk to them about aches and pains that they always, *always*, attribute to your weight but that you know have nothing to do with numbers on the scale. (You know that "weight" and "health" and "mobility" aren't the same thing, but you know they can correlate, and have no idea how to differentiate and find a peaceful relationship with one of those things in your body, let alone all of them, without falling prey to the same diet culture that fucked you up for decades of your life.) But you're not saying any of this out loud, and it doesn't seem like anyone else is either.

You feel ashamed, not ashamed of your weight, but because of how you think you may feel about your weight, and you know that feeling shame is the worst and not what you deserve at all!

You think you're the only one. And all alone, you're searching for a way for it all to make sense.

You're searching for answers to questions like the following:

- How can I love myself RIGHT NOW as I am?
- How can I give myself permission to change and grow in the future?

- Can I *want* to lose weight? What if I don't want to lose weight? What if I don't know what I want to do?

Someone needs to talk to you and tell you that you aren't alone. To reassure you that this, all of this, is totally normal; that you are a combination of years and years' worth of stories and experiences—some beautiful, some hard, some in between—that have shaped you into who you are right now. Someone has to tell you that it isn't your fault, and also remind you that how you feel is in your hands now. Someone has to meet you at your level, wherever you are right now. Maybe you are still that little girl tugging awkwardly at the clothes she *had to wear*, not the ones she *wanted to wear*. Wanting to be accepted by her peers and her parents, longing to feel anything but invisible. You may be forty or fifty or sixty, but you are still that girl deep down inside and LOOK AT YOU NOW, YOU EPIC BADASS! You have made it this far in life and have done SO fucking good! Whatever you had to do to get by, to feel loved, to feel safe, you did it. And your body has made it here. It has shown up for you every damn day, whether you were fat or thin or in between. You want someone to see that and understand that and look you in the eye and sit next to you and take a deep breath and exhale with you and tell you that you aren't alone and that your life can be more, and that you can become the epicenter of your own self-esteem and that all the conflicted emotions you have are not too heavy, they are not too sticky, and they are not too ugly.

Well, I will. If there's an empty space next to you, I'm coming to sit down. Can you feel my presence? Take a deep breath.

You are good.

You can do whatever the hell you want to do.

You can feel however you want to feel.

Your feelings are okay.

Your struggles are okay.

Your desires are okay.

You can find your way through the murky maze of feelings.

Whatever you have been will always be inside you. But you are so much more than that. You are everything about to unfurl before you. Like a sailboat about to catch the wind and glide across the water. Even if the water is not clear. Even if you have yet to chart the course. Because you have yourself. You have your Ultimate You. And with that, you have everything.

DIG SITE: BODY LIBERATION IS SOCIOPOLITICAL

Before we go further, it needs to be said that any conversation about "body liberation" will get deep and complex fast. Fatness is an economic, political, social, and racial issue. And, while I live in a marginalized body—I'm a larger plus-size woman, and a Jewish woman—I am also a white woman, and so there are elements of this depth I can be aware of but cannot claim experience with. *I am not a woman of color. I am not trans or gender nonconforming. I am not disabled. Outside of my fatness, my age, and my religious identity, I do not live with any of the major markers that society uses to stigmatize people. I cannot have a conversation about the idea of body liberation without acknowledging this.*

This book focuses on the SELF—and how we relate to ourselves—and it does so through my personal lens. There are many amazing teachers, writers, and advocates who can speak more about the body as it relates to society and systems and who do so from their unique lens. Black women, in particular, have been leaders in issues of fatness and social, economic, and racial justice—they deserve to be heard. Visit my website SarahSapora.com/Soul to find their valuable voices and explore issues of weight stigma, fatphobia, diet culture, social justice, and more!

A TALE OF TWO FAT WOMEN—THE CHOICES AVAILABLE TO US

Outside of our family structure, before social media, we learned a lot about what roles in life were available to fat people from TV and the movies; we could be the joke, or we could be diminished and subordinate. We learned that Carnie Wilson could sing on the beach but only if she covered herself in black from head to toe. In *Designing Women*, Suzanne Sugarbaker (played by Delta Burke) could be fat and glamorous, but it was okay only because her sister leaped to her defense. Black women could be fat as long as they served a purpose—they kept house, were foils for white women, made music, or entertained people. They had to be "sassy" to earn their place in comedy. Roseanne could have her own show but only because she was funny and, in many ways, made a name off the fact that people could both relate to her and say, "Well, at least I'm not like that." A fat woman could be the reliable best friend (like Mare Winningham in *St. Elmo's Fire*) and could have sex with a high-value, good-looking guy like Rob Lowe but only if she lent him money, let him make fun of her girdle and mock her for being a virgin, and hang in there long enough for him to momentarily see how loyal and special she was. We were Andrea Zuckerman, the smart and faithful, pining away for Brandon on *90210*. We were Mimi on *The Drew Carey Show*. Minnie Driver in *Circle of Friends*. The cast of *Living Single* told by network heads that they had to lose weight. We were the sassy, funny ones, again and again and again. We were very rarely, if ever, allowed to be perceived as beautiful without being made a joke of first (cue every Ricki Lake movie); and if, for some crazy reason, we were allowed to be perceived as a valuable, powerful person, it was only because another character qualified us as such. For an entire generation of women who grew up in the '80s and '90s, it was television and the movies that told us just how far we could dare to dream and reach. Unless, of course, you were a fat woman who publicly lost weight—then you could escape the confines of chains and reach for the *real* greatness that came with being a "formerly fat" person who now deserved to be respected because of their weight loss. (*Sarcasm.*)

In many ways, the big screen has been replaced by the small screens of our handheld devices. Whereas before we learned our messages from actresses who were playing roles, we're now learning from "real" people who have taken to social platforms to share their lives and create content. Somehow this raises the stakes because if we're learning from real people, then what they share HAS to be real life, doesn't it? They aren't actresses cast in roles predetermined by focus groups and men in boardrooms—because of this, we believe that we're learning from people just like us... or so we think.

What I have noticed, from more than eighteen years spent working in social media and observing social conversations online, is that while some opinions are amplified, other perspectives are totally absent from conversation. Which is unfortunate because if you rely on social media to help you gauge your sense of self and you don't see your journey mirrored back to you in some way, you'll start to think that there is nobody else in the world who understands you. That you don't belong anywhere in real life. This is simply not true.

You belong. You just may not have heard the right people talking to you yet.

We grew up believing we could be either the Funny Fat or the Sad Fat. These days, if you observe conversations online, you'll start to notice two newer narratives plus-size people can claim. Each one an extreme stereotype lacking nuance. (*I'm exaggerating here on purpose to make a point, okay?*)

The first is to be a fat person that is proud of their size. If you take this route, your mission in life will be to be fat and happy, espouse sound bites from Health at Every Size, insist that your weight doesn't matter or impact your life in any way, and declare loudly that if something is hard for you, it is because society hates fat people.

The second is to be a fat person aching to be thin, someone who lives in the false promise of Before-and-After weight loss. If you choose this, you must tie your happiness to a number on the scale and postpone every single dream you have ever dreamed until "after you lose the weight." You want to lose weight, and you need to lose weight in order to _____. There will be no love, no vacations, no bathing suits on the beach, no great sex, and no happiness, because happiness is exclusive to thinness. Every single thing that is wrong in your life is wrong because you are fat. Both of these tropes are incredibly harmful—but both have *elements* of truth to them.

You don't have to be either of these women, and their talking points don't have to be your own. But from them you *can* learn key things about what you value and how you feel about your own body. In order to do this, you have to pull back to the bigger picture and look at who you learned your body messages from in general, and what they taught you.

DIG DEEPER:
What Role Did Fat Characters Play in Your Life?

I polled my online community and asked them to share which fat characters they observed in the movies and on television while growing up. I asked them what those characters taught them about fat people, and how they internalized that for themselves. The reactions were immediate, raw, and revealed a communal hurt that so many of us are still carrying to this day. So, let's air this out. Because what you learned is NOT the truth.

Journaling Questions

Make a list of the plus-size characters you saw on TV and in the movies. For each, note how they were portrayed and positioned and how you were supposed to feel about them. Also, be clear about how they really made you feel; what did these characters teach you about your value as a person? For example:

Character	How they were portrayed	What message did that character give you about your worth?
Andrea Zuckerman on *Beverly Hills, 90210.* →	Chubby, geeky, but well-intentioned. People reluctantly allowed her to be in their social circle. →	Made me feel like it was my "job" in life to be a guy's best friend when I really had feelings for him.

As always, this exercise helps you do your own inquiry so you can simply start SEEING. There is nothing to solve or judge, just things to unearth. And unearthing leads to growth.

THE PARENTAL ZONE . . . WHERE INFLUENCE BEGINS

I recently saw an old home video of myself. I was in that fleshy, awkward stage of childhood—preteen years overshadowed by headbands, mustard-yellow sweater vests, and red zits—but I saw an eager, young

Sarah, whose eyes showed that she was wild to please everyone. Behind the video camera my uncle was prompting the conversation: "It's August and Sarah is back from camp—you've lost how much weight?" he asked, and I replied, smiling, that I had lost over thirty pounds. "She looks great, doesn't she?" he asked, and a chorus of voices sounded in agreement. "She's turning thirteen soon...Edith, what birthday wish do you have for your granddaughter?"

The camera turns to face my grandmother, who is clearly overwhelmed with love and pride. She chokes back tears as she tells me how beautiful I am and how proud of me she is for my weight loss and how precious I am to her. One by one the camera captured each of my family members speaking in turn, sharing some form of praise. And then something happens, the conversation shifts, and we're talking about peanut butter. I'm explaining that I can eat peanut butter, but only two tablespoons of it. "You can eat peanut butter?" someone asks.

I nod, rolling my eyes. "You can eat anything as long as it's on the plan," I say.

I wondered, at that moment, watching this video, whose idea it was for twelve-year-old Sarah to go to weight loss summer camp. So I called my mother and asked, "Whose idea was it for me to go to fat camp." She was silent. "I'm just wondering, was it my idea?" I asked. "Like, did I see it in a magazine and tell you I wanted to—"

"It was my idea," she said. And, as she spoke, I realized that only a person struggling with a lot of their own shit would decide it was a good idea to send a girl off to weight loss camp before she was old enough to get her period.

My mother was never happy with how she looked. Because of this, she never felt excited to love herself and put the energy into herself that she truly deserved. But doing that made her more unhappy...It was a vicious cycle, each feeling feeding the other until it became impossible to tell which was first, and which feeling was really in charge—the unhappiness, or the lack of deserving. I watched this from the time I was a child. I never understood it, but I accepted it as her normal. What is crazy is that anyone who has ever been in my mother's presence can see the truth—she is radiant and warm and a force of nature and lights up the room with her laughter. And yet even now, in her mid-seventies, she is uncapable of seeing these things. I'm not sure when or why my mother concluded that she wasn't worthy of her dreams, but at some point it happened, and I know it shaped her life and mine.

Contrary to what it may seem, this chapter is NOT about my mother. I love my mother. For sure there's big stuff to deconstruct here, but Mom is not the bad guy in my story (spoiler: there is no bad guy) in any way. However, this little moment right here *is* about illuminating a huge truth—that my complex relationship to my weight and my body was first and foremost influenced by the most important person in my entire life. I would bet it was the same for you; your mom, or another parental figure, might have influenced you in their own way.

Mothers and daughters can make a complicated pair. The source of love. The source of anxiety. The source of life. All of this makes me want to understand and pour love into my own mother. But more so, it illuminates just how few of the thoughts I had growing up about myself were actually my own and how many must have belonged to her.

It makes sense that the first and most formidable messages you learn about your body and, in turn, your worth, come from your mother or your parents.[2] For a long time, our parents are our main source of identity, right? Seeking their approval is our North Star—we share every discovery and look to them to explain to us how things work and where we fit in the world. We mirror, mimic, and absorb. In general, our parents are our primary influence in life until sometime between ages twelve and fourteen,[3] when the approval of peers becomes a greater dominating force.

I was seven when my parents divorced; admittedly, though I deeply craved my dad's approval and affection, he wasn't incredibly present in my daily life. While my relationship with my father would deeply impact my self-esteem as I grew up, the "body messages" I picked up were primarily from my mom.

DIG DEEPER:
The Influence of What THEY Said

Soul Archaeology is all about your ability to observe without passing judgment on what you see and how you feel while making the observations. The following questions will help you to see who the primary source of "body messaging" was for you as a child, what the messages you received were, and how they impacted you.

Journaling Questions

- Who was the primary source of "body inspiration" while you were growing up (for example, your mother, your father, your grandmother, a sibling, or someone else)?
- How did THEY feel about THEIR body? How do you know how they felt?
- What did they say, or do, that showed you how THEY felt about YOUR body?
- How did it make you feel when they did this?
- Do you still receive the same messages from them now that you did when you were younger? If not, when and how did they change?

If there is more than one person you can think of here, answer the set of questions for each person.

Remember, after you answer these questions, you don't have to "do" anything. Just sit with the information and let it breathe!

. . . AND THEN THERE WAS SOCIAL MEDIA

As children, our sphere of influence, or "life bubble," is pretty controlled. We see our family, we go to school, and we do activities—all of this, for the most part, keeps us in the same neighborhood, exposed to the same stuff and the same people. As we age, our bubble gets bigger, and we start being shaped by more and more things. Maybe we change schools, go to camp, seek community in church, or start to travel. My bubble remained pretty small throughout high school.

Once you hit college (if you went) or otherwise left home, your world started to broaden. Whatever you did, as your life got larger, so did the sources of influence in your life. The degree to which each source impacts us varies from person to person based on how we are raised and the type of communities and cultures we inhabit. Things that were really influential to one group of people were maybe of little consequence to another.

And then, social media happened.

I'm not going to get into a history of the internet and social media, but I'll share how using social media started to emerge in my own life—see if this tracks with your own experience. It started off on AOL, in chat rooms and on message boards where I used a screen name that had a dizzying mix of punctuation. Then AIM took over, and I became obsessed with having the right "away message" to let my friends and family know where I was at all times. In 2004 I created a Myspace page—it wasn't a personal thing; my job at the time (I was working as the marketing gal for the Chippendales, the global brand in female entertainment) wanted to be the first male revue to use social media, and I was tasked with making this happen. I eventually caved and created my own Myspace page with lots of glitter letters and automatically playing music—like Fergie's "London Bridge." In 2007 I joined Facebook, and I created an Instagram account several years later. In 2014, my Instagram became "public." I have worked with social media since 2004, and it's a tool that even helped me create this book. I have a love-hate relationship with it, as do many people.

This is all to illustrate how social media platforms have started to play a larger and larger role in our lives as time goes on. You don't have to work in social media to feel the impact of its growth. In 2012, people spent ninety minutes a day using social media;[4] in 2020, they spent 145 minutes every day on social media,[5] and that was before the pandemic and sheltering in place changed our lives forever.

Today, 98 percent of adults in the US ages thirty to forty-nine are online;[6] 96 percent of people ages fifty to sixty-four are online; and 81 percent of adults in the US ages thirty to forty-nine are using social media.[7] If we're spending over two hours a day on social media, it is safe to assume that we are shaped by the content we consume.

For many, social platforms have become the main sources of influence shaping their lives. It is no longer those closest to us, but rather the conversations we see online that impact how we feel about ourselves and how we relate to the world. The Instagram posts, the celebrity shout-outs, all of it. Whether or not we want to admit it, what we see on social media matters.

When the Loudest Talkers Aren't Talking to You

Conversation online is shaped by people with influence. To have this "influence," you must have a significant number of people following you. Influencers serve as gatekeepers to their followers; they curate what content and messages they share that best suit their agenda. People of influence online can include celebrities, politicians, and journalists, among others.

An influencer is defined as someone who has "the power to affect the purchasing decisions of others because of his or her authority, knowledge, position, or relationship with his or her audience" and someone who has "a following in a distinct niche, with whom he or she actively engages."[8]

Eighty-five percent of Instagram influencers are between eighteen and thirty-four years of age. Of that group, 31 percent are between eighteen and twenty-four, and 54 percent are between the ages of twenty-five and thirty-four.[9]

You read that correctly: Of the influencers building community on Instagram, 85 percent are between eighteen and thirty-four years of age (my bet is that you don't fall into this age range).

Eleven percent of Instagram influencers are ages thirty-five to forty-nine. Over fifty? You're shit out of luck. You have only a 1 percent chance of finding someone like you creating social conversation online.

It is safe to say that you, reading this right now, are consuming content online that wasn't created for you. If you've ever felt like you don't "fit in" online, that's a big reason why.

Let's put this in perspective with some more numbers. In 2021,

- 32.99 percent of women in the US were ages twenty to thirty-four;
- 31.46 were ages thirty-five to forty-nine; and
- 32.31 women were ages fifty to sixty-nine.[10]

And, just as a reminder,

- 98 percent of adults in the US ages thirty to forty-nine are online;
- 96 percent of US adults ages fifty to sixty-four are online;
- 81 percent of adults in the US ages thirty to forty-nine are using social media; and[11]
- 73 percent ages fifty to sixty-four use it.[12]

What do you deduce from that? When it comes to online conversation, there's a big discrepancy between those talking and those listening.

This is one of many reasons we feel excluded from conversations on social media. You may be listening to people who weren't even talking to you in the first place—people who can't understand your perspective and your lived experiences. This can leave you feeling invisible and unrepresented and questioning who you are and what you think you feel. Can you imagine how much harder it must be to find "visibility" in social conversations when you are a person of color or someone with alternative abilities? Representation matters!

BODY LIBERATION AND YOUR ULTIMATE YOU—FINDING YOUR OWN ANSWERS

Your body is magical.

It is epochs of scientific and evolutionary wizardry packaged together in one perfect place: 78 organs, 600 muscles, 7 trillion nerves, 37.2 trillion cells. And every day that you wake up, the magical machine that is your body works for YOU. It shows up for YOU.

Yet, if I asked you right now, "How do you feel about your body?" I'm going to assume you would have a hard time formulating some compassionate, concrete thoughts. Approximately 80 percent of women in the US are unhappy with their bodies.[13] And 97 percent of women will have at least one negative thought about their bodies every day.[14]

How many of the opinions we have about our bodies are actually our own and not the opinions and feelings of others that we've picked up along the way? Only *you* get to decide how you feel about your body and your weight. Your thoughts should not be limited by what your mother thought, or what your peers thought, or what people online think. Other people's feelings are not parameters that define you. It is your opportunity, your gift, to break free from the narratives so that you can make yourself the center of your own personal value system. This is an ultimate act of self-love on the path to creating your Ultimate You.

With this process, the goal is to empower you to do the thinking for yourself. Have you ever asked the following questions?

Can I lose weight?

Is it okay if I don't want to lose weight?

If I really loved myself, I would lose weight . . . Right?

If I really loved myself, I'd never diet again . . . Right?

I am not going to tell you to lose weight, and I am not going to tell you to gain weight or stay exactly where you are. Learning to think for yourself concerning these issues allows you to find true body liberation as it relates to *who you want to be* in your own life and *how you want to feel*, so you can learn how to move past the thoughts of others, and so that you can go through this thought process again and again throughout your life as needed to make sure you are connecting and aligning with yourself at each chapter of your life. Because you are going to have a relationship with your body for the rest of your life. Even though this work is hard to do, it's okay. Not only is it okay, but it's GREAT. It means you are awakening.

> ### DIG SITE: BODY LIBERATION—GOING BEYOND LOVE TO FREEDOM
>
> My favorite definition of body "liberation" comes from Jes Baker, an amazing teacher and writer. She says, "Liberation is freedom from *all* outside expectations, even our own. Liberation is not having to love your body all the time. Liberation is not asking permission to be included in society's ideal of beauty. Liberation is bucking the concept of beauty as currency altogether. Liberation is recognizing the systemic issues that surround us and acknowledging that perhaps we're not able to fix them all on our own. Liberation is personally giving ourselves permission to live life."[15]

NOW, COME BACK TO YOURSELF

As I shared earlier, my greatest wish for you is not that you should seek perfection, but that you should work to uncover your Ultimate You. The version of you that is deeply, intimately connected to yourself.

Life does not reward us for free thought. Human nature, like a social media algorithm, likes to rely on someone else to do the work—it's easier to make the familiar or popular opinions your own than it is to find the path that works for you. But "easy" doesn't necessarily mean "true." Easy choices aren't always the ones that are the most self-loving. The "easy" path isn't always the one that makes us feel the most whole.

It is only when we do the actual work for ourselves that we can define ourselves for ourselves and liberate our self-esteem from the permission of others. The specific decisions you make to support your body are less important, for our purposes, than your being deeply honest with yourself when you ask the questions and do the self-discovery that gives you the answers. You need to be so honest with yourself that you leave no room for ambiguity when you ask yourself what you really want, because your Ultimate You listens to herself. She does not need to be "influenced" by people who may or may not understand her. She acknowledges that her personal feelings are her own, and they do not exist to please other people. Just as I say about all actions of self-love, your feelings about your body can change. Your feelings will be relative to you, based on your needs and nuances. Your feelings about your body will be different from other people's feelings about their bodies. Your feelings can be sticky and complex. Your feelings will not always be easy. Most importantly, your feelings will not always need a resolution. Sometimes the healthiest thing any of us can do is simply acknowledge the feelings we have about our bodies, and then surrender into them with compassion and awareness.

Soul Archaeology will help you define life on your terms and also help you uncover your personal values so you can calibrate life to work for you. It will give you a vehicle to weed through other people's crap so you can be the epicenter of your own joy.

It will help you use your pain to illuminate how it is you really want to feel. Then, it will guide you to identifying and taking tangible action so that you can start to uncover who you truly are and who you want to be. No fancy gimmicks. Just a road map you can refer to whenever you feel stuck.

 ## DIG DEEPER INTO WHAT SHAPES YOU BY BUILDING YOUR OWN MAP OF INFLUENCE

This journaling activity may take you some time but it's great for Soul Archaeology. It is a wonderful exercise to excavate the things that have shaped how you feel about your body so that you can start separating your feelings from other people's feelings.

Creating Your Influence Map

As with any process of discovery, acknowledgment is half the growth journey. Creating an influence map is a great way to start bringing awareness to things that impact how you feel about your own body.

Step One: One by one, think about how each of the following impacts your personal feelings about your weight and your body. Just do a quick pass here—no need to stew over it.

- Your family
- Your friends
- Your intimate relationships
- Your religious institutions
- The media
- Social media
- Your community
- Your feelings about yourself

Step Two: Replicate the following chart and plot each of the above influences, noting whether the influence is one you currently feel or *used* to feel, and whether it is more or less influential (see my example on page 54 for guidance). Remember, go with your gut when you take this first pass.

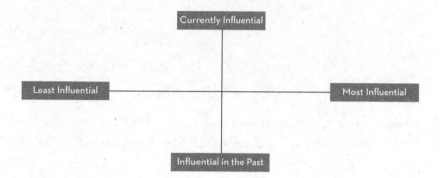

Step Three: Think about anything else that might be influential in shaping your personal feelings about your body and weight and add those to the chart as well.

Step Four: Get detailed. In your journal, answer the following questions for each influence:

1. What messages does this influence give you about your body?
2. When do you get these messages?
3. Is this an "optional" influence? (Meaning, do you have control over whether you are exposed to this influence or not?)

Step Five: Once you're done, take a deep breath and put the chart away. You don't need to do anything here other than open your eyes.

This is an exercise you can do anytime you are looking to see something with more clarity. Remember, the goal is simply to see, not to look for a solution.

Example: Sarah

Here's an example of how this map looked for me on the day I wrote this:

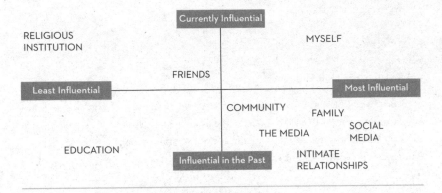

SURVEYING THE SITE:
WHAT WE DUG UP IN THIS CHAPTER

Uncovering your Ultimate You also means deciding how you feel about your own body based on *your* values and not based on the influencing forces that shape you.

There's a good chance that you are a child of the '80s and '90s; you graduated high school before the internet became a "thing." Our generation was exposed to a whole range of cultural markers about dieting and weight loss, from Weight Watchers and Richard Simmons to skinny Oprah wheeling her cart of fat out in front of a television audience.

There are lots of things that have shaped how we feel about our bodies. Growing up, our parental figures were most likely the greatest source of our body influence. This evolved as we aged. These days, it's very likely that social media are one of the main sources of body influence in your life.

If you are influenced by the media, there are only two main "narratives" that fat people can have in their lives: to be the Happy Fat (a person who is proud of their size and advocates for fat rights, oftentimes guided by Health at Every Size); or to be a Sad Fat, obsessed with dieting and full of self-loathing for her larger body. These tropes leave no room for people to find a way of approaching their own personal body liberation.

The key is to observe and note how all the influencing forces in your life tell you that you should feel about your body—from your parents to your friends to your community to social media and everything in between—and then do the work to find out how YOU feel about your body.

If you want to lose weight, you can. If you want to stay the same weight, you can. The essential thing is that you are honest when you ask yourself the questions *How do I feel in my body right now?* and *How do I want to feel in order to create my Ultimate You?*

Body liberation is an act of self-love. It is nuanced and sticky, but it is beautiful work.

II

CREATING LIFELOVE:
THE STEPS AND STRATEGY
TO UNEARTHING YOU

Learning to Create a Self-Love To-Do
List and How to Use the List to Guide
Your Soul Archaeology

Chapter 4

HOW THIS IS GOING TO WORK

Setting It Up So It All Makes Sense

Something is off in your life. Maybe you know what it is; maybe you just feel like a tangled human, flailing around and throwing shit at the wall and hoping something sticks.

Maybe you hate your body. Maybe you hate your job. Maybe you hate your kids (not really, but you know), or maybe some days you can't stand to look at your partner's face. Maybe you don't have a partner and you feel like a failure because of it. Maybe you feel like everyone else has their shit together and you're still waiting to "be a grown-up" even though you are four decades old. You think you weigh too much. You don't have enough sex, or you have too much sex for all the "wrong" reasons but not the "right" ones. You are worried life is passing you by. This is the part of the book where we get to work. Where we move from feeling something is off to making change. Welcome to the party (**grin**).

Have you been chasing some big, illusive *After* that you're sure will be the magical fix? If yes, it's time to do this. You are starting at the top of your Soul Archaeology and have no idea where to go or what to do next, but don't freak out—we're going to walk through this together. We'll move from theory to action; we'll take ideas and make them practical. Personal growth is great, but have you ever thought about how much of it seems totally intangible? Like ideas floating around the ether. Ideas are fun to talk about and exciting to discuss, but if we stop short of going from an idea to its execution, we can fall flat. We get caught up in the romance of learning new things and constantly look out for new solutions instead of putting our feet to the pavement and getting practical where we are RIGHT NOW.

You won't experience change by talking about things. You will experience it if you start *doing* things, because doing leads to more doing. Doing clears the path. If we focus on the *process* and not the outcome, we can let the doing be our guide. You don't need a special key to unlock what comes next. You don't need a $29.95 monthly membership or a fancy outfit or a new app. You need your brain and a piece of paper, maybe even a journal, and something to write with. Above all, you need to be willing to get real with yourself. You need to start doing shit you haven't done before. It is going to take practice. You may swim right away, or you may feel like you're treading water. But if you keep practicing the strategies I'm about to teach you, things will get easier. This approach to your life can be used time and time and time again.

DIG SITE: A REMINDER ABOUT "ABILITY"

All of us come to the table with different abilities. Some people have anxiety; some have depression. Some have chronic illness. There are hundreds of thousands of ways and reasons why we are all different—as we should be. We have the opportunity to remember that there is no one single baseline of what "mental health" is and all of us will come to the table in different ways and at different depths and levels based on what we are individually capable of. Personal growth that doesn't make room for people to have their own chemical makeup and physical needs is exclusive and, therefore, crappy. There. I said it. (*Grin.*)

PERSONAL GROWTH AS A WAY OF LIFE

I have never kept a single New Year's resolution in my entire life. In fact, I stopped making them years ago for that specific reason. Every year I would make myself a huge promise that usually involved me doing something that would lead to my "happy ending," and I'd psych myself up for all the awesome things I was going to do and then I'd never do a single one of them. By the time my birthday would roll around the next year, I'd come brutally face-to-face with all the things I said I'd do but didn't do and all the ways my life was still exactly the same as it was the year before and all the reasons my life was therefore a failure going nowhere. *I literally used to think this every birthday* . . . And then I would do it all over again the next New Year's.

New Year's resolutions suck and yet we make them because they're kind of sexy. It's seductive to think about all the ways our lives would be better if only we could slay the dragon guarding our castle to find the perfect job and the perfect partner and reach our "goal weight"—or whatever would be THE ANSWER to making everything better. A recent survey tells us that over 74 percent of women make New Year's resolutions[1]— that's a lot of women looking for a magic solution to everything they think is wrong with their lives.

The challenge is that growth itself is not a single event; it's a way to live your life. Life is continuously in flux. Wouldn't a better way to approach your ever-changing life be to find a strategy that throws out the big, one-time goals and, instead, guides you with continuous evolution?

This book offers you a new strategy to *approach* your life, to shape it and guide it. I was using this approach before I had a name for it. It's been my practice for over eight years. At first, it was really hard for me to adjust from fulfilling short-term goals to seeking longer-term evolution. At first, to be honest, my instant-gratification ADHD brain really sucked at the process. Over time, it got easier. Now it flows through me with ease and agility. While the things I uncover are not always easy, the process itself is second nature to me now.

Every time you feel stuck or off balance, you can come back to this strategy. It will help you to untangle and get clarity, and will offer you a tangible and concrete plan for moving forward when you can't find one any other way. There is no limit to how many times you can do this, or how few. You know those times you catch yourself saying, "What the fuck am I doing?" That's when you whip this bad boy out to help give you direction.

When you need help, it's normal to search for direction, and you can find it in many places. Religion, a relationship, your parents or loved ones, the media—anywhere. All of these things can influence the road you take. But many of these things have some kind of agenda, and that agenda is not necessarily you. The key to unearthing your Ultimate You is found in *your feelings* and *your values*. This is about learning how to become your own navigational beacon when the fog rolls in or the water becomes rough. When you allow what matters to you to shape you, you are creating a life for *you*.

You may be thinking, *Wow, that's a whole lotta "me." This sounds kinda selfish. Shouldn't I care about other people?*

I see how someone could say that, but it's not true. This strategy doesn't suggest that you ignore others or stop caring about people or that you make the world ALL ABOUT HOW AWESOME YOU ARE. This strategy is about keeping a hold on your self-worth and your self-perception instead of giving it away for someone else to shape or juggle. It is about being good to yourself and, in turn, being good to those you love as companions, caretakers, or colleagues, for example. It is about how to maintain your own agency instead of handing it off to someone or something else.

You can be of service to others while maintaining boundaries. You can be loving to others without cockblocking yourself in the process. In fact, the clearer your boundaries are and the more aware you are of what it means to show up fully for yourself, the more you are capable of supporting and loving others without blurring the lines and becoming enmeshed or codependent—without letting someone else decide how you feel about yourself,[2] and without compromising your autonomy and identity.[3] Doing the work to craft a life that places you as the main character is not selfish; rather, it's healthful and allows you to give to others in a balanced way.

YOUR LIFE IS A WINDING ROAD

This road represents my life since 2015. Each stop illustrates a time when I have felt stuck and I've intentionally used Soul Archaeology to help me reconnect to myself and move forward. Each time I hit a roadblock, I turned to the tactics we're exploring to help me "unstick my stuck" and continue on my path to my Ultimate You.

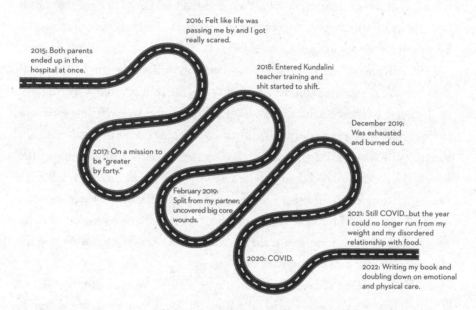

2016: Felt like life was passing me by and I got really scared.

2015: Both parents ended up in the hospital at once.

2018: Entered Kundalini teacher training and shit started to shift.

December 2019: Was exhausted and burned out.

2017: On a mission to be "greater by forty."

February 2019: Split from my partner; uncovered big core wounds.

2021: Still COVID...but the year I could no longer run from my weight and my disordered relationship with food.

2020: COVID.

2022: Writing my book and doubling down on emotional and physical care.

It is normal to search for direction to tell you where to go. Many things can direct you—God, a relationship, or media, for example. I believe the path to unearthing your Ultimate You can be found in YOUR feelings and YOUR values. Each time you feel stuck, if you reconnect with YOURSELF as a compass, you can move yourself forward. There is no limit to how many times you can ask, and answer, "What is the most self-loving thing I can do for my Ultimate You right now?"

Each of these times I was stuck; I felt lost and needed direction but had no idea how to move forward. So I worked the strategy to create a door leading to the other side of the stickiness; I moved myself forward, living, experiencing, and learning, just to do it all over again when I needed to. You can do the same.

GOALS SUCK, EVEN WHEN YOU DON'T

What happens when we don't keep our resolutions? Every year, 91 percent of people fail to achieve their New Year's resolutions,[4] and 80 percent abandon their resolutions entirely by February.[5]

I want you to imagine a group of one hundred mothers standing on the sidewalk of a busy city street with their toddler children. Each mother holds out her hand, as mothers do, and takes her child's hand in hers because she knows that without her guidance, it won't be safe for that small child to cross a wide, bustling street. The traffic pauses and, in unison, the mothers step off the curb and the children follow suit. Two steps into crossing the street, eighty of the hundred mothers drop their children's hands and keep walking, leaving their children to stand confused and scared, wondering what happened. By the time the whole group of mothers has crossed the street, ninety-one of the hundred have abandoned their children—only nine of the children will have been safely guided to the other side of the street, protected, and cared for. The rest? Maybe they'll make it safely; maybe they won't—who knows. But as the traffic begins to barrel down the street again, it's not looking too good for those ninety-one kids crying their eyes out…

Each time we make a resolution to ourselves and we abandon it (whether it is on New Year's or any other day), we become that small child standing confused in the street. We make a promise and pick up our own hand. We enter the year like we are crossing the street, with every intention of making it safely to the other side. And then we drop our own hands. *We drop ourselves.* We abandon our promises, endangering the hopes and dreams and the belief in ourselves that we can accomplish what we set out to do. If we do that enough times, sooner or later we'll stop trusting the hands we extend to ourselves in the first place—we'll stop listening to that voice inside us that says we want something more entirely. And one day, we won't even bother wanting to cross the street anymore. We'll just stay in one place, because staying in one place is familiar and safe. This is one way we get stuck.

I have a few big problems with resolution-type goals. First, a lot of the goals we make are enormous. Like a single person saying, "This is the year I'm getting married" when they have nobody special in their life, or someone else declaring, "This is the year I get rich" when they have no financial foundation. Second, on the opposite end of the pendulum, there are people who make goals that are SUPER specific. Folks who say, "I'm going to lose a hundred pounds this year" or "I'm going to fit into my size 6 goal jeans" or "I'm going to make ten thousand dollars a month in revenue after taxes." Third, you get the goals that people can't even define but they make anyway because doing so sounds good or makes them feel better. Like saying, "I want to be happier this year" or "I'm going to get into better shape." They are lovely ideas but relatively ambiguous. And finally, you have goals that are decoys—they say one thing but really mean something else. For example, saying, "This year I'm going to fit into the same size I wore in high school" may be more about reclaiming feelings of youth, hope, and vibrancy than about a pant size. (FYI, statistics tell us that the top resolutions people make every year usually have a few common themes, like getting more fit, losing weight, or saving money.[6])

The way I see it, any of these four kinds of goals are setting you up to fail in some way or another. If you make goals that are too big to hold, it's almost impossible to achieve them in the first place, so when you don't get there, you feel like you suck. In the second scenario, it's like trying to hit the bull's-eye with an arrow, and then splice the same arrow with another arrow in the exact same bull's-eye—so when you don't hit the super-specific mark exactly as you need to, you feel like you suck. When your goals are undefinable, you'll never be reaching for anything, so you'll flail around and grasp for anything—and when you don't get "anything," you will feel like you suck. If your goals are really secret decoys for feelings you can't articulate, there's a chance you'll actually accomplish what you wanted to but still be feeling like shit because it was never about the specific goal in the first place—which means you will still feel like you suck. Are you seeing the pattern?

You can't grow in life if you are weighed down by the feeling of your own suckage. If you are feeling trapped under a pile of shit that you are positive is of your own making, it is almost impossible to want to keep trying new things—why should you, when it only results in more shit piled on top in the future?

If you want to feel something different in life, you have to be willing to do something different and to try something different. Simple. (Not easy, but simple.)

"If I'm not supposed to chase goals that I'm pretty, totally, almost entirely sure will be the key to making me happy, what am I supposed to do?"

One day, my boyfriend—I call him "Man Candy"—and I were debating the idea of personal growth. He was frustrated because, understandably, he had goals he hadn't met in his life. (He's not at all into self-reflection, by the way. We're very different in that respect.)

"Why are you making goals anyway?" I asked. "Goals are terrible!"

He looked at me like I had four heads. "What am I supposed to do if I don't have goals? Like, what's the point of life if you don't have goals?" he said with an incredulous tone in his voice that warned me he is, in fact, a general contractor and therefore a creature of logic, so I better come at him with some logic or else . . .

And then I said something to him that made him as (faux) crazy as it's probably going to make you right now: "You don't do things for the end result; you do things for the sake of doing them. You do things because in the process of doing you bring something to life that's probably truer than what you could have imagined if you just went straight to home base right away. You do things because life is about just DOING. That's how you stay present."

I wish I could tell you he got it. Maybe he did, but he looked at me like I was Gwyneth Paltrow trying to sell him a This Smells Like My Vagina candle for seventy-five dollars, so I'm going to assume he didn't.

I'll say the exact same thing to you right now. You do things because doing them is a journey and that, itself, is what reveals life to you. Just doing is the reward. You point your ship in the direction you want to go, you navigate guided by your own compass, and you see where it takes you! You let your feelings guide you, let the sails fill up with wind, and open your life to possibility.

SEEING IT IN ACTION—THE SELF-LOVE TO-DO LIST IN REAL LIFE

Throughout this section, I'll be sharing examples from my process to guide you, but we're also going to look at other women doing the same work. I'll be sharing real-life examples from three women in my community who have agreed to let me share their Self-Love To-Do Lists with you so that you have more examples of how everyday women are doing this work for themselves (*the names and identifying details of each of these women have been changed to protect their privacy*). The work they have done and what we're doing together here is the same process I teach in my online mentoring groups, and also at live events and retreats.

You'll see the Self-Love To-Do List road maps these women created to help unstick their stuck and move forward in living a Self-Loving Life. You'll see some of the common challenges people have when creating their lists. All of what you see will be an example of how you can use self-love to guide your Soul Archaeology and create a truthful and vibrant life based on your own values and needs. How you can create your Ultimate You.

Anna, 39, South Carolina

"Fat girls can't wear Uggs," Anna told me once. It's not that anybody ever explicitly told her plus-size women couldn't wear Uggs; it's just that Anna had spent a long time carefully observing the type of girls who did wear them—they were wealthy and thin and the boys wanted to date them— and she was none of those things, so in an attempt to stave off the inevitable unwanted attention that would come when she was caught trying to color outside her social lines by wearing Uggs herself, Anna came to this conclusion on her own.

Anna has spent most of her life adjusting as a precursor to interactions with friends, family, loved ones, and basically anyone in the world around her. She would give nobody any fuel to make her feel bad about herself, because she already did that well enough on her own; her brain made rules based on what she saw, and Anna was acutely tuned in to what she felt like she needed to be. She has been a fixer and an encourager. She has felt "fucked over" by the diet industry and gone from being on the diet hamster wheel to having no tolerance for anything at all related to weight loss, dieting, or the system she has felt harmed by since she was a child. Recently, she realized she is no longer interested in living her life on the offense, prepared with her shield for battle every day so she won't be attacked or devalued.

If you were to ask her what she loves, she'd say it's the feeling of the sand between her toes and the breeze coming off the ocean. If she had to describe herself, she'd admit she wants to "write words out like poetry," and include a hearty "fuck the patriarchy" for good measure.

Anna wears Uggs now. I have seen a picture of her beaming face and her feet, enveloped in bright pink suede and wool. Because coloring inside the lines is no way to live your life.

Chloe, 38, Tennessee

When she was fifteen, Chloe's youth pastor began to sexually abuse her. But he was nice and said things like "God thinks you're very special," which made Chloe think what she was experiencing couldn't have been a big deal; even though she knew it wasn't right, it couldn't have been *that* wrong. It went on for two years. The patterns of chronic self-abandonment that she learned at his hands stayed with her for the rest of her life, and she never kicked the feeling that whatever man was in her life would automatically know more than she did and that his opinions were far more valuable and reliable than hers could ever be.

In her early twenties, Chloe began to experience bouts of depression, alternating with manic periods; she was diagnosed and treated for bipolar II disorder. During this time, she knew her judgment couldn't be trusted, and would often find herself on the other side of a depressive or manic episode, looking at a decision she'd made when she was influenced, and think, *Man, you should have just done what your mother said instead.* Chloe self-medicated with alcohol for years and would later struggle with bulimia. She admits she had "dozens and dozens of relationships" prior to being married, because she always felt she needed a man, a relationship, where someone else would know best.

Chloe is so much more than any diagnosis she has ever received. It would be easy to label her as a shy and anxious woman who just wants everyone to get along. But if you scratch one inch beneath the surface, you quickly see how wrong that shortsighted assessment is. Chloe is a tigress and self-aware—she is very deep, and she loves to laugh.

Chloe has been sober for years and her bipolar II is under control, but she still doesn't trust herself. She continues to be frustrated that she never did anything to stop the abuse she experienced, because she "was fifteen and should have known better and should have been able to stop it." She undermines her own judgment and regularly turns to other people for solutions when she knows she really has them. She doesn't trust herself, but she wants to and she's ready to.

Lindsay, 44, Colorado

Lindsay is a bighearted, straight-talking woman who works an intense job in a male-dominated field. She married her college sweetheart when she was twenty-three; they divorced ten years later. He was the first man she'd ever had sex with when they tied the knot. Recognizing how sexually repressed she'd been and now discovering and prioritizing her desire has been a huge part of her Soul Archaeology.

Lindsay self-soothes with food and shopping online. She chronically overcommits to doing things so she can avoid the discomfort of being alone and because she wants to appear busy. She knows these behaviors are a tell, and one of the signs that she's not doing well.

I ask her if it's really that she's uncomfortable with being alone, or if it's the weight of society's discomfort with single women that bothers her the most. "The weight of society," she says clearly and without apology. "It's the expectation . . . No—it's *my* perception of the weight that society puts on being a single woman that I'm trying to avoid."

As a younger adult, Lindsay lived with her head in the sand—she expresses this freely and thinks it's important to know this when understanding who she is now. "Although I'm a strong and bubbly person, I struggle with anxiety and depression because I try to balance my life—I don't know that it's possible. As women in our forties, we get to this point where we don't have any 'fucks' left to give anymore, and I'm trying to find out, What serves me now? Where am I filling up my bucket? Because it needs filling."

Lindsay struggles with "the body stuff." Additionally, when she turned forty, she faced unanticipated medical issues. "My body freaked out and told me, *Hey, you need to take care of me*, and now I wonder, *Do I need to lose weight? Do I want to?* I don't know," she says. "I've just gotten to the place that I know it's okay to love yourself at any size but fuck, man, it's just going to get harder and harder as I get older and closer to menopause." Since Lindsay is an extrovert, her greatest joy is forming deep connections to others. She also loves traveling and trying new things . . . but she's aware of how her body and weight are starting to eat away at the joy that traveling brings her. "I'm just learning to be who I am *as I am*."

Are you able to see common connections among these three women? While they are different in so many ways, they share key challenges. While the challenges are not something we will explore in depth here, all three women are currently or were previously on a body journey that has impacted their self-esteem and perception of self. Each of these women is a deeply intricate creature deserving of understanding in her unique experiences. That being said, at even a surface-level glance it is easy to see that Anna, Chloe, and Lindsay have all spent the majority of their lives seeking answers outside of themselves such that, walking into (or in) their forties, they lack self-trust. This lack of self-trust keeps them from feeling centered and at home in themselves, their bodies, and their lives.

Whether it's Anna, who has preemptively shape-shifted in order to create an identity apart from encouraging and being useful to others, Chloe's deference to men she perceives to be all-knowing, or Lindsay's years spent intentionally sweeping aside hard things, each of these women longs to meet herself where she is so she can grow into who she knows she is on the inside. They all know the answers are inside themselves, but they have struggled to listen to themselves and build the solid foundation of self-trust that can fuel their growth.

Creating a Self-Love To-Do List will help each of these women home in on her own voice and build a tangible road map to uncovering who she is and living a more empowered, authentic life based on values she didn't even realize she had!

THE PLAN IS IN THE DETAILS

To get shit done and open the closed doors blocking your way, you need a strategy, and you need tactics (those are two different things). One without the other is lovely but useless. Here's what I mean:

Strategy	Tactics
Helps us know how to guide ourselves; it's the overarching way we are going to approach our growth.	Tell us what shit we need to get done—the how and the when. They are a playbook for execution.
Is overarching.	Are detailed.
Tells us what road we are taking to get somewhere.	Tell us what car to drive, how fast, when and where to get gas, what music to listen to, and where and how and what to acquire for road snacks.

Sun Tzu, Chinese general and author of *The Art of War*, wrote, "Strategy without tactics is the slowest route to victory. Tactics without strategy is the noise before defeat." And while we are not at war, this idea translates well when we think about what it truly takes to face the big and scary stuff in life. Great businesspeople understand this as well—ideas without plans to execute fail to produce, and executing haphazardly for the sake of doing will lead to inefficiency and chaos.

You need to have what James Clear, the author of *Atomic Habits*, describes as "systems." "The purpose of setting goals is to win the game," he writes. "The purpose of building systems is to continue playing the game."[7]

Stop Trying to Get Things Right

When you set out on the path of Soul Archaeology, you're going to feel compelled to "get it right." There is no such thing. You don't begin the process of peeling back your layers with a specific end point in mind. You don't let the analysis paralysis of trying to do something perfectly stop you from taking the first steps. Instead, you commit to the process, start it, and see where it leads you next, because you know the process itself (where the magic happens) will move you forward.

Everything that happens as a result of your action can be used for your growth. It's all data. Every time you start. Every time you stop. Every time you feel successful when something clicks into place. Every time it makes no sense and you bang your head into the wall. The alternative is to sit it out—to put your life on cruise control without your participation. But that isn't you anymore. Remember, your Ultimate You requires that you do two things: First, be as real and honest with yourself as you can be at any given time; and second, be committed enough to yourself that you take self-loving action. You don't need perfection; you just have to be honest with yourself and show up for the process.

THE STEPS AHEAD OF US

I've told you how the process works and why you need one. In the next few chapters, I'll be sharing the three actual steps you can take to start living your own Self-Loving Life. These will cover the strategy and the tactics. Whatever you want to call it, *this is the good stuff.*

- In Step One, we'll start where it hurts, because being able to see your pain is the best place to begin.
- In Step Two, you'll do the work to uncover the feelings that fuel you, and these will serve as the starting value points for your Soul Archaeology. We're going to explore why FEELINGS, and not "goals," are your lighthouse.
- In Step Three, we'll "back it up and flip it around" and turn challenges into opportunities to create your very own Self-Love To-Do List.

By the time you complete this section, you will have a list of tangible tiny points of entry (TPEs) to your Self-Loving Life. These are *totally doable* things that you can start practicing TODAY to facilitate change. You will have your strategy and your tactics. You will have your game plan for RIGHT NOW, to unstick your stuck. And you will have learned what to do so you can call upon the process whenever you need it in the future.

SURVEYING THE SITE: WHAT WE DUG UP IN THIS CHAPTER

In this chapter, we talked about how truly effective personal growth work needs to be rooted in the practical. Ideas and new concepts are enticing, but the rubber has to hit the road for you to start to work through your shit. You don't need a special key to access your own personal development, and there is nothing elite about wanting to be a more active participant in your life—you just need commitment, willingness, and an open mind.

Therapy, education, and all the tools and professionals who do the work to help people are awesome and very needed in this world. I hope you will empower yourself to seek help as it feels relevant for you! I also

want each of us to be accountable for our own growth as well. It is important to remember that mental health matters and we should never assume
that "healing" is accessible to all persons in the same way. Progress is not
the same for everyone and empathy is essential here.

Personal growth is slow work; it may feel awkward when you begin,
but keep practicing. It also requires some structure—or you may meander a bit aimlessly. Growth requires strategies and tactics, each serving a
different purpose. Strategy is the overarching approach we take to address
something. Tactics are covered in our detailed playbook for executing.

In the next three chapters, I will talk you through my own personal
strategy for how to live a Self-Loving Life that will help you unfurl into
your Ultimate You. This strategy is one you can use again and again,
including whenever you fall off course and need to find direction.

As I mentioned above, I'll be teaching you the steps to create your very
own Self-Love To-Do List. I'll also share examples of three women from
my community, whom you met earlier, who have also been doing the
work for themselves. So, buckle up, buttercup! It's time to do this. Grab
a journal or notebook and something to write with. Maybe some tissues.
Get comfy. We're going to start where it hurts the most.

Chapter 5

___

STEP ONE: START WHERE IT HURTS

An Ode to Cockroaches and Pain

The only way to really start changing your life is to become honest with yourself about what hurts you right now.

I know you don't want to do this. I know that forcing yourself to acknowledge your pain comes with a fuck-ton of shame, because if you actually have to see the reality of what hurts, then the things you are feeling are real. And if they are real, then you may feel like the pain is really yours, and so it's all your fault. Right? I hear you, but that's not so self-loving, is it?

My job is to get you to commit to loving yourself—to pick up your hand and lovingly tell you the difficult stuff you probably know deep in your heart but you don't want to accept.

I *won't* coddle you, but I *will* tell you that hard things are okay and reassure you that you can absolutely do hard things. And it starts here. So, I am asking you, *What are you pretending not to know in your own life? What are you pretending not to see? What are you pretending not to feel?*[1]

Your answers to all three of these questions are the doorway to what's next, and the path to living your Self-Loving Life. If you cannot identify the ways that pain is showing up in your life, you cannot heal through them. If you can't see how pain plays a role in your life, you will keep hurting yourself, again and again.

Take a deep breath if you need to. If, while you read this, tears start to flow, that's okay too; you can be choking on the possibility of your own pain for a long time before you allow yourself to swallow it whole. We all have hurt, and we all have pain, but ignoring that pain doesn't actually make life better. In fact, it delays the growth and the healing work we *are* capable of. Ultimately, it makes things harder. With that in mind, we're going to do a few things: We'll talk about what pain can look like in life, then we'll talk about shifting our relationship to pain—so we stop thinking about pain as being our enemy and start seeing it as a flashlight that cuts through the dark. Last, we will open ourselves to explore and identify our own pain.

Pain has an uncanny ability to adapt over time, much like cockroaches do. (Yes, cockroaches.) Cockroaches can survive any climate and, just when you think you've exterminated them for good, can come scampering out of a hidden crack in the floor. *Pain, like cockroaches, is a natural part of life.*

The best way for me to talk about pain, and to open the door for you to see your own pain, is to share some of mine with you. Pain has many faces; some of them are dramatic and some are quiet. Some pain looks like everyday life from the outside, while some looks like an epic shitfest. You may not even be able to see pain when it looks you in the eye—it is only in the rearview mirror that you can see its form taking shape.

To understand why I'm writing this book and how the lessons I've learned can be applied to your life, I'm holding my pain up like a mirror for you to look deeply into. Maybe you'll see yourself in some of the things I share. A different shade or color, perhaps, but the root might feel familiar.

PAIN ONE: THE PAIN THAT IS ALL-ENCOMPASSING

There are times when pain is a blanket that covers everything. You can't see where it starts and you can't see where it ends, because everything you experience is in reaction to something else. Whether or not you know it, many things you do in this instance are strategic ways to avoid something that hurts. The following is an example (totally not exaggerated) of my life on a single given day in the year 2015. With the exception of some variables, this is how most of my days passed then.

I wake up in the morning around eight or nine; my shih tzu, Winston, is curled up in the small of my back. I stretch because my body hurts before I've even left the bed. My back is hyperextended, and I'm exhausted even though I was in bed for nine hours, as sleep apnea has kept me from actually getting rest.

I haul myself out of bed, and when I stand up, everything is tight and sore. I walk into the kitchen and open the fridge, even though I'm not hungry or thirsty. I grab a Diet Coke and bring it back to the bedroom and cuddle with Winston. I contemplate my day and then throw on comfy pants, a T-shirt, and some flip-flops and head outside for Winston's "walk."

I live on the second floor of an apartment building and take the elevator rather than walk down the single flight of stairs. Winston is pulling at his leash and I know he wants to run free. I open the door to my building and release the extendable leash as far as it will go; he runs a few feet and yanks the leash at the front. This is the extent of our walk; I groan but he demands that I move halfway down the block to where there's a little scrap of grass he can poop on. There's a patch around the corner he really likes, but I don't have the energy to get there…The extendable leash does its work while he prances in a circle around me and finally does his business.

I stand firmly in place and he eventually gets the message—we're not going any farther. If I'm being honest, I want to go farther but that isn't an option for me; I've been awake for less than half an hour and standing for only ten minutes, but my lower back is already starting to throb.

It's not a sharp pain in my back. It's pressing, like someone with big hands has put my body in a vise and keeps tightening it. My left knee is starting to go numb, so I take careful steps because it could buckle. That's a nightmare I've feared before—being on a walk with Winston when my knee buckles and I drop the leash and he runs off and I can't get up to catch him before he's gone in a whizzing ball of fluff, dodging between cars on the busy Los Angeles streets.

Inside the building, I catch the elevator and I take it one flight up. Part of me is embarrassed I use it to go up less than nineteen stairs, but the other part of me doesn't give a fuck. I'm always aware of how cliché it must seem to be a fat girl relying on the elevator; I know this kind of shaming self-talk is bad for me, but it happens just the same. If someone gets in the elevator with me, I make small talk about throwing out my back, as if to justify my existence. I've even taken the elevator to the fourth floor and then walked down three sets of steps so someone else didn't judge me for the lack of mobility I clearly judge myself for.

I get back to my apartment and bend down to unclip the leash—I have to lean on the wall. Winston scampers over to the water bowl, and I (quite literally) collapse back into bed or onto the sofa. I sit there for a few minutes while I wait for my body to stop screaming.

I know I've got enough in me to do one big thing every day. I could do the laundry. I could wash the dishes. I could clean. I could go to the supermarket. If it's Tuesday, I could go to choir practice. But I can't do all of those things in one day, because my body just doesn't let me. Doing laundry means going up and down to the basement a few times, bending and walking, and then I have to have enough stamina to fold the laundry and put it away. Doing the dishes means I have to stand long enough to rinse and clean everything and then load it in the dishwasher by bending over. The supermarket means I have to go there and then come back and unpack everything. If I go to choir, I have to leave with enough time so I can take the walk from the parking lot on the UCLA campus up the slight hill and stop as I need to, and then enter the building on the lower level and take the elevator up one flight so I can catch my breath and lean against the wall before walking into the choir room. There are four steps up to my seat in the soprano section, and each time I walk up one, I say a silent little prayer that my knees let me do it.

But this particular day is a Monday so there is no choir tonight. In general, there isn't really a great demarcation between my nights and days—they all sort of run into each other. There is a lot I think I WANT to do in my head, but I mostly stay home. Today I sit on the couch with my laptop and answer emails, surf the web, and get on social media for a few hours. In between all of this, I mess around on dating websites and scare up conversations with guys; I run a few of them at once, and I am always swiping and searching for something because none of this ever yields anything.

I've been chatting with one guy who seems decent and he lives nearby; we had a long and honest text exchange a few days back, but I haven't heard anything from him since. I wonder what I did that he lost interest in me, so I ante up and send him a picture of my hands clutching my breasts together with the message "Care to lend a hand?"

He answers back, almost right away, and I know I've got him back on the hook, except now he wants to make the conversation a bit more risqué, which I gather is my fault because I took it there first. I wanted to connect but I really just wanted to talk—which is clearly something I'm not going to get from him now, but I'm always hopeful that someone will come along and prove me wrong.

Here's my (not so) secret confession—I want someone to take me seriously so bad it hurts, but the only way men pay attention to me is if I offer up my sexuality as a bargaining chip. "Well, don't do it, stupid," you probably want to say. And I get it. But the truth is I rarely meet up with anyone. I play with the idea that I might and somehow that helps.

I decide to take a trip to Costco and lean on the cart as I walk through the store. I buy the kind of bullshit everyone buys, meat, vegetables, and a bag of cheddar cheese and caramel popcorn. I haven't eaten anything since breakfast, and I grab a hot dog on the way out. I load everything into the car and fall into my seat; I've been standing for a while. I lift my left leg up by the knee in order to get it into the car, because it's just kind of hanging there tingling. I sit in the car and decompress. I play on my phone and get on social media, text, and do a run-through on the dating apps before heading home.

On the way home I decide to stop off and grab some fast food since I'm already out. At home, I try to decide what from my Costco haul is perishable and needs to be brought upstairs, because I can't make more than one trip and there's no way I'm carrying all of this in a single shot. It's like the Hunger Games of sundries, and I leave behind the bleach wipes, the garbage bags, and a few other items that don't require refrigeration. I carry the rest up in a heavy cardboard box while balancing my fountain soda on top. When I get into my apartment, I throw everything on the dining room table.

I take my dinner over to the couch and I eat it quickly while I watch TV. I'll unpack as little as possible when I'm done; there are fruits and vegetables in the fridge that need to be thrown out, but I don't have the energy. And now Winston needs to go out. Fuck.

I repeat the walking process from earlier today, except I go only as far as the front door of the building. I let the leash do the work, and then pull him back in and get upstairs as fast as I can.

I curse my back a lot. I spend the night doing almost nothing... I watch *Rocky IV* (which is the best one, duh), and I talk to guys. A few weeks ago, this guy I really like, the Sales Guy from San Diego, said we might meet up, but we haven't talked since. I wonder what's wrong with me.

I do the math. I moved away from Brooklyn at twenty-four; I multiply 365 by the number of years since I left home. I take out thirty days each year with the occasional sleepover or company, and it still leaves a shocking number of nights that I've spent alone. There are people out there who sleep with someone every night. They would laugh if they knew I was sitting around counting the nights right now. What is it like to sleep with someone every night? How much different would my life be? Why don't I get that feeling? What's wrong with me? Why did the Sales Guy not text me back? You know what they say—if he's not sleeping with you, he's sleeping with someone else...

My bottom lip starts to quiver, and I feel tears in my eyes. This happens a lot. A moment of complete loneliness and despair passes through my body. Everyone has their life and I have a dog. I am unlovable. I am untouchable. I am fuckable and that's all. If something happened tonight, who would find me? How would someone know I was dead? Would anyone miss me? Besides my mom—I'm sorry, but you don't count here, Mom. I start to wail-cry and it's good that my part-time roomie isn't around to hear. I grab Winston and, bless his pliable little heart, he lets me drag him into my arms and cry into his fur as I thank him out loud. I'm scared this is it. I'm scared this is all there will ever be. I'm so fucking scared...

I'm hungry.

I get out of the bed and walk into the kitchen in my underwear and nothing else. I go straight for the caramel and cheddar cheese popcorn and I pour a bowl and eat it standing up in the kitchen. I put two frozen hamburger patties in a pan to cook and put two English muffins in the toaster and pour a second bowl of popcorn while I'm waiting. I put the TV on and watch reruns of *Columbo* on Netflix...then bowl three. The hamburgers are done, so I put them on the English muffins and put both on a plate and fill bowl four with the popcorn and go into the bedroom to eat everything in bed while I finish the Netflix show. I'm not sure I even taste any of it as I eat, but I'm eating and I'm filling myself and I'm distracted and I'm not texting and I'm not crying...

I let Winston lick the plate. I put the plate on the table next to me. And I go to sleep.

I share this example for you to get a sense of my stressor + coping mechanism pattern. During this day you can see a bunch of times where I was uncomfortable—physically or emotionally—and, in an effort to not feel the pain, I used strategies to self-soothe, both emotionally and physically. Unfortunately, in most of these cases, the things I did to dampen the hurt feelings would only delay the pain for another day or, in some instances, create more pain. There were so many chances I had to lean into my raw feelings...Instead, I covered them up.

When you start to think about your own pain, you have an opportunity to see where in life you are seeking to numb out and the ways that you do it. It is normal to want to self-soothe and minimize our pain, but if the way we do it serves as a crutch and not a "tool for navigation," our coping mechanisms may be harmful to our well-being. When we lean on maladaptive coping mechanisms so much that they become second nature, these behaviors can become compulsive and ultimately cause more harm than good.

DIG DEEPER:
Recognize Your Pain

This exercise will help you look at everyday experiences to identify what in those experiences could be a sign, symptom, or result of pain. This will also help you see possible "stressor + coping mechanism" patterns in your life. First, we'll use my life as an example. Then you'll turn the lens toward yourself to look objectively at what your patterns may be.

Revisit my narrative above and, in your journal, answer the following questions:

- What are some common themes you noticed in this day in my life?
- What feelings did it seem I was trying to avoid?
- What tools was I using to self-soothe and cope?
- Did it seem as if the tools I used to feel better actually worked?
- How did it appear to make me feel when I used those tools?
- Did you see me as being an active participant in creating my pain or someone who was feeling pain because of what others had done to her?

Now, let's think about you. How has life been for you in the past month? Think about how you have spent your time. Have there been times where you have felt stressed, uneasy, unhappy, any other hard emotion?

If you immediately have a yes answer, ask yourself what you did in response to these feelings the moment you felt them. Was it something you do a lot, or did it just happen once? Did doing this make you feel a "release" or ease the hard feelings?

If you can't identify stressors in your life, but you still felt a sense of general discontent, ask yourself if you have done any of the following recently:

- Used a substance—like alcohol or drugs or food—not for casual enjoyment and appreciation, but because it "made things feel better."
- Shut down to avoid feelings.
- Daydreamed or escaped into your own thoughts because it was more pleasant than the present moment.
- Self-harmed, like picking your hair or skin, cutting, or binge eating.

- Did stuff people you love might consider "risky" actions or behavior.
- Self-blamed for everything possible.

These are all examples of maladaptive and unhealthy coping techniques.[2] If you are doing any of these things, there's a good chance that something is stressing you out or painful to you, even if you aren't able to acknowledge it! Research suggests there are three main reasons that people turn to maladaptive coping mechanisms—overwhelming stress, poor treatment, or emotional invalidation.[3] Are you currently feeling any of these things?

The purpose of this exercise is not to get you to "fix" anything. It's simply to open your eyes to what may be hurting you right now.

PAIN TWO: THE PAIN THAT DOESN'T ALWAYS LOOK LIKE PAIN

Sometimes, pain is hardly noticeable—not to yourself in the moment or to others looking in from the outside. You may see your patterns as random, unconnected bad habits. Friends and loved ones may notice things that seem out of the ordinary but write your behaviors off as harmless quirks. But if you were to read carefully between the lines, pain is often the root cause of your actions. This is especially possible when you stack your patterns and habits on top of one another. On their own they may appear benign—but when you look at them together, it cannot be denied that something is...*off*.

These are some of the things that flew under my radar for years, but looking back, I can see how disordered these behaviors were:

- Bags of scented candles sitting in the trunk of my car, totally melted from the hot Las Vegas sun.
- Drawers stuffed full of things I can't identify.
- Discarded clothes still bearing tags.
- Burger King bags speckled with oily spots covering the nightstand, spilling onto the floor like a crawling ivy plant.
- Food wrappers cluttering the passenger seat of the car, leaving no room for anyone to sit.

- Laundry, sitting undone in a pile and eventually lost, thrown out, or simply replaced with brand-new garments.
- A single pistachio-green Christian Louboutin slingback with a lost mate probably accidentally thrown away.
- A $900 pale aqua Marc Jacobs purse, splotched with blue pen ink, basically unused.
- Cuticles picked till they are bloody.
- Dirty dishes "hidden" in the freezer and cabinet.
- Bugs hovering around kitchen trash bags that have sat unattended for weeks.
- Bills unopened, stuffed into drawers.
- Defaulted credit cards.
- A drive-through run at six in the morning on the way home from a night out, food eaten in bed, followed by an hour of sleep, a shower and dress, and another drive-through run on the way to work.

What I didn't know then but know now is that none of these actions by themselves might be an alert of major issues; for example, plenty of young people mismanage their money, live in a messy apartment, or treat their belongings poorly. But, when considered cumulatively, each helps to tell the story of a person who is anxious, insecure, living in denial, and uninterested in showing themselves respect.

We assume pain will announce itself with flashing lights, but sometimes it's insidious. Like carbon monoxide, it has no smell or taste, and you don't know it's killing you till you start to choke and vomit. This is why it's important to know that pain can hide in plain sight.

PAIN THREE: THE PAIN WHEN YOU KNOW WHAT YOU'RE DOING IS WRONG BUT YOU DO IT ANYWAY

There are times when you don't know. There are times when you do know. And then there are times that you *know* you are wrong, but you don't care, and you do things anyway because doing *something* is the *only thing* that drowns out the hurt.

I was twenty-six years old and sitting in my bathtub. I was crying. Earlier that evening, a little girl had padded down a flight of steps and caught me making out with her father. "Daddy, what's going on?" she asked.

I don't blame her for being confused. Her dad had a girlfriend—who took the little girl to Disney World—and I wasn't her. What was I doing at her house?

I was trying to make something work. Wiggling my foot into a tiny crack of an open door I shouldn't have been walking through in the first place. I'd met Elvis on a dating website, where he was actively looking for a girlfriend. We'd chatted for a bit, and it was only when we talked about meeting up that he finally told me he already had a girlfriend.

But she didn't understand him . . . And he was *so unhappy* . . . So, I kept talking to him.

He was constantly listing all the things wrong with their relationship like it was an invitation for me to improve upon it, and I listened. I didn't understand why, if he was so unhappy, he didn't just break up with her. I wasn't stupid; I knew it wasn't cool to talk to a guy who was already in a relationship, but I did it anyway.

Whatever she was, I knew I could be the opposite. *I understood.* If he gave me the chance—which I could tell he totally was going to do—I could be better than she was. Making things work was my superpower. Maybe "something" could turn into something great, right?

Instead of giving me an invitation for a proper date, he invited me over to his house one night. I could come over after his daughter had gone to bed, but we had to be quiet. I don't know where his girlfriend was or what she was doing that night, because I didn't want to know. Getting dressed, I focused on my victory. I felt high, but it didn't feel exciting. It felt unauthorized.

I took my shoes off and settled onto the couch. I posed. I made my point. I was delicious. I was *everything* . . . We ended up kissing a little, which turned into kissing a lot, which might have turned into even more, but that's when her little voice called out, "Daddy, what's going on?" I froze. I was sitting on his lap with my back facing the staircase. I buried my face in his shoulder and closed my eyes. "Who is that?" she asked.

The space between question and answer felt like forever. I thought I heard him mutter a "Fuck" under his breath.

"It's nobody, sweetie," he said. "Daddy's friend is sad, and he's making her feel better." There was calm panic in his voice; I think I stopped breathing. "Go back to bed."

I waited while she padded back up the carpeted steps and then until I heard the bedroom door close. He exhaled, loud. Avoiding all eye contact, I stood up, grabbed my bag, and silently walked out the front door.

I made it home and into the bathroom before the tears came. He'd said I was "*nobody*" . . .

I hadn't won anything. It was all wrong. I was all wrong. That's what I got. Who does that? What kind of person was I?

An ember of awareness simmered inside me and I didn't like the burn.

It's been said that desire is your brain's way of telling you that you're missing something in life.

Desire is Machiavellian. Without a mindful system of checks and balances in place, desire plays whack-a-mole with your judgment. What you think you want pops up in one hole and disappears just as you move to smash it. When desire is a mask for pain, it's an illusion. But it feels so good. The string of names entered into my phone reads like this:

"Mike POF, Mike J.Date, Mike OK Cupid" because there was always more than one Mike from more than one website because I was on them all.

The last names that I can't remember.

The last names that I never asked for.

The first names I may have known at one point.

The first names I never remembered to begin with.

The threesomes that went bad, with partners who got caught in the middle, and the feelings I didn't care about sparing because I got what I needed to feel like the victor.

The Older Guy I created an indoor picnic for in my living room to celebrate his birthday, and made Ina Garten's potato-fennel gratin for, grating till my hands smelled like Gruyère cheese, who never called again after that night.

The Bell Hop.

The Sensitive Man who cried and said my dog was high maintenance.

Clubfoot Guy.

The Magnum.

The Nice Jewish Boy with the great hair.

The Chef.

The Pop Singer's Cousin.

The Lumberjack.

Massage Therapist Steve.

The Cowboy Viking who was big and blond, with whom I spent so much time that his son once asked, "Why don't you like my dad? He's so happy with you and I really like hanging out with you," because his thirteen-year-old brain couldn't imagine why we weren't together except that I must have not wanted his dad. *If only he really knew I was there, wanting him and waiting as he came in and out of my life before falling for someone else who must have been everything I was not and more.*

There were times I knew I was younger and more fun than their girlfriends could ever be, and I made sure they knew it.

There was the fear of loneliness. The fear of what I was not. The fear of unknowing. The fear of not possessing. All of which I could pretend never existed if I could persuade whoever it was to acknowledge me.

All the things I couldn't remember doing that I ignored. The bargaining with myself. The times I feigned indifference and told myself it didn't matter. *It did.* All of the times I made someone's shortcomings my responsibility. *I adapted, and in the process, I abandoned myself, time and time again.*

Yeah, that was pain. All of it.

THE PAIN OF THE FROG IN BOILING WATER

There's an urban myth you've probably heard. It suggests that if you take a frog and throw it into a pot of boiling water, it's going to immediately jump out to save its life. But if you put the frog in a pot of cool water and turn the temperature up slowly, it will fail to notice the rising heat—its body temperature will rise along with the water temperature—so by the time the frog realizes the water is boiling, it's too late and it dies. The frog literally sits in a pot of pain and becomes so used to it that its biological survival mechanisms fail to protect it.

Except this isn't true. While scientists haven't thrown a frog in boiling water for shits and giggles (it would scald and die, they've said), they have tested to see what happens if a frog gets placed in slowly warming water. The result? A short 4.2 seconds into rising temperature, that amphibious little creature bolted out of the pot, leaping twenty-four centimeters of "Fuck this shit" into the air to save its life.[4]

When I was in my twenties and very blond and very tan, at a pool party dangling my legs into the crystal clear water, I was having a conversation with someone I thought was my friend about random life-related topics, including his recent weight loss, when he sneered at me and said, "You can't tell me you're really happy?" and I wanted to throat-punch him for implying that my confidence and my happiness were all a lie. Of course I was happy! I had a great life, had done some cool jobs, had left my home in NYC and moved to Las Vegas and had lots of sex (some of which was with men who had an ass you could crack a walnut on), and that was all awesome, right? Sure, I was always tying myself in knots trying to get some guy to take me seriously. Sure, I was always on edge trying to find out what other people were doing so I could come along, because nobody ever remembered to invite me, but I just knew they meant to so I showed up anyway. Sure, my bank account was overdrawn (again), but that was what overdraft protection was for, wasn't it? And when I went to the gynecologist and weighed in, the scale said I was

295 pounds, and that seemed like a lot but my knees didn't bother me, so it wasn't a big deal that I'd gained so much weight in the last year, right?

There was such a state of chaos in the seemingly surface-level things of my life that it drowned out the real baseline of unhappiness and perpetual discomfort I felt underneath. I couldn't remember a time that I wasn't longing for something, scrambling for another thing, or making excuses—so how could I ever imagine life was supposed to be any other way? And, if I didn't feel overtly happy, at least I thought I wasn't UNhappy, so that was good, right?

Wrong.

I didn't feel happy. I didn't feel unhappy. In retrospect, I spent so much energy *getting by* that I wasn't present enough to feel in general. This is how I spent several decades of my life, experiencing but not actually feeling. Avoiding. Responding. Reacting. Doing what I needed to do to survive.

In 2015, both my mother and my father ended up in two separate hospitals for two different reasons. My dad, who had been undergoing cancer treatment, had fallen down the stairs backward. My mother had a totally unexpected heart episode; doctors told her she was lucky to have survived. I realized that I couldn't walk a single city block from the parking garage to my mother's hospital bed without stopping in pain again and again.

Staring at my mother hooked up to tubes and machines, I thought, *Maybe you're not doing as great as you think you are, Sarah*. In that moment I realized my life was one big loop playing out in circles, like in the movie *Groundhog Day*; I wasn't evolving, growing, or experiencing the things I really dreamed about. I knew I was going to die—I had no idea when, but the idea of death became really real really fast. Along with that came one big, icky, messy truth: If I never did anything different, this was all my life would ever be. I would age, things would happen around me, and I would stay exactly where I was... and that scared the absolute shit out of me.

My life was working perfectly until I realized it wasn't working, and I could no longer pretend not to see how much my weight, my lack of real love, and my shortage of joy was actually making me miserable.

The truth is, sometimes you just get sick and tired of how things are. The fear of things staying the same begins to weigh more than the fear of moving forward into an unknown. And that's when I became that frog, leaping out of the pot in order to save my life. *Fuck this shit . . .*

CREATING A KINDER RELATIONSHIP WITH PAIN

Pain is a natural part of life, yet, as humans, we hate it. For the most part, we will do anything we can to avoid it. However, by paying attention to our pain—by observing it objectively—we can see where our lives are out of alignment. When we make choices that go against our greater good, pain gives us clues and shows us where we are stuck. In order for it to do this, we can't be blind to pain. We must acknowledge it.

Pain as a Flashlight

About a year into my Soul Archaeology, I began to see that in my greater attempt to circumvent feelings like rejection, isolation, and feeling invisible, I created more hurt for myself in the long run. Had I allowed myself to feel hurt, I might have been able to see myself with more clarity and I might have been able to let that pain teach me something. It could have shown me WHERE I was stuck so I could focus my time and energy on what I'd been doing.

For example:

Action:	In the moment . . .	But later . . .	The flashlight would have illuminated . . .
I maxed out credit cards buying random shit and fancy shoes and handbags I couldn't afford.	It was exciting and gratifying; I could be "like other people" and buy cool designer-brand stuff.	I scrambled for money and put myself in debt. I avoided bills, which went into collections, and I was in a constant state of anxiety waiting for the bottom to fall out from under me.	That I really needed to focus on my self-worth and identity so I could see MYSELF as the source of acceptance and not other people.

Action:	In the moment...	But later...	The flashlight would have illuminated...
I continually entered into casual, sex-based relationships with guys.	It made me feel valuable and seen and gave me instant gratification that I was desirable and worthy. It kept me from feeling lonely.	I felt crappy. I would try to get the men to take me seriously outside of the bedroom. I was obsessed with fighting to prove my value to guys who weren't interested in caring about me.	How I presented myself and engaged with men set the tone for my relationships. If I wanted to find what I truly desired—healthy intimacy—I would have to approach relationships differently.
I invited myself into social circles, but I didn't bother to see if my values were aligned with those in the circles, because I had no values for myself, just a desire to fit in and be deemed acceptable by other people.	It was cool to be included where the "cool" people were.	I was never sure if I really fit in. They rarely returned my calls or proactively invited me to gatherings and often did things socially that I didn't align with, like snorting cocaine in the bathrooms of Vegas nightclubs.	That I was hanging out with people who didn't share the same values and interests as me; I had an opportunity to find friends who energetically matched me and valued me. I didn't have to change my identity to get people to like me. I could have focused on MY uniqueness vs. being liked.

Back then, I paid more attention to covering up what hurt than to the possibility of using the hurt as a guidebook. I was caught up in a cycle of self-abandonment, and because it all felt "normal" to me, I didn't perceive any of it as pain. I lived moment to moment, doing things that made my life feel better right then and there. And I did this without any self-awareness that there was a big discrepancy between how I perceived my life and what was actually true.

When the discrepancy became clear—when I started to see the gap between how I had perceived my life and how it actually was—I had a choice: to freak the fuck out, or to lean in. I chose the latter and learned two key things about how to navigate my pain with more ease.

Stand in the Eye of the Storm

There's a scene in the 1996 Jan de Bont classic film, *Twister,* when the protagonists—Helen Hunt and an epic Bill Paxton—are facing off against a huge tornado from the front seat of a Dodge Ram. Barreling down a rural road, the pair start to come in contact with the debris a large tornado is uprooting in its path. Trees. Dirt. A large gas truck. And . . . cows. *Close-up of the poor cow, who has no fucking idea what's happening, as it rips past the truck.*

"Cow . . . ," Hunt says dryly. "Another cow," she continues, as a second cow circles the vehicle with a despondent *moo.*

"Actually," Paxton corrects, "I think that was the same one."

Twister illustrated the damage that occurs in the swirl of a tornado, but also the extreme calm inside its eye. While cows get tossed about in the violent core that rotates around the eye, it's possible to stand in the center and be totally safe while witnessing the pain that would surely consume you if you got too close.

Pain is like a tornado. You can let it sweep you up or you can decide to stand in the eye of the twister and observe it, knowing you are safe where you stand. It doesn't matter whether it's cows being flung or one-night stands and disordered eating. You can observe the storm without stepping into its path—without letting the shame and self-judgment eat you alive. Understanding this gave me the ability to feel emotions without being overwhelmed by them.

In order to observe the storm without stepping into its path, I started to say this to myself when confronted with something difficult I'd done in my past: *I have done this. This is my pain. This was the best I could do in that moment. What I did in the past does not have to be what I do in the future. I see it, I acknowledge it, and I have faith that in the future I will make a different choice.*

DIG DEEPER
INTO YOUR DEBRIS

Visualize if you will that you are in the center of your own storm, and the painful debris of your past and present starts to fly by. Can you identify what the debris is? What is the vice? The coping mechanism? Ask yourself, *What are the "cows" of pain I can see in the storm in front of my eyes?* If you had to label what was flying around, could you identify your pain? What are the "things" you can see when you reflect upon what hurts you right now or has hurt you in the past?

For an extra bit of fun, you can visit my website at SarahSapora.com/Soul for a downloadable printout of Twister-style cows you can label and write on to help you visualize and deconstruct your patterns!

Realize Your Pain Isn't Uniquely Yours

I'd always assumed that I was the only one feeling the feelings I felt. If this was true, then the pain really was about my shortcomings and my flaws. It was mine to carry alone, which made it all the heavier.

One day in 2018 I was looking at my boobs. *Seriously.* I had lost a significant amount of weight by then, and I happened to be looking down at my chest and my eyes caught a glimpse of the crepe wrinkle of my boob skin. I picked my left boob up in my hands, feeling shame and anger, while tears sprouted because, in my head, I was sure my tits looked like something out of the classic horror film *House of Wax*. But then I had a realization—breasts have been getting wrinkly for hundreds of thousands of years, and as long as humans survive on this planet, they will be getting wrinkly for hundreds of thousands of years more. My wrinkly breasts were not that unique, and neither were the crappy feelings I felt about them. Surely other women in history have felt unhappy with their wrinkling boobies, right?

Somehow, accepting that wrinkly breasts were a part of human existence made it hurt less. In that moment, I stopped owning the weight of my own pain. My pain was no longer mine, but a recognition of a common, shared human experience that was, quite literally, a part of life, because pain is a part of life.

I was not the first person in life to experience heartache. To be cheated on. To have a one-night stand. To make impulsive decisions. To numb myself out. I wouldn't be the last. The pain I was feeling was literally being felt by millions of people all over the world at any given time—it wasn't mine; it was OURS. It helped to tell myself this: I am not the first person to feel this feeling and I am not the last. This is a

HUMAN feeling, not only MY feeling. I can feel this feeling without carrying its weight.

The less I felt my pain was personal to me, the easier it became for me to look at it objectively. The more objective I could be when looking at it, the more I understood myself and the freer I felt. I still experienced pain, but pain didn't own me.

DIG SITE: THE DIFFERENCE BETWEEN DISCOMFORT AND DANGER

This must be said because your job is always to advocate for your mental and physical health above all things. Some pain is a sign of danger, and some is not. When you are doing Soul Archaeology and spending time reflecting and looking at yourself, it's important to know the difference between the two so you can lean into the things that are only *uncomfortable* and, if needed, find a qualified and licensed professional who can help you explore the dangerous stuff more safely.

Psychoanalysts explain that psychic pain is, among other things, the recognition that there is a discrepancy between how we perceive ourselves in relation to others, and how we are really existing in relation to others. It is the "loss" of what we feel is real that is emotional pain itself.[5] Pain is a stressor.

When we experience a stressor of some kind, it activates our sympathetic nervous system. This autonomic reflex system is hardwired to keep us safe from things that serve as an immediate and intense threat to us. It is what makes us avoid driving headfirst into a tornado full of sharks, run away from a burning car, or avoid walking down a dimly lit alleyway while being followed way too closely by a person wearing a ski mask and muttering sexual obscenities at you.

Sometimes, though, our nervous system is activated by something that feels threatening but isn't—it could be something that's just unpleasant. Like talking politics with a family member who has opposite beliefs, disagreeing with someone online, or having a clash with a former partner who took advantage of you. These things can be truly uncomfortable and even make you incredibly angry or sad, but unlike being chased by a raging, hungry predator, they are unlikely to pose an immediate danger to your actual life.

Something that is uncomfortable is not necessarily dangerous, so our job becomes understanding the difference between the two. It's important to note that, based on our personal history and our mental health, different things may be dangerous for some people and not others. In short, when you do Soul Archaeology, it's important to differentiate between what is discomfort and what is danger, so you know where to "dig deeper" and where to step back or call in reinforcements.

(ACTUALLY, LIKE, REALLY) STARTING WHERE IT HURTS

This step is about OBSERVATION and not ACTION. It is about seeing the things that have hurt you in the past, or are hurting you right now, and examining them. This layer of our Soul Archaeology asks us to look at ourselves as honestly as we can at this given moment. Why do we start with this, before doing anything else? Two reasons:

1. If you bought this book, something is hurting you or feels off in your life. We want to honor that and give it some attention so it doesn't have to take up precious real estate in your heart and mind.
2. Sometimes we don't know what we want in life, but we definitely know what we don't want. That's great information to work with.

Many times, the simplest questions are the most powerful. In order to get clear about what is hurting you in your life right now, we'll go back to three simple questions (revisit the questions on page 75 and come back here to continue).

Take some time to answer each. If you already did those, or if you still don't want to, and you are sitting in a whole messy pile of uncomfortable emotions right now, let's just do some observation. After you address those questions in your journal, answer the following:

- What do you feel right now?
- Is there a specific scenario or instance that is running in your mind?
- What is "screaming" inside your head that you cannot ignore?

As you look at your stuff, your inclination may be to clean up immediately. I don't want you to do that. I want you to lean into it. As long as what you are experiencing is discomfort and not real danger, then running away is a bad idea. Just hang out here for a few minutes. Cry if it feels right. Sit on your hands to keep yourself from reaching for your cell phone or a remote control. *Don't tap out; just be.*

It is essential that you remember you are totally okay right now.

Discomfort is okay, and strength is knowing that you can experience discomfort and still be present and here and you can still be you. You can stand on the beach while the waves ebb in and out—your feet may sink a little in the sand, but you'll still be standing.

SURVEYING THE SITE:
WHAT WE DUG UP IN THIS CHAPTER

The more you try to ignore pain, the heavier it gets. Pain doesn't go away, but the role pain plays in your life can get smaller and smaller. It's like one of those plastic water snakes you might have played with as a kid; you can let it wiggle and slide through your hands, and you can displace the water from side to side, but if you squish it, the plastic will expand to compensate for the pressure because the water needs to go *somewhere*. In the same way, pain from one area of your life will bleed into other areas.

It's not about "fixing" what hurts you, because *pain just is*. It *is* about getting better at listening to your pain and using it as a messenger to show you where in life you are stuck, or where you need to go in order to return to a more self-loving place. For example, not all pain results in a coping mechanism (and not all coping mechanisms are bad!), but all coping mechanisms are born from a desire to avoid some degree of pain. And when you can identify and observe coping mechanisms as you are using them, it can help you lift the lid and uncover what is really beneath the surface.

You can push pain down for a long time—ignore it, drown it out, or dress it up and make it look pretty—but eventually, it's going to have its moment in the spotlight. The longer it sits there claiming real estate in your heart, the more powerful it grows.

Seeing what hurts you is hard. It's especially hard when you realize that you are perpetuating your own pain or creating it with your own actions. The things that have hurt you in life are not your fault; I'm not blaming you for the things you have done. What I am saying is that I know nobody *in my life* can hurt me more than I have subconsciously hurt myself again and again. If you feel that way too, I want you to know you are not alone.

You cannot outrun what hurts you; I'm sorry. But eventually you will feel ready to move forward. When this happens, you want to do something that will help the feelings to FLOW THROUGH you.

Open the window and let in some fresh air. Get outside and take a walk. Move your body. Masturbate. Soak in a bubble bath. Pray. Play some music. Hug a pet. Color or draw.

Notice I didn't suggest you have a drink or do drugs or eat? Or gamble or play video games? You are allowed to self-soothe, of course, but there is a difference between doing that and numbing out.

When you are done, my suggestion is you go to bed and close your eyes and sleep a good, deep sleep, and wake up for another day tomorrow.

We've given a lot of attention to seeing the things we don't want to see in this chapter. Next, we'll step into owning what we *do* want to see.

Chapter 6

STEP TWO: PUT A STAKE IN YOUR FEELINGS AND CLAIM THEM

The Chapter Where You Decide How You Want to Feel

My alarm goes off at 5:30 in the morning, playing soft tones to wake me; I've learned I need to put my phone away from my bed when it's time to sleep, so I got an actual alarm clock. I'm already half-awake because my body wakes up naturally around this time. In bed, I can stretch deeply before getting out and pulling up the sheet and blankets (I make the bed no matter what, every day, because it makes my room look put together and the order helps me feel calmer).

In the kitchen I bump into Man Candy, and we share a smooshy hug. We have separate rooms and sometimes we sleep together, sometimes apart—we both like personal space and value sleeping well, and honestly, we just sleep better apart. I make my iced coffee—no sugar with some almond milk—and hold off on breakfast because my body doesn't like eating first thing in the morning and I have a Pilates class in an hour, and I prefer to eat after.

In my room, I grab leggings and a top; getting dressed is easy because the clothes in my drawers are folded—once a month when my drawers get messy, I take things out and fold them again so I can more easily keep track of what I own so I stress less getting dressed. I do Pilates three times a week because my body deserves love and attention. I want to add more activity to my day—I'd like to begin strength training again—but with the extra weight I gained from sheltering in place during the COVID pandemic, I want to make sure I'm doing activity that is safe for my joints. I love Pilates; it helps me quiet down and connect to my body and helps me get stronger—I have to listen to myself and constantly adjust and it feels meditative to me.

At home, I scoop a big glob of Greek yogurt into a bowl and top it with a spoon of homemade granola—I use a measuring cup because granola is one of those things I can overeat without thinking and I want to be mindful of how much I consume. I enjoy the morning sun while I have breakfast in the quiet. During the day I will work, do laundry, stop to defrost some flank steak, eat an orange, eat some turkey breast, have a can of Diet Coke, work more, put another load of laundry in, do more work, and fold the laundry and put it away.

I do some window-shopping online and make a mental note to purchase something when it goes on sale. I pay my bills early because the money is in my bank account and I want to make sure it's done and off my plate. I investigate a cabin rental for a month in Montana since I've made a promise to myself to leave Las Vegas regularly and get out and see the sky and country. I spend a little time thinking about the meal I'm cooking for Passover Seder, which I've never made before but felt called to do so this year. Before I get more work done, I mix olive oil, garlic, and some spices and let the flank steak marinate for a few hours.

When I finish with work later, I take some quiet time to cuddle with Eliza (my 105-pound American bulldog) without television on because it helps me transition from "work mode" into "me mode." Man Candy comes home and we make dinner together; we sit at an actual dining room table and play music quietly and talk while we eat. I remind him that we're doing Speaking Snapple on Sunday, and I remind myself I want to talk about something that's important to me when we do; it's not a fun topic and it'll be a sticky conversation, but it needs to come up and it's been on my mind. I eat a scrumptious homemade peanut butter cookie for dessert.

After dinner we do the dishes so they don't sit in the sink overnight. Then we sit and watch television, and I crochet some rows of a large blanket I've been working on. Somewhere around nine, I make myself a cup of Sleepytime Extra tea because I sometimes need some help falling asleep and, if I stay awake anxious in bed, I am more likely to toss and turn, watch television, or get a snack for comfort.

While I am lying in bed with my eyes closed, I dance in my head—ballet. I go through the five positions and imagine my limbs and fingers extending gracefully. I dance to *Swan Lake* and think about fluttering feet doing entrechat jumps. Somehow this is comforting to me, like a hug or the feeling of my mother patting my back in small circles with her soft hands. Eventually, I fall asleep.

My life isn't fancy—it doesn't make for great videos or social media content. It feels pretty peaceful; even though I have a *lot* of big stuff going on, I don't feel chaotic. My life is mine, and I like how unfussy it feels. For the first time in my life, I don't feel like I'm fighting anything, especially myself. I don't feel like I have to prove anything to anyone. And while, yes, I want to be successful and I want to do well in life . . . I don't feel an underlying hum of noise in the back of my head at all times. I used to feel that if you were to scratch the surface to get under the calm I tried to maintain, a confetti of innards and guts would explode out. *Everything that happened felt like it happened to me. Now . . . it just happens.*

My life is no longer one big reaction to other people. Do I still care about what other people think? Of course! I always will. But these days, I am the nucleus of my own identity. Because of this, I know my source of value and strength sits firmly in me. For example:

- *If this book went away, I would still be a writer . . .*
- *If I stopped doing kinky, fun things with my partner, I'd still be a kinky and fun person . . .*
- *If nobody was there to laugh at my jokes, I'd still be silly and "adorkable" on my own.*
- *If my social media went away overnight, and I no longer had a platform with which to speak to people, I would still be a teacher at heart.*
- *If Man Candy and I split up, I would still be a well of love.*

It wasn't always this way for me—I didn't always know who I was. When I woke up in a hotel room on the morning of my forty-first birthday, I was ripe with the awareness that I felt totally untethered. After three years straight of Soul Archaeology, one epic breakup of a relationship that crumbled from the inside out and forged me into iron, and a shit-ton of realizations about my dad, my self-worth, and my choices—I saw one thing loud and clear...I had no idea who I was.

Everything I knew about myself was evidentiary. It was based on feedback I received from other people about who I was and what I was worth—none of it came from ME. This could have scared the shit out of me or made me sad thinking about "lost" years. Instead, it lit me up because it meant there was possibility. There was space for me to LEARN myself and decide WHO I was. There was room for me to put a stake in the ground and claim myself on my own terms. There was *life*.

Every single thing I have practiced since that time has been in service of getting to know myself. Now, my life flows. Is it easy? No. Perfect? No. Fuck all of that. But I flow in the direction of my life and I feel centering calm from the inside out.

In this chapter we're going to put that stake in the ground and help you to CLAIM who you are on YOUR terms. We're going to help you start the journey to own your experiences in life for YOU.

RECLAIMING YOUR SELF

My bet is that you've kept yourself small by fitting yourself into boxes and roles that were determined for you by someone else. Or else you've shaped the idea of who you are...based on evidence you've collected from other people. That doesn't sound like you...That sounds like You According to Everyone Else. Now, stack on to that the reality that most people in your life are doing the exact same thing—living their lives as one big reaction to the shit that life throws their way—and we can surmise one crappy but incredibly powerful thought: That this is how you end up living life on someone else's terms.

When you cobble together your identity as it relates to other people who are, in turn, cobbling their identities based on people in their lives, you're not actually YOU. You are You in Response to Other People. That is a surefire way to go through your life constantly chasing things you think will make you happy but always leave you cold, because every hope you grasp at is just a Band-Aid covering a cut someone else gave you.

I want you to know who YOU are, because the greatest gift you can give yourself is the ability to live a life based on your values and your own North Star (this doesn't mean you won't care about other people and consider them; it simply means you take other people's weight off your ankles so you can dance unencumbered).

When you are living life according to your own values, you will no longer feel at odds with yourself. You will swim with the current, not against it. In doing this, you'll feel more ease, more clarity, and a fuck-ton less anxiety. You will feel more at home in your own life than you do right now.

IN ACTION: CHLOE IS LUMINOUS

Twenty women are sitting around a U-shaped table in a meeting room at a beachside resort in the Dominican Republic. We are at my LIFE-LOVE Vatreat. Most of the women are wearing bathing suits—which might not seem unusual given the destination, but the average member of this group is a larger plus-size woman around the age of forty-two. This is NOT a population that likes "showing skin," so padding around bare-foot, wrapped in diaphanous cover-ups, means something serious—these women feel comfortable and free, feelings they don't embody easily in their daily lives.

Their heads are down, and their fingers move swiftly over loose-leaf notebook pages as they write. Coldplay's "Magic" is playing softly over the speaker.

"Okay, guys," I say, turning the volume down. "Anyone want to share their 'feeling' word and freewrite with us?" For a split second, there are crickets as the room goes quiet, and then one hand shoots up.

"Me! I'll go," Chloe says, her blond hair bobbing in its ponytail.

I'm a bit shocked. This is Chloe, who appears to live in a shell most of the time. Chloe, who speaks in a quiet, Southern-accented voice. Chloe, who sent me no less than eight emails asking questions for which answers could easily be found online . . . And here she was. First. Bright smile. Hand shooting up in the air. Go on, *girl; get it,* I think. "What's your word?" I ask.

I asked the participants to identify a word describing the feeling they selected from a big, long list of adjectives—it will serve as the basis for the Self-Love To-Do List they will be working on later this week.

"Luminous," Chloe says, without an ounce of hesitancy.

I ask her to read aloud her "three-minute freewrite" for us, the exercise the group just completed, where they riff and let their minds wander on what life would actually FEEL like if they lived their words.

A smile washes over Chloe's face and she speaks: "When I feel Luminous I will feel light. I feel like a shining light. I feel open to be myself. I feel loud and messy. I feel happy. I take up as much space as I want. I am free. I can laugh and not take myself seriously. I am not too much, I am just the right amount of me." Chloe looks up from her paper and makes direct eye contact with me. She is proud. She is present. She has arrived.

ONE ARROW, ONE BULL'S-EYE, ONE "CHANCE" FOR HAPPINESS . . . *NO, THANKS*

Raise your hand if you have ever wanted something SO BAD it hurt—you chased it; you dreamed of it; you fixated on it. It would solve everything if you could just have that one specific thing. It would make you feel whole and perfect. And you got it.

Raise your hand if that magic solution did not, in fact, make everything in your life better. Maybe you didn't accomplish what you felt you needed, which only added to the shame and the pile of shit you felt you were under . . . Maybe you did get whatever that magic solution was, but the solution was different than what you imagined it would be . . . Maybe you "got it" and it was everything you wanted it to be . . . but STILL you didn't feel whole.

There are a few reasons for this. Life itself is not about arriving at a specific destination. Life is more like a road we travel and experience with stops along the way, and we create meaning in our lives based on how we experience the journeying process. Philosophers, therapists, religious teachers, and teachers of all kinds know this to be true and have taught this for thousands of years. Happiness is not a target you hit. Rather, it's a feeling that blossoms from inside you as you work to create the "states of being" you want to experience in your life. In other words, you don't LAND on the feeling of happiness; you *bring it to life* by doing things that will actually make you happy.

In 1991, the glorious cinematic achievement *Robin Hood: Prince of Thieves* hit movie screens. One iconic scene from the movie involves Robin Hood (as played by Kevin Costner, with majestic flowing locks) firing a flaming arrow into an executioner about to chop off the head of Will Scarlet (portrayed by Christian Slater). Of course, Kevin's arrow hit exactly where it needed to, thanks to Hollywood magic, but what if that one arrow had missed? *Peace out, Christian Slater.* But let's just say, instead of that *one* Kevin Costner firing *one* arrow, you had *multiple* Kevins firing a bunch of different arrows all traveling different paths with the same action in mind—to free Christian. There is no way that at least one of them wouldn't land somewhere helpful and, no matter how you painted it, Christian Slater would live to see another day!

The same thing applies for your goals. If you identify only one thing that will make you happy in life, ONE path with ONE result—you are setting yourself up to either succeed or fail. However, if you identify the direction you want to go but fire a whole bunch of arrows, you're bound to make contact with joy in some way.

Hard-and-fast goals can strangle the creative ways in which life might work for us. They cause us to focus on the result of the goal and not the Soul Archaeology of uncovering US. If we believe that only one thing can make us happy, we close ourselves off to the possibility of all the beautiful and interesting ways that life can create happiness for us.

CHASING ONE GOAL AS A WAY TO CREATE HAPPINESS

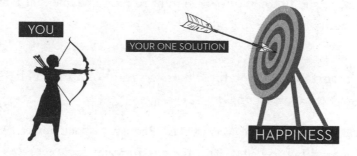

CREATING FEELINGS AS A WAY TO CREATE HAPPINESS

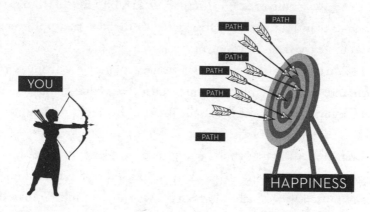

I am an expert at strangling. I put my hands around the neck of a dream and grip tighter and tighter, until the life is forced out. I decide a thing must happen, and it must be a certain way or not at all, and rather than giving it space to form and take shape, I remove its oxygen with anxiety and my desperation such that it is smothered before it ever has a chance to live. I have done this with relationships and jobs and decisions to move cross-country and almost everything else I can think of. My stubborn insistence to smash my round peg into a square hole has, without a doubt, made my life harder than it has had to be, forced me to swim upstream, and to miss opportunities to grow in beautiful ways, because I

NEEDED something specific to be a certain way in order for me to be the kind of person I thought I needed to be to please people that I don't even know really mattered to begin with.

The Importance of God (or Whatever You Want to Call It)— Because It's Not All on Us

Universe. God. System. Master plan. Energy. Higher power. Whatever. Are you willing to believe that there is a greater force working its hand in life? Are you willing to believe that this force works on our behalf? I am. I don't have a very formal relationship with God, but I like to think we can have a conversation; I respect WHATEVER IT IS out there that is bigger than I am. I have surrendered to the idea that not everything in life is mine to shape and control.

I wasn't always this way. As a nonpracticing Jew from NYC, I was born and raised a cynic who questioned everything and was taught to seek empirical proof for life itself; if I couldn't see it, touch it, taste it, or fuck it, then it didn't exist.

I remember the first time I questioned this, back in 2016. In a moment of getting real with my pain (like you just did in the previous chapter), I had admitted how much it hurt that I was always finding myself in these awful relationships with guys who wanted to have sex with me, but not actually care about me as a person. I let that pain be my flashlight and turned my observations to seeing where I was stuck and why. Rather than be ashamed of myself, I used the experiences as data.

What I saw was that no matter how much I would have liked to blame every man I'd ever dated, *I* was the common thread in every relationship I'd ever had. Some of that had to be because of what I was bringing to the table, right?

I wanted a healthy relationship so bad it hurt. But I had no idea what that was. I asked myself, *How can you actually know what a healthy relationship looks like if you've never had one before, Sarah? You never saw one mirrored to you with your parents either. You have no proof. Is that something that's even possible for you?*

I had no history to call upon, nothing that I could use to guide me. I just had to be willing to believe it was possible. Simple as that. I had to believe that if I did something BESIDES strangle every relationship I entered into, something else could happen. I had no idea what that was, but I knew if I did something differently, it would end in something different. I had to have faith, a belief and confidence in *something*.

In that moment, I made myself a promise. I was going to guide myself by my feelings, not my *expectations* of what I thought I needed, but by how I wanted to feel.

I wanted to feel love. That was all I knew. I knew, in my life, I wanted to feel and experience LOVE. So, I created a mantra to guide me:

I am willing to allow love into my life.
Love for myself, from myself, and love from others.

This would be my road map. If something made me feel love, I would pursue it. If something didn't, I would walk away from it. I didn't know it then, but when I did that, I was creating my very first Self-Love To-Do List. I had identified a feeling that was important to me—love—and decided that I was going to guide myself by prioritizing actions and thoughts and experiences that created love for me. I couldn't imagine what would come from it, but I knew I had to cultivate love if I wanted to feel love. I was open to all the different possible ways that love could come into my life.

IN ACTION: ANNA, WHO IS BRILLIANT

It is just after sunrise, and our small group is gathered on the patio of a house on Myrtle Beach. We are wrapped in yoga blankets and wind flicks through our hair; you can walk directly onto the sand from the back of the house, and the waves are coming in loud and clear with lots of white foam. It's January—not an ideal time for lying out on the beach, but the perfect time for an intimate retreat with nine women, all wearing some form of comfy clothes with lots of fuzzy slippers in sight.

Anna has her hands wrapped around a mug of hot tea, and a journal sits open in front of her on the wooden table. Her brunette, shoulder-length hair is loose, and she appears to be deep in thought. She looks out at the water and then back at her journal.

"Do you want to talk it out?" I ask her. She says no but that she can share if I'd like her to.

She tells me her word is "brilliant," and as she says the word, her eyes spark a bit. She takes a deep breath and begins, "When I feel brilliant I don't apologize for being smart. I have an agile mind; I am clever and resourceful and ensure my own success. I trust myself."

She doesn't know it just yet, but in less than a month Anna will enroll in college to get her bachelor's degree in psychology—something she's been wanting to do but has been scared to. In just a few years more, she'll go for a master's. Because Anna is ready to ensure her success. She is ready to trust herself. And the road is wide open ahead . . .

YOUR LIFE IN BUCKETS

Like a perfectly cut gemstone, you have many facets. Likewise, the feelings you have aren't flat either—they are multidimensional. It is very rare that feelings can stay specifically within the boundaries of one facet of life; rather, feelings have a tendency to creep into the different facets of your life at the same time. Very few feelings can exist in a vacuum.

It might help to think of your "life-facets" like different buckets, with each representing a different area of your general well-being. This is important to understand, because when you think about how you want to feel in your life, it's good to know that one feeling can have a multi-dimensional impact on your life. While a feeling can primarily live in one bucket, it will most likely spill over into the others as well.

Dr. Peggy Swarbrick, associate director of the Center of Alcohol and Substance Use Studies at Rutgers, shares that our overall wellness can be divided into eight pillars: emotional wellness, environmental wellness, intellectual wellness, physical wellness, occupational wellness, spiritual wellness, social wellness, and financial wellness. While I love these divisions, I've adapted the idea to fit our needs a bit more specifically.

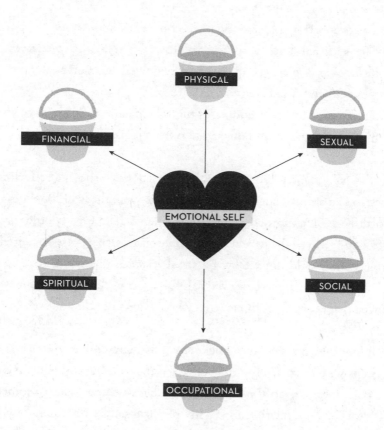

In this diagram, you are your Emotional Self. It represents you as you are, with all your feelings and experiences. You are surrounded by your facets, each one represented by a bucket.

- The physical bucket reflects how we relate to the (physical) experiences we are having in our bodies. It's all about how we create self-care for ourselves physically, including movement, nourishment, and our relationships to food, sleep, and exercise.
- The sexuality bucket addresses how we relate to ourselves as sexual, intimate beings and, in turn, how we relate to others sexually.

- The social bucket reflects how we relate to others in the world around us, with a focus on our interpersonal relationships and how we express ourselves socially.
- The occupational bucket relates to our work and/or our passions.
- The spiritual bucket speaks to how we relate to ourselves and includes any relationship to a higher power, our personal value system, and our connectedness to self.
- The financial bucket addresses the relationship that we have to our money, our spending habits, and our financial value systems.

In the last chapter, you probably noticed how the main feelings I seemed to experience in an average day in life were those of loneliness and unworthiness—I expressed how "unlovable" I felt. One would assume that feeling "unlovable" would impact my social bucket, yes? Because feeling unlovable would impact my personal relationships and my social life. That's a given. But if you observed carefully and without judgment, you'd have seen that this feeling impacted a whole bunch of other buckets as well.

- It impacted my sexuality bucket by influencing my intimate relationships with men; feeling unlovable led me to using my body as a tool to get instant gratification and proof that I was desirable to someone.
- It touched my relationship to my physical self by impacting my ability to self-care and, more dramatically, my relationship with food. All of which impacted my weight, which limited my physical ability and mobility even more.
- Feeling unlovable also impacted my financial bucket because I compensated for my feelings by spending lots of money I didn't have on things I didn't need.
- The idea that I was unlovable impacted every inch of my spiritual bucket. It impacted my self-worth, my ability to believe in good things, and my sense of hope and overall excitement about my life experience.
- Feeling unlovable also touched my occupational bucket by causing

me to take jobs that I could shape my (nonexistent) identity around. I worked for bosses who asked me to sacrifice and I did, because doing this gave me a sense of worth and purpose.

In the last chapter, we explored different kinds of pain and what those looked like. While I would have never picked "unlovable" as a feeling I would want to be my North Star, it subconsciously became my guiding light because it was what felt familiar and I didn't know there was any other way I could feel. All my choices and actions were shaped by feeling unlovable in my life, and the result was a whole lot of pain.

The Feeling of Alignment in Action

As I write this book, the feeling I am using to guide myself through this chapter of my life is "aligned." Can you see that translated into my daily activities as I described at the beginning of the chapter? Can you observe differences between the way my day is shaped now and the way it was shaped by my feeling unlovable?

Flip back to the beginning of the chapter and read through my recent day one more time. That example day, and all days lately, I do my best to listen to my actual needs. I see them and I try to serve them—I don't run or numb out when something scares me. For example:

When I was guided by feeling UNLOVABLE...	When I am guided by ALIGNMENT...
I reacted to what I felt in my body and did what I wanted to do.	I listen to my body and try to give it what it needs rather than what I want immediately.
I avoided having hard conversations with people.	I acknowledge that I need to talk about something difficult and set up a framework in which to safely do so.

As you move into this next exercise, you'll start to see how different feelings shape your life experience. When we start to flesh out your Self-Love To-Do List in the next chapter, you'll begin to see how your feelings can impact different buckets too!

IN ACTION: LINDSAY, WHO IS INTENTIONAL

We are eight months into a pandemic, and it feels like everyone in America has mastered the art of Zoom. The seventeen women floating in small boxes on the screen in front of me are no exception—this is my 2021 Love and Action group, a five-week online group focused on moving AWAY from New Year's resolutions. In the last hour we've done Alternate Nostril Breathing, had a Whitney Houston Dance Break, and also had a group meditation where everyone was supposed to keep their eyes closed but I caught a few people opening their eyes and peeking around, as if to double-check that they were "doing it right."

But not Lindsay—she never opens her eyes. She goes "all in" with everything we do. When the time comes to share, everyone (unsurprisingly) goes quiet. So, I call on her because I've learned that Lindsay never shies away from a challenge and she thrives when she's held to task. She smiles and doesn't pause and gets right down to business.

"My word is 'intentional,' " she says, her voice professional and put together. "When I am living Intentionally, I am purposeful. I am grounded and clear on my Why, Want, and Needs. I take care of myself and practice self-care. I pray to God and meditate. I am honoring my desires and being firm with who I am and true to who I am in my choices. I am brave and act with intent, living in my truth. I am open to new experiences. I am trusting and vulnerable."

Lindsay is decisive and committed and I see why she is so successful in the male-dominated environment she works in. But there's even more underneath. Blossoming. Warm. She has bright eyes that make you want to hug her. She is ready to discover herself.

PICKING FEELINGS TO SERVE AS YOUR COMPASS

This is the moment you've been waiting for. In the previous chapter, you got honest with yourself about what hurts you right now in life. Now, we're going to explore what you truly long for. What an authentic life is like for your Ultimate You—how she feels and what she experiences. **You're going to do the work of picking the feeling that will be the compass in your life right now.**

On the next few pages, you'll see a big list of words. By the time you complete this chapter, you'll have picked one word to focus on. This is the word we'll turn into your Self-Love To-Do List.

As we begin this process, remember a few things:

1. This is not about getting anything right; it's more about opening the window and letting the sun shine all over your soul. We're going to find what radiates to you.
2. You're working in the present tense, with how you are experiencing life right now. The word you end up working with today is what you feel pulled to right now. Because of that...
3. You can, and will, change your mind about your word in the future. Just the same, if you start to "work" the word you've chosen, and it doesn't speak to you, you can pick another and try again.
4. The word you pick does not have to represent every bucket of your life! It can specifically speak to certain parts of your life at any given time.

Find a cozy place to sit. Someplace that feels safe and comfortable. Turn off the TV; maybe light a candle. Play some soft music. Take off your bra if that makes you feel free (*grin*) and settle in. Take a deep breath, in and out.

Finding Your Feelings

1. **Take your first look.** Welcome to the Big List of Feelings. Sweep over it quickly. Do you see anything that pops out at you? If you do, put a little mark next to whatever feeling sticks out.

ABUNDANCE	ADMIRATION	AFFECTION
ACCEPTANCE	ADORABLE	AFFLUENCE
ACCOMPLISHED	ADORED	ALIVE
ACKNOWLEDGED	ADVENTUROUS	ALLURING

AMAZEMENT

AMAZING

AMOROUS

ANCHORED

ANEW

ANIMATED

APPRECIATED

APPRECIATION

ASSERTIVE

AT EASE

AT HOME

ATTRACTED

ATTRACTIVE

AUTHENTIC

AWAKE

AWESOME

BALANCED

BEAMING

BEAUTIFUL

BLESSED

BLOSSOMING

BOLD

BOUNDLESSNESS

BOUNTIFUL

BRAVE

BRIGHT

BRILLIANCE

CALM

CAPABLE

CAPTIVATED

CELEBRATED

CENTERED

CERTAINTY

CHALLENGED

CHARISMATIC

CHEERFUL

CHERISHED

CLARITY

CLEANSED

CLEVER

CLOSENESS

COMFORTABLE

COMFORTED

COMPASSIONATE

CONFIDENT

CONNECTION

CONSCIOUS

CONSIDERATE

CONTENT

COSMIC

COURAGE

COURAGEOUS

COZY

CREATIVE

CURIOSITY

CURRENT

DARING

DECISIVE

DEEP-ROOTED

DELIGHT

DELIGHTFUL

DESERVING

DESIRE

DESIRED

DETERMINATION

DEVOTED

DIRECT

DREAMY

DYNAMIC

EAGER

EASE

EASYGOING

EBULLIENT

ECSTASY

ECSTATIC

EFFECTIVE

EFFERVESCENT

ELATED

ELECTRIC

ELEGANT

ELEVATED

EMBODIED

EMBOLDENED

EMERGENT

EMPOWERED

ENAMORED

ENCOURAGED

ENERGETIC

ENGAGED

ENGROSSED

ENLIGHTENED

ENRICHED

ENTERPRISING

ENTHUSED

ENTHUSIASTIC

EQUANIMITY

EUPHORIC	GLAMOROUS	INNOVATING
EXCITED	GLEEFUL	INQUISITIVE
EXCITEMENT	GLOWING	INSIGHTFUL
EXHILARATED	GOLDEN	INSPIRED
EXPANSIVE	GRACE	INTEGRITY
EXPECTANT	GRACEFUL	INTENTIONAL
EXPRESSIVE	GRACIOUS	INTERESTED
EXQUISITE	GRATEFUL	INTRIGUED
FABULOUS	GREAT	INTUITIVE
FANTASTIC	GROUNDED	INVIGORATED
FANTASY	GUIDED	INVITING
FASCINATED	HAPPINESS	JOYFUL
FEISTY	HAPPY	JUBILANT
FEMININE	HARMONIOUS	KEEN
FESTIVE	HARMONY	KIND
FIERCE	HEALING	KINDNESS
FLEXIBLE	HEALTHY	LAVISH
FLUID	HELD	LIBERAL
FOCUSED	HOLY	LIBERATED
FORTUNATE	HOME	LIGHT
FREE	HOPE	LIGHTHEARTED
FRESH	HOPEFUL	LIMITLESS
FRIENDSHIP	HYPNOTIC	LION-HEARTED
FRUITFUL	ILLUMINATED	LIT UP
FULFILLED	IMAGINATIVE	LOVE
FULL	IMPASSIONED	LOVED
GENEROUS	IMPORTANT	LOVELY
GENIUS	IN AWE	LOVING
GENTLE	IN LOVE	LOYAL
GENUINE	INDEPENDENT	LUCENT
GIFTED	INFINITE	LUCID
GLAD	INFLUENTIAL	LUCKY

LUCRATIVE

LUMINOUS

LUSCIOUS

LUXURIOUS

MAGIC

MAGICAL

MAGNETIC

MAJESTIC

MASTERFUL

MESMERIZING

MINDFUL

MIRACULOUS

MOMENTUM

NATURAL

NEW

NOURISHED

NURTURED

ON PURPOSE

ONE

ONENESS

OPEN

OPENHEARTED

OPEN-MINDED

OPEN-

   MINDEDNESS

OPENNESS

OPTIMISM

OPULENT

ORGANIC

OVERFLOWING

OVERJOYED

PAMPERED

PASSIONATE

PEACEFUL

PHILANTHROPIC

PLAYFUL

PLEASANT

PLEASURED

POETIC

POSITIVE

POWERFUL

PROACTIVE

PROSPERING

PROUD

PURE

PURPOSEFUL

QUIET

SAFE

SATISFIED

SECURE

SEEN

SENSE OF PRIDE

SENSITIVE

SENSUAL

SERENITY

SETTLED

SEXUAL

SEXY

SHIMMERING

SINCERE

SOFT

SOLID

SOUL-FUELED

SOULFUL

SPIRITED

SPIRITUAL

SPONTANEOUS

STEADY

STRENGTHENED

STRONG

SULTRY

SUPPORTED

SURE

SURPRISED

SWEET

TENACIOUS

TENACITY

TENDER

THANKFUL

THOUGHTFUL

THRILLED

TOUCHED

TRAILBLAZING

TRANSFORMED

TREASURED

TRIUMPHANT

TUNED-IN

UNDERSTOOD

UNFORGETTABLE

UNIFIED

UNION

UNIQUE

UNLIMITED

UNSHACKLED

UNSTOPPABLE

UNTAMED

UNTANGLED	VIVACIOUS	WHOLENESS
USEFUL	VULNERABLE	WILD
VALUABLE	WARMHEARTED	WONDER
VALUED	WARMTH	WONDERFUL
VAST	WEALTH	YEARNING
VIBRANT	WEIGHTLESS	ZEAL
VIBRATING	WELCOMED	ZEST
VIGOR	WELL-OFF	
VITALITY	WHOLE	

2. **Clear your head quickly.** Do your best to be as present with yourself as you can be. If you feel like a breath work or meditation practice is accessible to you, try one! (You can find some on my website at SarahSapora.com/Soul.) Sing. Stretch. Whatever. We're doubling down on the focusing here so you can slow down and connect to your own intuition and voice as clearly as possible.

3. **Make your initial list.** By hand on a separate clean piece of paper (*not* on a computer or your mobile device), make a list of all the words you were initially attracted to. Pay attention to what it feels like to write them out; don't go too fast or too slow. Spend perhaps one second per word. If a word you were initially attracted to feels lifeless as you write it out, put a scratch through it and eliminate it.

   Note: Feel free to write and make notes in this book as much as you want. Really. But if you don't want to, you can visit my website at SarahSapora.com/Soul and download a copy of the list to print out.

4. **Step away for a few minutes, then come back and let your mind dance.** Go to the bathroom or make a cup of tea or stretch. Break things up for a few minutes and come back. When you come back, take a closer look at your list. Let your mind dance over each of the words. There is no formal process required here; the idea is that you listen to yourself and observe where you are feeling the most pull. Cross out words that don't radiate as strongly. Write the

list again. Review it again. Cross out words. Write the list again. Put it down. Go pee again. Pick it back up. Repeat the process till you have a maximum of three words left.

5. **Pick one word and explore it.** You may not be used to asserting what feels good for you. It may feel scary for you to make a decision and own it. This is a place where it is 100 percent safe to start practicing doing what you want for you and not what anyone else wants for you. Pick one. Whichever one excites you the most. Circle it. Now take a blank piece of paper and write your word in big letters across the top.

   Congratulations! This is more than just a word. This is a feeling that speaks to you. This is you listening to yourself. This is the start of your sails unfurling. This is you starting to meet your Ultimate You.

6. **Now we're going to get our hands dirty.** If you have your phone nearby, set a timer for three minutes, or else use a clock, the timer on your microwave... whatever works. You can also choose a song you love that's around three minutes long and use that as your timer. For those three minutes, answer one of the following questions in a freewrite:

   When I feel [word], I am...

   or

   When I am living [word], I am...

   There is no right answer here and no wrong answer. It doesn't have to be in full paragraphs, but it can be. It could be a list, or a diagram—anything that works for you.

7. **Turn your freewrite into a power statement!** Look carefully at what you've written. Is there a common theme to everything you shared? Your final step for today is to take your freewrite and condense it into a single phrase, a nugget that crystallizes what you just wrote and condenses it into something powerful and memorable.

   In order to do this, ask yourself, *What am I* really *saying here?* The answer will be your mantra, your self-love battle cry!

Here's how Lindsay, Chloe, Anna, and I transitioned our free-writes into our power statements.

Person	Freewrite	Power Statement
Sarah	When I am aligned, I . . . can listen to myself really clearly. I give myself the direction I need to make choices that support me. I don't stress over things that aren't essential to my development.	When I am ALIGNED, I am calm and centered. I have clarity and confidence because I am dialed in to me.
Lindsay	When I am living Intentionally . . . I am purposeful. I am grounded and clear on my Why, Want, and Needs.	When I am INTENTIONAL, I listen to myself and practice self-care.
Anna	When I feel brilliant, I don't apologize for being smart. I have an agile mind; I am clever and resourceful and ensure my own success.	When I am BRILLIANT, I have an innate wisdom and discernment that allow me to operate in my gifts.
Chloe	When I feel luminous, I will feel luminous and I will feel light. I feel like a shining light. I feel open to be myself . . . I am free.	When I am LUMINOUS, I am unapologetically free to be my authentic self, no matter who I am with or where I am at.

Your power statement will be your best friend. You will live it and breathe it. When you are unsure of which direction to go, you will consult it and call upon it. Make sure it speaks to you. Make sure it IS you. Keep it short and strong and descriptive, and make sure it answers the question "What am I REALLY saying here?" Begin your statement with "When I am" and use your word, and then finish it in one or two sentences—nothing more.

Now that you've done that, take a deep breath and be done for the moment. You've done what you need to for now.

DON'T WORRY IF YOU SUCK

As you start to dig into this work, you may feel compelled to "get it right" the first time. Stop. This isn't math class; you aren't being quizzed. What you are being invited to do is listen to yourself and interpret and identify your own feelings and desires. Nobody can tell you that your feelings are right and nobody can tell you that they are wrong, because only YOU know the truth.

You may suck at this right now. If you have spent most of your life looking to other people for cues on how to live and how to feel, it is totally acceptable for you to be bad at it. You'll get better, I promise.

You also need to know that feelings are subjective. Cookies-and-cream ice cream tastes different to everyone. Some people love George Strait, and some people think he's boring (they would be wrong, but okay, fine...); some graphic designers think "minimalist design" is about negative space, while others see it as a hodgepodge of colors and text. It's the same with feelings.

The point is, don't stress, because your answer is the right answer for you right now. The key to feeling greater is to live a life that is shaped by your value system and your preferences. But you don't necessarily know what that is until you start to do the discovery work.

SURVEYING THE SITE:
WHAT WE DUG UP IN THIS CHAPTER

In this chapter we focused on the second step to creating your own Self-Love To-Do List: claiming the feeling you are going to use as your North Star for this part of your journey! We talked about why goals suck and how they position us to have a "succeed or fail" mentality, which can ultimately leave us feeling like we're standing under a mountain of our own perceived failures. Using the example of a mother crossing the street and holding the hand of her child, we talked about how so many of us abandon our resolutions and how that leaves us feeling—stranded and alone. Rather than goals, we should aim to create feelings in our lives—but rather than focus on a specific outcome, we focus on the DOING of actions that help to create feelings and leave the end result to play out and interpret itself as best serves our lives.

Chapter 7

STEP THREE: CREATING YOUR SELF-LOVE TO-DO LIST

This Is How You'll Feel Your Feeling

According to Urban Dictionary, a cockblock is "one who prevents another from scoring sexually." So, I need to tell you that you... are...a cockblock. But instead of sex, you're preventing *yourself* from scoring at living a Self-Loving Life, big-time. Put the sex part aside and think about it this way: Every time you thwart your own growth, every time you do something that stops you from connecting to your Ultimate You, you are cutting yourself off from the good stuff. From an orgasm of awesomeness. In essence, you become a big cockblock.

Fear not, my friend! We are going to use this to our advantage! In this chapter, you're going to get a prescription for creating your Ultimate You. By the time we're done, you will have a list of things you can start doing today to create change. It's not enough to simply *want* to feel a certain way in life—we actually have to DO things to create those feelings.

"If you want to be happier, why don't you just do stuff that makes you happy?" asks every person ever who doesn't really *get it*.

I cannot tell you all the ways I despise that question. If I really knew what would make me happy, wouldn't I just do it? And if it was that easy to do the things that made me happy once I knew what they were, wouldn't I just do them?

In college, I studied logic and was taught that there are two ways to approach reasoning—inductively and deductively. With **inductive reasoning**, you draw a general conclusion based on a set of examples—you start with an observation, see patterns in the observations, and develop a hypothesis as a general description of the observation.[1] With **deductive reasoning**, you start with a given set of premises and use that to draw a conclusion—the conclusions that are drawn are only as valid as the premises we draw from.[2]

I failed every quiz and assignment about inductive reasoning—for the life of me, I could not wrap my head around it. But deductive reasoning always made sense. Mostly because it started with facts, something tangible I could use as a departure point.[3]

Personal growth is the same way. A lot of what we see in personal growth asks us to use a kind of inductive reasoning—to make our decisions and steer our course based on circumstantial evidence that we collect about ourselves and then apply. We gather our evidence and then leap forward to our conclusion. It is a bottom-up way of thinking.

But what happens when you just don't fucking know WHY things are the way they are? You don't know what evidence to collect, you have no idea where to begin, and it's all just so overwhelming that you can't even begin to pull a logical conclusion out of your asshole in any way, shape, or form. It's like being asked to pluck random things out of the air when solutions are intangible and unimaginable. "Just do things that make you happy!" people say, to which I say…"FUCKIFIKNEWWHATTHAT WASANDIFICOULDDOITDONTYOUTHINKIDBEDOINGIT ALREADYFORFUCKSSAKE?!"

I use deductive reasoning. I start with a fact and then I move forward using that fact to navigate; it's top-down thinking based on shit I actually know and understand, which, to me, makes solution-finding so much more accessible. Which means that big ideas like "How can I be happier in life?" don't have to be so huge and scary anymore.

So, let's go find some solutions, shall we?

BE LIKE JUVENILE AND BACK THAT (AZZ) UP

When I was growing up, my dad used to tell me that if I didn't know what I wanted, I could move forward by avoiding the things I knew that I *didn't* want. "Sarah," he'd say, "you don't have to know where to go next; just start with where you don't want to go and see where that takes you. You know"—he moved his hand around in the air—"just back up into what's next. It makes sense."

He was right. It does make sense. There is no need to be crippled by analysis paralysis, trying to pick out magical solutions from the sky. Instead, back up into what's next by using what you don't want as the starting point. Back up into your feelings. Back up into action.

We've established that doing things for the sake of doing them is where the beautiful stuff happens (and not because we expect or *need* a specific outcome to make us whole). With this in mind, we can venture confidently into the unknown toward our Ultimate You knowing it's okay to take steps without being exactly sure where they will lead, because we have faith in ourselves, in the strategy, and in a greater power at play. We know that the more we do things that lean in the general direction of our Ultimate You, the more we learn in the process. Each time we absorb new information, it becomes data we can use to home in on the road ahead.

We move forward by turning around and walking backward. We refer to what we understand and see as facts, and we use those facts to guide us. The reliable data, the "facts" that we know are our truth, in this case, are our experiences of what hurts us. Our hurt can be the data we construct our logic around. Once I see it and acknowledge it, it's evidence. And evidence is what allows us to "back that azz up," and go.

IN ACTION: CHLOE, WHO IS LUMINOUS

"How are you cockblocking yourself?" I ask all the women in the room. They look around at one another, unsure they've heard me say what they actually think they heard me say. "Yes, you heard me," I confirm, "and don't pretend like you don't know what I'm talking about."

It's the third day of my LIFELOVE Vatreat, and everyone laughs out loud at my offensive joke. But, at the same time, they know exactly what I mean. They know, in some way, shape, or form, they are doing things that are keeping them from feeling happier, but they don't know exactly what they are or why they should care.

"Think about your word and your nugget," I instruct the group, and on cue, they open their notebooks and turn to their notes. "Now, make a list of everything you do that is keeping you from feeling your word. If you picked that word, it's probably because you *want* to feel that way, but you currently do not. So, tell me why you don't. What are you doing in your life right now that cockblocks you from feeling that way? But don't actually *tell me*—make a list."

I turn the music back up as their heads go down and their fingers start to work. Nina Simone's "Here Comes the Sun" plays, because I want them to remember that the sunshine always comes after the storm. After a few minutes, their heads start to pop up.

"Each thing you just identified on your list is a challenge that is keeping you from feeling how you want to feel," I explain. "Now we're going to turn each challenge into an opportunity. Because on the flip side of every challenge is an opportunity, right? The flip side of 'death' is 'birth,' the flip side of 'love' is 'hurt,' and each of those dualities can live together at the exact same time." They are following me, but I pick my words carefully because I want them to see how clear the road is in front of them, and not to get easily overwhelmed. "You are literally flipping your challenge upside down—the reverse of your challenge is your opportunity."

They look a little lost, so I call for Chloe so we can do an example together. I ask her to repeat her word and her "nugget."

"My word is 'Luminous,' and when I feel Luminous I am unapologetically free to be my authentic self, no matter who I am with or where I am at."

"Okay," I begin, "what do you do right now in life that prevents you from feeling Luminous?" Chloe looks down at her paper and cautiously reads aloud:

> *I worry about what other people will think of me.*
> *I get stuck in an idea of being the perfect mother and perfect wife.*
> *I look to others for my sense of self.*
> *I act the opposite of my real self. I am quiet and reserved instead of loud and open.*
> *I overanalyze my every action.*
> *I hide my real self.*

I always ask my husband, mother, or therapist what I should do.
I make jokes about myself to make other people laugh.
My husband calls me "crazy." I call myself "crazy." I thought it was okay and that I was fine with it, but I'm not.

There is quiet in the room as Chloe shares herself. "Those are big things," I say. "Those first few—can we make those more detailed? I get that you worry, but what do you actually DO in your life because of that?" I ask Chloe to think about it again, but this time to get more granular and specific. And when she raises her hand to speak again, she says . . .

I spend hours doing my hair and makeup when I don't want to.
I wear uncomfortable clothing just so I fit in.
I hold back on my ideas because I don't want to put myself out there.
I'm quiet because I don't want people to think I'm stupid.
I look at Instagram and compare myself to others. I look to the women in my neighborhood and daughter's school for my self-image.
I constantly question myself and my actions.

You could hear a pin drop. We are all dialed in to Chloe.

"Let's flip those 'challenges' into 'opportunities.' " I walk over to where she sits and ask for her paper. I say, "What's the opposite of 'I spend hours doing my hair and makeup when I don't want to'? Let's flip that."

"I wear my hair in a ponytail or bun with frizzy hair all day long," Chloe says. I smile.

" 'I wear uncomfortable clothing just so I fit in'?" I ask.

"I wear comfortable clothes like leggings and a T-shirt when I take my daughter to school." Chloe goes on. I read her list out loud, and one by one, she flips each challenge into an opportunity to do something different:

I am as loud as I want.
I laugh out loud, literally. I snort and cackle.
I stop replaying situations with my husband and mother and asking them what other people's actions mean.
I make my own decisions. I don't need my husband's or my mom's permission.

It is as if we've all watched a flower bloom. Her face shines. I ask her to make a list of things that she can do to start making these flips real. She takes a minute, head down and pen scribbling. "Will you do me a favor and read your word and nugget again?" I ask.

"My word is 'Luminous,' and when I feel Luminous I am unapologetically free to be my authentic self, no matter who I am with or where I am at."

"Now read that list you just made . . . ," I encourage her.

"I can do these things to make my flip possible," Chloe reads. "Wear my hair in a ponytail or bun, with frizzy hair and all. Wear comfortable clothes like leggings and a T-shirt. Speak up with my thoughts and ideas at room parent meetings. Speak up with my opinions in conversations with other people. Stop asking my husband or mother for permission on what I should do. When a problem arises, try to see the solution myself. Stop replaying situations with my husband and mom. Use social media less," she finishes.

I look around the room to gauge everyone's face. They have smiles on their faces, and their love beams straight to Chloe like a Care Bear stare.

"Everything you just read on that list," I explain, "that is all self-love. That is your Self-Love To-Do List. That is what you focus on *right now* to start removing yourself from pain and start moving toward feeling Luminous in your life. Each one of those actions is self-love to YOU."

Chloe has her action plan, and she is ready to take it on.

CHLOE'S Self-Love To-Do List

1. Wear my hair in a ponytail or bun with frizzy hair and all.
2. Wear comfortable clothing like leggings and a T-shirt.
3. Speak up with thoughts and ideas at room parent meetings.
4. Speak up with my opinions in conversations with other people.
5. Stop asking my husband or mother for permission or opinions on what I should do when a problem arises—try to see the solution myself.
6. Stop asking my husband or mother for advice or permission on situations.
7. Stop replaying situations with my husband and mom!
8. Use social media less—Instagram, FB, Pinterest.

HOW TO CREATE YOUR SELF-LOVE
TO-DO LIST

In Step One, we got clarity around the things that are hurting us right now. We saw ourselves with honesty and compassion and had the bravery to admit our pain. In Step Two, we reclaimed how we want to feel in our lives. What speaks to us, and who we know we are inside. We owned this and defined it and brought it to life with a visceral power statement. Now, in Step Three, we'll create a Self-Love To-Do List that serves as a personal road map to unfurling into your Ultimate You. (If you are someone who likes checkboxes and lists, this is going to rock your world!) This is a tangible list you can write out or print out and stick to your wall or leave in a notebook and refer to whenever you feel lost. It works because it takes the way you want to feel and turns it into digestible nuggets of action, so you can use those actions as your North Star.

Using your Self-Love To-Do List is simple. If something is on the list, do it—it is a priority. If something is not on the list, it is not a priority. If an action helps connect you to the feelings you want to feel, do it. If it detracts from the feelings, don't do it. This is a definitive way for you to figure out "what is good for you" and what is not. If you are confronted with a choice and neither answer is on your Self-Love To-Do List, you can simply say to yourself, *Does this help me to feel my word? If it does, I'll do it! If it does not, I won't.*

You don't need to meander in this gray zone of *wanting* without *doing*. This is why you have a word. You have a nugget and a power phrase. And you have your Self-Love To-Do List. You have multiple checks and balances to help unstick your stuck and guide you forward.

Keep Things Simple

We've talked a lot about how big goals can lead to the "before-after" and "success-failure" mentality. We've also talked about how little changes can add up over time and create BIG shifts in the long run.

The items on your Self-Love To-Do List (SLTDL) should be doable things. They may not be easy, but they must be clear and actionable. If you find yourself coming up with "flips," and the action items to create those "flips" are too broad, you must break them down into actions that are smaller and more bite-sized. If you don't, you'll never do them. Remember:

Be specific.
Be granular.
Get to the heart of it.

Instead of saying...	Say this:
Make time for self-care.	Take five minutes every morning to breathe and apply skincare without touching my phone.
Spend less time on social media.	Set the alarm on my phone for thirty minutes when going on Instagram. Stop using it when the alarm goes off.
Exercise more.	Walk outside for ten minutes on Tuesday, Thursday, and Saturday mornings.
Don't buy lunch out at work.	Add sandwich fixings and fruit to my shopping list. Make a sandwich at night before bed for the next day.
Be mindful of how much TV I watch.	Set the DVR to record the shows I like. Only watch shows that have been recorded, and don't turn the TV on when I'm bored or feel like I need background noise.
Spend less money.	Go to Starbucks two days a week—on Monday and Friday—instead of five. Download budget-tracking software and review my budget from the last month. Pick ONE expense to eliminate.
Go out more and do more fun stuff.	Plan a "solo date" once a month. Subscribe to my city's events calendar to see what's going on locally. Start a "wish list" on Pinterest. Commit to one trip every quarter—pick the dates and put them on the calendar.

If the actions you put on your SLTDL are vague or too sweepingly large, you will not do them, or you will do them when you feel "motivated" but drop your hand halfway through crossing the street.

Remember: No big goals. Go for small, quantifiable changes.

Do One Thing at a Time

Once you have created your SLTDL, you may feel an urge to do everything on it at once. Don't. Pick a few things—two or three at the most—and commit to those and do them regularly for a month before adding on new items.

This process can be magical if you trust it. Once you commit to an action item and do it regularly, it clears out some space in your brain and life for the next thing, for what comes next. Once this action becomes regular to you, it will no longer be a challenge, and you will naturally gravitate toward doing something else and creating more change.

You may not get to everything on your SLTDL. What matters is that you start, you incorporate the changes into your life, and you let them take you where you need to go next.

"But Nothing Is Happening . . ." Do It Anyway!

We've been conditioned to live a Before-and-After life, which means we're told that once we do the thing that we think is the key to unlocking happiness, we're in the AFTER phase and everything will be magically awesome!

But that is not how it works. We have to *do* the things on our SLTDL regularly. For months at a time. We have to do them enough that they become normal for us. Even if it doesn't feel like doing the list is making anything magical, we still need to do it. You know why? Because by the time the shit hits the fan, our new patterns will be so ingrained, we won't fall back on the harmful coping mechanisms we're used to.

We don't practice self-love for all the times when everything feels great and easy! We work the muscle of our own self-love so that when we hit DEFCON 2, we have strategies and ways to navigate that are loving and supportive of us.

Do the items on your SLTDL long enough to fully integrate the actions into your life—so that it won't be challenging to do them when weathering a storm in your life. When your entire sense of reality is turned upside down, that's when your new "action items" will make all the difference.

The SLTDL is a vehicle for change. No matter what is on that list, if the action items are different than what you normally do, and you do those action items regularly, you will experience change.

The magic is not just in creating the list and executing the items on your list once, one at a time. The real magic comes from the adjusting, negotiating, and listening to yourself that come naturally when you are doing something different. In the process of just *doing* what is on the list, you will grow and evolve.

Once you've done something from your SLTDL long enough to have made it part of your life naturally, you'll find yourself in a different place—and then you can move on to what's next. Let's jump right into the process:

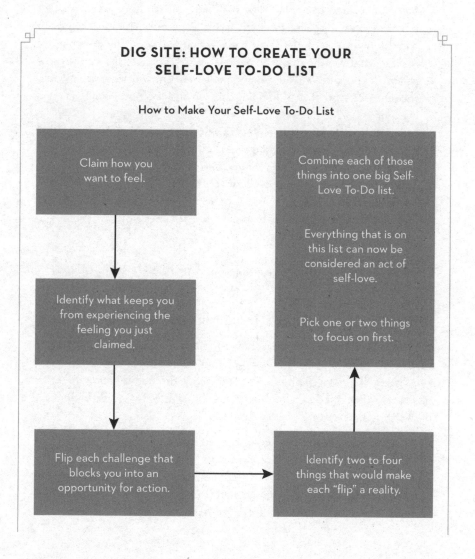

**DIG SITE: HOW TO CREATE YOUR
SELF-LOVE TO-DO LIST**

How to Make Your Self-Love To-Do List

Claim how you want to feel.

Identify what keeps you from experiencing the feeling you just claimed.

Flip each challenge that blocks you into an opportunity for action.

Identify two to four things that would make each "flip" a reality.

Combine each of those things into one big Self-Love To-Do list.

Everything that is on this list can now be considered an act of self-love.

Pick one or two things to focus on first.

1. **Claim how you want to feel!** You did this in the previous chapter. You have a word, a freewrite, a "nugget," and a power phrase that encapsulates how you want to feel.

2. **Make a list of all the things you currently do that PREVENT you from feeling your word.** Get really clear on how you cockblock yourself. List each thing individually. All of these things that you do that get in your way are your CHALLENGES.

3. **"Flip" each challenge that blocks you into an opportunity for ACTION.** Draw an arrow next to each challenge and, next to it, write out your flip (an example follows). This is, most often, just the exact opposite of the challenge. Each flip is your opportunity for growth and self-love! You've identified the way you play a part in creating this reality—what are the opposite actions? We're going to flip into reverse gear. Ask yourself, "If what is happening now isn't working, what would the opposite of that be?" In doing this, we find the opportunity in each challenge.

4. **Identify two to four things you can do that would make this "flip" a reality.** What are a few things you can do to start taking action that would make this flip happen for you in real life?

5. **Take every action item and add it to one list. This is your Self-Love To-Do List!** Everything on this list can be considered an act of self-love because it helps you to create the feelings your Ultimate You wants to experience in life!

Bam! You've done it! You've created your first Self-Love To-Do List!

Hitting Roadblocks? Let's Troubleshoot.

If you are working the strategy but it feels really hard . . . keep going. It gets easier each time. Do a little bit of your list at a time, take breaks, and keep going. If you've "flipped a challenge" but the coordinating opportunity feels like a dead end you can't possibly figure out . . . it's either one of two things:

- An invitation for you to break the "opportunity" down into smaller pieces. Can you get more detailed with this task?
- A sign that you've hit a place where you need to get help from someone (a professional) in order to better understand how to help yourself. Make sure to add something like "Get help for XXX" to your list!

It's okay if challenges and opportunities are resulting in a really long list. Get it all out on paper to create your SLTDL and remember you will focus on only a few things at once (just get it out of your brain!). If you start digging into your list and it doesn't feel like you, that's great data. Go back and pick a new word guided by what you just learned.

Want to see more examples of real SLTDLs? Visit my website at SarahSapora.com/Soul for more!

SELF-LOVE AND ALIGNMENT —MY LIST IN ACTION

In the last two chapters you've heard me describe a day of my life that was shaped by feeling unlovable. You then saw me describe a day shaped by the feeling of being aligned. I didn't just wake up one morning with everything falling into place. This is a strategy I have been working on for years: asking myself what I need, how I want to feel, and then doing things to create those feelings.

A few months ago, I knew I was walking into the next chapter in my life. With that, I would need guidance and a road map that was relevant for me now. So, I went through the process again—the very same one you are doing right now—and this is the SLTDL I actively use in order to help me feel aligned in my life.

Is there anything you see on my SLTDL that you can recognize from my "day in the life" in the previous chapter? Can you see how doing things on this list can help me feel calm and centered? How they can give me clarity and confidence because these actions help me to dial into myself?

My SLTDL is a reflection of *me*. Anything that does not contribute to my feeling calm and centered, I avoid. This includes personal relationships, jobs, and activities. Whatever contributes to keeping me calm and centered, and helps me LISTEN to myself and create a greater sense of flow, I'm all about it. I have my North Star. I know how to guide myself.

Now, it's your turn. Use a notebook or paper with plenty of room to write. You can also visit my website and download some blank SLTDL sheets for free. *Visit SarahSapora.com/Soul to find them.*

ALIGNED

THREE-MINUTE FREEWRITE	*When I am ALIGNED* . . . I can listen to myself clearly. I give myself the direction I need to make choices. I don't stress over things that aren't essential to my development, and I don't let myself get distracted by shiny new things. I pay my bills on time, and I don't put off doing things that are important but not fun or glamorous. I put my attention and energy into the things that are the most healthful for me, emotionally and physically. I ask myself, *Do I need this? Do I want this? Does this serve me?* before I make choices, and I liberate myself from the things that are not a "yes." My voice comes through clearly. I do what is most beneficial and not what is easiest. I feel at ease because I am not fighting against the current of my life. I am flowing and present.
NUGGET/ POWER STATEMENT	**When I am aligned, I am calm and centered. I have clarity and confidence because I am dialed in to me.**
"BACKING IT UP"	What is keeping me from feeling ALIGNED (more aligned) in my life right now? • I fight doing things that I don't enjoy but are important for me. • I think about "boring but necessary" stuff as a punishment. • I avoid thinking about money and spend haphazardly. • I wait till the last minute. • I spend time doing bullshit on my phone when I should be doing other things. • I don't have a set schedule.

"FLIPPING IT"

THE CHALLENGE	THE OPPORTUNITY
• I fight doing things that I don't enjoy but that are important to me.	→ • I embrace things that I don't enjoy but that are important.
• I think about "boring but necessary" stuff as a punishment.	→ • I "shift my mindset" to see doing "boring but necessary" things as an honor.
• I avoid thinking about money and spend haphazardly.	→ • I make friends with my money and spend mindfully.
• I wait till the last minute.	→ • I do things early.
• I spend time on my phone when I should be doing other things.	→ • I am more intentional with my phone.

TWO TO FOUR THINGS YOU CAN DO TO CREATE THE FLIP

- I embrace things that I don't enjoy but that are important.
  - Take medication every day.
  - Schedule appointments with doctors.
  - Do the dishes at night before bed.
- I "shift my mindset" to see doing "boring but necessary" things as an honor.
  - Tell myself self-care makes me better!
  - Get clear about what I NEED to do every day vs. every week. Make a list.
  - Put it on the bathroom mirror.
- I make friends with my money and spend mindfully.
  - Use an app to track my budget.
  - Buy coffee out only once a week.
  - Return clothes! (Actually do it!)

- I do things early.
  - Schedule bills to be paid a week before their due date.
  - Use money from a paycheck when I have it, before I need it.
  - Put deadlines for payments and big things on my calendar and on my phone.
- I am more intentional with my phone.
  - PUT IT DOWN IN THE OTHER ROOM.
  - Wake up to something else besides the phone.
  - Download a tracking app to monitor my usage.

MY SELF-LOVE TO-DO LIST TO HELP FEEL ALIGNED

- Take medication every day.
- Schedule appointments with doctors.
- Do the dishes at night before bed.
- Tell myself self-care makes me better!
- Get clear about what I NEED to do every day vs. every week. Make a list. Put it on the bathroom mirror.
- Use an app to track my budget.
- Buy coffee out only once a week.
- Return clothes! (Actually do it!)

- Schedule bills to be paid a week before their due date.
- Use money from a paycheck when I have it, before I need it.
- Put deadlines for payments and big things on my calendar and on my phone.
- Put my phone down in the other room.
- Wake up to something else besides the phone.
- Download a tracking app to monitor usage.

IN ACTION: ANNA, THREE YEARS LATER

In the years since our small retreat in Myrtle Beach, Anna has made massive changes in her life. She's expressed boundaries between her and her parents, she's embraced speaking up for herself more, and, most importantly, she has gone to school to get her bachelor's, and soon her master's degree, in psychology. She is stepping into her dreams and her purpose. Anna has also worked her Self-Love To-Do List several times, updating it with new words each time she's felt a little lost . . . By the time we're sitting around the table in our room at the Vatreat, Anna is a pro.

She knows the process. Where once the idea of claiming a feeling made her nervous, she now does it with ease—it's exciting and it means NEW opportunities ahead! She works the steps without hesitation.

"It gets easier," she says with assurance when one of her Vatreat sisters expresses confusion. "I know, the first time it feels really weird, but

I promise you the more times you do it, it does get easier. Now it's like second nature to me."

I ask her if she will share her process with everyone, and she does it with confidence. With the self-awareness of a woman who has spent a few years learning how to listen to herself.

Her word now is "expansive." She says, "When I feel expansive, I embrace my path, prioritizing space, alignment, and flow." We are all impressed with the ease she feels in herself and her thought process. When I ask if I can look at her notebook, what she shares with me is beautiful.

EXPANSIVE

When I feel expansive, I embrace my path—prioritizing space, alignment, and flow.

The Challenges: What is keeping me from feeling this way? (BACK IT UP)
1. I allow my father's opinion to influence my decisions.
2. My home is full of things that don't serve me.
3. My schedule is full—job, school—without fun/levity and connection for balance.
4. Debt has been weighing me down, limiting my choices that are in alignment.

The Opportunities: What is my opportunity for growth? (FLIPPING IT)
1. I will make decisions and inform my father—not ask for his opinion.
2. I am selling my house and will only take with me things that I love or need.
3. I will make time to intentionally connect and have fun:
   • Movie dates.
   • Try new restaurants w/ Sam or Jen.
   • Schedule weekly FT with Annie.
   • Make a new list of what is fun for me.
4. I will use the house money to pay off debt and prioritize financial literacy by:
   • Following the 50/20/20/10 plan.
   • Read a book on building wealth.
   • Monthly financial check-in with trusted peers.
   • Make a list of trusted people.
   • Reach out for permission.

Anna's Self-Love To-Do List

1. I make decisions and then inform.
2. Put everything on my sell list in storage.
3. Call Aunt Jo to set a time for pickup of things to sell.
4. Throw out everything not coming with me.
5. Try new restaurants with Sam or Jen.
6. Schedule weekly FaceTime with Annie.
7. Make a list of what I find fun.
8. Use house $$ to pay off debt.
9. Follow the 50/20/20/10 plan.
10. Read the Rachel Rodgers book.
11. Make a list of people I trust to help me (monthly check-ins on $$).
12. Reach out to see if ↑ are willing to meet monthly.
13. I will be mindful and intentional about what I bring into my space.

Creating a Self-Love To-Do List is a way to give yourself clarity. In times when you (respectfully) feel like your head is up your ass, it is a graceful way to pluck that same head out of your crevice and screw it back on straight where it belongs.

SURVEYING THE SITE: WHAT WE DUG UP IN THIS CHAPTER

In this chapter, we went from thinking to action by learning the process of creating our very own Self-Love To-Do List. Instead of basing your actions on obtuse ideas that can be hard to visualize, let alone do, your SLTDL is based on facts and your personal truth. If you are willing to listen to yourself with honesty and see yourself as clearly as you can, you will be able to utilize this strategy for growth.

We talked about how to actually use your SLTDL. You can revisit this process whenever you feel like you are wandering without direction, whenever you feel stuck, or whenever you feel disconnected to yourself. You can print your list out, keep it on your phone, or use sticky notes or whatever vehicle helps you to stay committed!

When we think about getting clarity on what it is we want, there are two important questions it's necessary to remember from this chapter. The first question is, ***What am I REALLY saying here?*** This is a question you can ask yourself when you feel confused, when you find yourself talking in circles, or when you are having a problem giving yourself an answer to a question you are asking yourself. For example, if you say, "I want to feel happier," what you might really mean is "I want to be brave and travel more" or "I want to worry less about what other people are thinking of me" or "I feel sexually frustrated." Sometimes we struggle to express things in a finite way, so instead, we default to using more general and safe words because we aren't always comfortable being as truthful with ourselves as we can be. That's okay. Keep asking yourself, *What am I really saying?* until you get to a nugget of truth that resonates. Like this:

Statement: *I want to lose weight.*

What am I really saying here?

I'm saying that I'm not comfortable in my body anymore.

I'm saying that my body hurts, and it keeps me from doing things I want to do.

I'm saying that my poor mobility is getting in the way; I want to be more mobile so I can feel freer and do more things.

The second question is, ***How detailed can I get?*** When it comes to your SLTDL, generalities and sweeping statements are not your friend. Specificity is liberating, especially when it comes to taking action; humans don't like change, and we are experts at thwarting ourselves, so the more detail we can give ourselves and the smaller the action is we ask ourselves to do, the easier it will be for us. Earlier in this chapter, on page 129, I shared some examples of what this can look like for reference.

Most importantly, we used this chapter to illustrate a simple idea: Sometimes you don't have to know what you want, because it's enough to know what you DON'T want. You can "back up" into creating happiness in your life and on your terms!

III

SELF-LOVE OUT IN THE WORLD

The Importance of Owning Your Shit, Seeing
Your Story, and Loving into It When the
Rubber Hits the Road

Chapter 8

SELF-ABANDONMENT

That Thing You Do You Don't Know You Do

You're a six, but your personality makes you an eight."

I am in my living room when this guy I sleep with and I'm kinda-sorta in a relationship with named George says this to me over the phone all casual and glib. I'm not sure I hear him correctly at first, because that doesn't seem like the kind of thing you expect to hear from someone you've been sleeping with for a year and a half, does it?

"I'm a six... but my personality makes me an eight?" I ask rhetorically.

I'm a little taken aback but, logically, I can't argue. I mean, I *am* average. I'm not exciting or sexy. I'm just... a cool chick to be around, which, I gather, makes me a six. So, I don't protest. Instead, I laugh.

A few breaths later, George tells me about this other woman he sleeps with sometimes, who is apparently perfect. *They met in London. They used to swing dance together. She has great tits.* I make a joke about it and call her "the Ten" because she's clearly everything I am not and will never be and a whole lot more. I joke because jokes are better than hurt feelings, right? A few months later, when George comes to visit, the Ten also happens to be in Los Angeles and, in the middle of our weekend together, I encourage him to visit with her as well. I tell him it's okay when really, inside, I'm screaming because I feel like I know that I am certain—yes, totally certain—that I could never be exciting enough to make the trip worth it for him on my own and it sucks that the Ten has to be the one to bring it all home... When he comes back after their night together, I make sure to blow him really hard and show him (and myself, I guess) that I may be a six, but I still have *something* going for me.

This is one of thousands of times I'd self-abandoned in my life. It wouldn't be the last. Self-abandoning was my currency. It's how I maneuvered people into getting what I felt I needed in order to feel loved and valuable and needed. Constantly and chronically diminishing myself for other people was my identity, and I had, quite literally, no idea how much of myself I'd shaped around doing just that.

There is a question I ask the women who gather with me in workshops. It seems simple: "Do you trust yourself?"

The answer usually comes with a robust chorus of "Yes!" Of *course* they trust themselves! I note this silently before moving on.

I continue, "Do you trust yourself to always have your own back? Can you really, truly say that you support yourself fully every day?" The "yes" answers get a little softer. "We're going to talk about self-abandonment today," I say next. "Self-abandonment is that thing you do that you probably don't even realize you do and it's what is keeping you from living the life you really want to live. It's time to start seeing how we play an active role in NOT getting the things we really truly want." The room gets quiet. And shit gets real.

The thing is, you have to be willing to see the part you play in the process of living. Nobody *wants* to feel responsible for their unhappiness, but seeing how your actions and decisions have contributed to shaping your life into what it is right now is a necessary part of learning how to evolve and do things differently. Doing things differently is what is required of us if we want to experience something we've never experienced before. So, we're going to do it together, as gracefully and compassionately as possible.

I am going to say something to you now: Nobody is coming to save you...but you. If you are unhappy with something in your life, you are the only one who can (and will) do something about it.

This may be a hard truth, but it's incredibly liberating. It's natural to want to hold everyone and everything else accountable for our happiness, especially when we are unsatisfied in our lives. To believe that everything "happens to you" because you are bad or unworthy or that you are a victim being punished for some reason can be strangely soothing; if you can put the onus for everything on other people, you don't have to accept, or be responsible for, yourself. But you are your own bottom line.

If you want to experience something differently in your life, only YOU can make changes. If there is another version of you that you know exists, or if there is another way you know in your heart you are supposed to be living—this is, quite literally, in your hands. Unfurling into your Ultimate You is work for you and you alone. You may interact with other people and your relationships may be opportunities for you to experience yourself, but the work is your divine assignment.

In this chapter we're going to explore self-abandonment and (lovingly) open our eyes to the ways that we self-abandon. We're then going to talk about how the patterns of self-abandonment keep us from growing. And, as we move through the rest of this section of Soul Archaeology, we're going to keep talking about what happens when our self-love journey to unfurling into our Ultimate You hits the pavement of the *real world,* because growth can occur only within the context of actual life, and not in a bubble. So, it has to be *practical.* If it isn't based in the practical, it's not sustainable.

I want you to be the truest and most unabashedly vibrant version of you that you can be. I want you to feel liberated from others' expectations and from your own self-doubt. I want you to experience life in Technicolor. I want things to feel easier and more in flow to you. But the only way any of that happens is if you "go there" with the icky stuff. Very few things I've done in the moment to avoiding feeling uncomfortable, consciously or subconsciously, have ever really made my life better in the long run. Consciously or subconsciously avoiding anything so I wouldn't feel uncomfortable in the moment has not made my life better in the long run.

To create change in your life, you have to have faith and the ability to trust yourself. If you want to trust yourself, you have to honor yourself. If you want to honor yourself, you have to do your best to avoid self-abandoning.

DIG SITE: DISCLAIMER—PERSONAL RESPONSIBILITY, TRAUMA, AND BIG STUFF

We are not responsible for traumatic things we have experienced in our lives. Sometimes, really shitty things happen and it's not because we asked for them or deserved them. There are terrible things that happen to people that are *not* their fault; it is not our place to blame ourselves or blame victims. It also needs to be said that, sometimes, forces outside of our control shape things, and those forces can cause people a lot of pain—systemic racism, for example, or capitalism or organized religion, or the reality of socioeconomics. These are big things no single person can be responsible for changing. That being said, what we can be responsible for is how we treat ourselves, see ourselves, and experience ourselves as we relate to the things that happen to us and around us. When we talk about "personal accountability," we must allow for nuance and accept that there are limits to what people can, and should, consider themselves responsible for.

DEFINING "SELF-ABANDONMENT" AND WHY IT MATTERS

As you move through the items on your Self-Love To-Do List in your everyday life and start doing things differently than you did before, you'll encounter a million little moments (and some big ones) where you are given a choice either to do what serves you or to fall back into old patterns. In order to learn how to avoid bringing our past missteps into the future, we have to look at where we're misstepping in the present.

When we think of the word "abandon," we often think of things that have been left behind. Things get abandoned all the time, but what happens when what is abandoned isn't an inanimate object, but ourselves? Do we, like that rusty old car left on the side of the road, gather dust and begin to fall apart until a tow truck comes to haul us away and take us to the dump? Kinda. But instead of pieces of debris being left behind, it's pieces of ourselves.

According to the National Alliance on Mental Illness, "self-abandonment is when you reject, suppress or ignore part of yourself in real-time." It explains that when we self-abandon, we have a need and are presented with a choice to meet it or not, and then we make a conscious or subconscious decision not to meet the need.[1] Basically, self-abandonment is the act of telling ourselves that our needs—and subsequently we—don't matter.

Each time we self-abandon, we reinforce to our subconscious that we are not worthy of our own trust and esteem. We take a little chisel and *tap tap* away at the bricks of our foundation—the stuff we need to feel safe in our own lives. We can do this so much and so often that it becomes our normal. We become so used to putting other people's comfort, needs, and feelings before our own that we stop realizing we even have feelings and needs; eventually, we find ourselves so disconnected from our own ability to listen to ourselves and see ourselves that we feel powerless to the inertia of what is happening around us. We settle. We neglect. We repress. This becomes who we are. How can we possibly ever find the self-love to be greater if our entire identity is based on being as un-great as possible?

The Ten Ways We Self-Abandon

Let's make this as clear as possible. PsychCentral online has identified ten of the most common ways we self-abandon.[2] I'll share them here:

1. **Perfectionism.** If you have sky-high expectations for yourself and feel like you will never be good enough—regardless of what you do and how awesome you do it.

2. **You don't trust yourself and you second-guess yourself.** Do you ignore your own instincts? Are you capable of even hearing them to begin with? You may disregard your instincts entirely and, eventually, may even stop recognizing them. This is when you believe everyone knows more than you, or you allow them to make decisions for you.

3. **Criticizing and judging yourself.** If you say mean, crappy, and hurtful things to yourself—stuff you would never say to anyone else you loved.

4. **People-pleasing.** When you crave validation from others, and you suppress and downplay your own needs in order to make other people happy.

5. **When you don't honor your own needs.** You have needs. You know they exist, and you either consciously or subconsciously decide not to meet them. You feel unworthy of self-care and may stop serving yourself entirely.

6. **Hiding yourself.** This may be your whole self or just parts of you. It could also be giving up your interests and hobbies or the things that make you happy. You may do this specifically for another person because your feelings and interests would not be welcome or enjoyable for them.

7. **Suppressing your own feelings.** When you tell yourself that your feelings don't matter or you are in denial of things. This *also* means anesthetizing your feelings so you can avoid them, using stuff that changes your physical and mental chemistry—like food, drugs, or alcohol.

8. **Not acting in a way that is aligned with your own values.** Abandoning your values and personal beliefs and standards—your personal guidelines that help you determine what is right or wrong.

9. **Being in codependent relationships.** Depending on someone else's perception of you to determine your own value and worth to the point that you deny yourself.

10. **When you fail to speak up for yourself.** When you know what you need but don't ask for it, don't enforce boundaries, and let others take advantage of you.

DIG DEEPER:
Figuring Out What Self-Abandoning (Actually) Looks Like for YOU

If you are still struggling to see the ways you self-abandon (or don't think you do it at all), that's totally okay. I've got a tool to help you see more clearly! Look, I don't *want* you to self-abandon, but if you *do*, I want you to see what you do so that you can learn how to do things differently moving forward.

This is my Big (hopefully not too scary) List of Self-Abandonment. It shows a bunch of ways that people can self-abandon in some real-world settings. Don't obsess over the details—I don't know your life and my examples can't be spot-on relevant for you, and they don't have to be. All you need to do when you review this is note which of the following feel familiar to you in some way, shape, or form.

In order to do this exercise, read each item on the list. Consider if it feels familiar to you. If you don't see yourself in an example, move on to the next one. Put an *X* through each checkbox that indicates a thing you are *currently* doing in life. Put a check mark in each box that indicates something you *used* to do but no longer identify with.

THE BIG LIST OF (HOPEFULLY NOT SO SCARY) SELF-ABANDONMENT

- ❑ I isolate myself from other people.
- ❑ I really want to be liked.
- ❑ It's my fault when people are upset.
- ❑ I spend a lot of energy trying to please people.
- ❑ I am super critical of myself.
- ❑ I feel like I have to prove that I am worthy to others.
- ❑ I need attention in order to feel valuable.
- ❑ I go along with what other people think or do, even though I don't agree.
- ❑ Other people's comfort is more important than my own.
- ❑ I regularly hide my feelings because I don't want to make other people uncomfortable.
- ❑ I complain a lot.
- ❑ I know my body is ugly.

- ❏ I compare myself to others a lot.
- ❏ I rarely think before responding or taking action; I am impulsive or reactive.
- ❏ In my heart, I know I'm "living the life" that someone else wants me to live.
- ❏ I rarely allow myself to get angry, even though I've been hurt by people before.
- ❏ I have a hard time speaking my truth.
- ❏ I am really good at doing something (talent, artistic gift) that I don't do anymore but that used to bring me joy.
- ❏ I know my health isn't great—I want to care but I don't.
- ❏ I spend a lot of money on stuff because I think it matters to other people.
- ❏ My bank account is always running low / I continually max out my credit cards.
- ❏ I don't focus on myself; I give all my energy to caring for others who need me.
- ❏ Doing things I like is a low priority in my busy life.
- ❏ I regularly schedule way too much and leave no time for me.
- ❏ I have to drink at the end of the day.
- ❏ I am always stressed out and too busy.
- ❏ I avoid doing things I know are good for me.
- ❏ I repeatedly make "mistakes" even though I know what I'm doing isn't good for me.
- ❏ I chronically pay bills late, miss deadlines, or put tasks off to the absolute last minute; I scramble and panic.
- ❏ I eat to calm down or when I'm bored.
- ❏ I know I have an eating disorder but I don't want help.
- ❏ My partner calls me names. I stay anyway because I don't want to lose them.
- ❏ I feel coerced into doing things sexually in order to keep my partner happy.
- ❏ I feel sexually unfulfilled because my partner doesn't have an interest in sex the way I do.
- ❏ I "play games" with people in order to get what I want.
- ❏ I am in a relationship where I feel like I can never breathe.
- ❏ I don't know where I end and my partner begins. (Or the same with a parent!)
- ❏ I trust people who let me down.
- ❏ I am in a relationship I value more than my dignity.

- ❏ I ignore red flags in relationships.
- ❏ I do activities my partner or friends want to do, even though I don't like doing them and they know it.
- ❏ I let people treat me poorly. I know it happens but I don't know how to stop it, or I don't want to stop it.
- ❏ I deal with other people's shit and not my own because it's easier to focus on other people than myself.
- ❏ I have never set boundaries in my relationships...I don't even really know what boundaries are.
- ❏ I've never had a serious disagreement with anyone.
- ❏ I pretend to like people I don't.

Now that you've made it through the list, let's do a bit of thinking and journaling to help us process what we just experienced.

Grab your notebook or journal and answer the following questions:

1. Was there anything you saw in that list that surprised you?
2. Do you notice a "theme" with the ways you self-abandon?
3. How did it feel to review that list and think about yourself?

If going through that list made you really uncomfortable or sad, you may want to do something *right now* to ease the discomfort and make it all better. I invite you...*to not*. Let's just stay here a second together. Do nothing. Sit on your hands if you have to. Just sit here. No matter how wonky you feel right now, you are totally okay. You are the exact same person you were a few minutes ago. Remember, the point of life is not to avoid your hard feelings, but to create a kinder relationship to them. You don't NEED to do a single thing. Just see.

Take the opportunity to practice self-compassion, and recognize that the ways you have self-abandoned as a protective coping mechanism in the past do not make you unworthy or less than. Your survival instincts are fierce magic. They told you what you needed to do in order to get your basic needs met, and they totally worked because they got you this far! That's badass! But now you can do different things to meet your own needs in different ways, ways that are more aligned with your values and who you want to be. These new things you can do will take practice but are totally possible. This is a chance for you to offer yourself some love as a caring parent would offer to a child. Most importantly...this is a chance to start rebuilding trust in yourself. And self-trust is the foundation for everything.

If you feel like you *need* to self-soothe right now (again, totally normal), I offer two suggestions:

1. Do something from your Self-Love To-Do List (the one you made in the last chapter)! This list is 100 percent about serving YOU, which is

the total opposite of self-abandoning. Use it. Feed your soul. You've got this.

2. Talk to yourself with fierce compassion. Try saying this: *I see that this is how I have self-abandoned in my past. I see this without judgment. I am human and I have done the best I could. I am safe. I hold my hand now, and I commit to a more self-loving course of action in the future. I am enough.*

That is all. You don't need to do anything else. Just see.

SELF-ABANDONMENT IN THE NAME OF (MY) LOVE

When it comes to men, I'm a champion self-abandoner. The most profound, clear example of how deeply I've self-abandoned might have been my long-term relationship with a guy we'll call Jake. He said he was recently divorced and hadn't been dating. He was coming to Las Vegas for a pool tournament with friends, and would I be willing to talk to him?

His online profile showed pictures of a tall, broad, and thick-looking man who was just my type. My heart (or was it my vagina?) skipped a beat and so I agreed to meet up. I promised myself it would be just once. I drew my line in the sand.

We met for dinner and when he stood to greet me, Jake towered over me; I felt small and feminine the minute he put his big arms around me. He had a soft, deep voice with a hint of Southern twang. We talked for hours, and at the end of the evening he walked me to the valet and waited while my car was brought around. He held the door as I got in, and kissed my cheek. "Text me when you get home," he said, and it wasn't a question.

The next night we went dancing. I drank too much. He kissed me on the dance floor as if nobody else was there. Later that night we giggled our way through awkward, intoxicated sex. And in the morning, we slept late and went for breakfast. *I felt alive.*

He went home to Kentucky, and even though I told myself we'd never talk again, we did. Every day. He was divorced with two kids, owned a gym and a liquor store, and was kind and funny. *He was my big Superman.*

Jake flew back into town just weeks later to see me. During that trip he told me he loved me. He said if he didn't have his businesses or kids, he'd come to Vegas and try to give it a real go with me. His words felt like the kind of love I'd been craving my whole life, so when he asked me to be in a relationship with him, I jumped in headfirst.

There were red flags, but I couldn't have spotted them if I tried and, if I could have, I certainly didn't *want* to see them. Once he sent me a picture of his kids; he said he'd just taken it, but there was a woman in the shot I'd assumed was their mother. There was a ring on her ring finger, and I tried not to vomit my heart out of my throat when I asked him about it. He told me it was a family ring, then picked a fight with me about something totally unrelated. When I finally convinced him to let me come and visit him in Louisville, he drove us to a hotel downtown and showed me the beautiful room he'd gotten us. "I got us a hotel room so we could be in the center of things," he said, and I thought it was odd but romantic in some way. I wanted to know why we couldn't stay at his place, but I didn't bother to ask. Later, he told me he wished we were living together, and that was all the permission I needed...A little over a year after we'd met, I moved to Louisville.

"Are you sure you want to do this, Sarah?" a girlfriend of mine asked. This friend had a way of finding things out about people; I gathered she'd found something she didn't like about Jake or else she wouldn't have asked me that. But I was ready. I was twenty-eight and moving cross-country into an apartment that overlooked a cornfield, and I was in love...with a man that turned out to be married. He had three kids, not two. And he still lived at home with his wife and family.

I barely saw Jake. Whenever he did visit, it was during a weekday and never (ever) at night. In the two years I lived in Kentucky, he slept less than three nights at my apartment with me. On Valentine's Day he bought me a fern that he dropped off in the morning. I bought him Christmas-themed flannel pajama pants, but I wasn't able to give them to him for Christmas, because, well, clearly Christmastime is meant for family and not your mistress, right? Not a Thanksgiving. Not a long weekend. Nothing. What I got was nothing like what I'd hoped it would be, nothing like what we talked about, and nothing like what I'd wanted at all.

I pulled away from my friends and family. Once or twice, I got to do "girlfriend things" for him. I threw him a Super Bowl party and I stood in my kitchen and watched him cheer with his friends and I thought, *Man, this is what it's supposed to be like, isn't it? I've waited my whole life for this.* At the end of the game they left, and I spent the rest of the evening doing dishes by myself.

I never complained. I believed if I could be cool and calm about everything, my willingness to go with the flow would show him I was dedicated, and it would motivate him to make changes. "Always be classy; never be crazy" was what I said to myself.

Except I felt alienated every day. I was embarrassed and ashamed. I told almost nobody in my life what I was really going through. I cried myself to sleep at night while all my friends and family thought I'd met the man of my dreams and we were living the life together in Kentucky. I tried to get involved with local activities, but nothing felt right. The weeks turned into months. The months turned into years. And by the time I was thirty, my eyes had lost their sparkle, and I had done nothing but make excuses to myself and everyone who loved me.

I did ask Jake to make changes. I would tell him, "No, this doesn't work for me," and I meant it in the moment. He made promises, but they were always broken. My "nos" dissolved into meaningless protests, time and time again. Neither of us could follow through with the promises we made. Every "I can't do this anymore." Every "If this doesn't happen by the end of the month, I can't be in this relationship." They all meant nothing, and I hated myself for it. I was fully aware that I was "the other woman," but I believed him when he said he was leaving. *I didn't ask for this, you know?* I believed him when he said they were miserable, and he slept in the garage. I wanted to fix it.

I hadn't lost my grip on reality. I was sane; I just . . . didn't care enough. I fixated on my (hopeful) relationship at the expense of everything else, and my only priority was hanging in long enough so that Jake would leave his wife and we could be together.

One night, I showed up at Jake's bar unannounced. He had been evading my calls, and when I did manage to get him on the phone, he was defensive and aggressive. He said he wasn't at the bar, but I knew he was there . . . I *knew* he was there; I wasn't fucking crazy. So, I just showed up to prove myself correct. Before I left home I sat in my parked car with my keys in my hand before starting the engine. *I knew I wasn't wrong.* I was tired of being shut out. I put the key in the ignition and drove the thirty minutes in silence.

I showed up without getting clearance first and he was mighty pissed off (when your boyfriend is married, there is no such thing as spontaneity; everything requires permission before it happens). I had no idea who he would be with or what I was walking into, and I didn't care. I needed him to SEE ME because I was tired of being completely invisible. *I needed to be seen.* I needed to talk to him.

As I got out of my car, all the words I had rehearsed during the drive vanished. Jake flung the bar's door open and light streamed from behind him. He was like an angry dog and I was mute. I stood there in the dark of the parking lot with my headlights beaming onto the gravel.

He yelled at me for showing up. He looked at me like I was a stranger. He was drunk. I tried to speak but he was louder. He said it was my fault that he'd been dodging my calls because he couldn't deal with me. I told him I just wanted to talk to him, and he hollered at me, "You're out of control!"

He turned his large back to me and walked away, the wooden bar door *thwacking* closed and bouncing on rusty springs. I got back into the car and drove home. I couldn't argue. What kind of person was I? I didn't recognize the person I was—whoever I was, I hated her.

At home, I spent the next few days crying. I thought about calling a friend for help, but who could I tell this to? I was alone. I didn't feel like I could talk to anyone. Alone was my penance for having stayed so long in a place I never should have been.

Eventually I would leave. It was, quite literally, a matter of saving myself. Like when Rose removes Jack's frozen, dead hand from hers at the end of *Titanic* before allowing him to sink into the depths of the icy North Atlantic. I had to let go or else I'd go down with Jake, and I knew it; I finally saw it.

I stepped back into the center of my life. Scared. Emotionally bruised. I had nothing to stand on and no trust to bolster and support me, but I was ready to fight for myself and that was all that mattered.

 DIG DEEPER:
Seeing the Most Common Ways You Self-Abandon

I'm going to bet something in this chapter has resonated deeply with you. Maybe you've had an "Oh, fuck" moment or two? If so, this short exercise is a great way for you to gain even more clarity about how you currently self-abandon and how you have done so in the past.

Back in chapter 6 we discussed how feelings rarely exist on their own; they can stretch out into other areas of life and, in turn, manifest and show up in unexpected ways. The same goes for self-abandoning; it is rare to self-abandon in only one way and in one specific situation. It's more likely for us to have a go-to style of self-abandonment that "works" because it helps us meet our immediate need (aka to remove ourselves from discomfort) and we utilize that go-to in lots of different ways.

Using the Big (not so scary) List of Self-Abandonment, review the items you've either checked off or circled. Each time you note something, think about which of the main categories of self-abandonment it fits in. For example, if you marked "I regularly hide my feelings because I don't want to make other people uncomfortable," you may feel it's an example of people-pleasing, suppressing your feelings, codependent relationships, and when you don't honor your own needs. For each of those, put a mark in their specific box.

The point of this exercise is to tally up in which areas you self-abandon the most, and which don't feel as familiar to you. There is no right answer here and no wrong answer. Again, this is just about starting to see our own patterns.

Self-criticism and judgment	Hiding parts of yourself	Suppressing your feelings	Not trusting instincts	Perfectionism
People-pleasing	Not acting according to values	Not speaking up for yourself	Not honoring your needs	Codependent relationships

Here is what it looks like when I fill out the boxes based on some of my past experiences:

Self-criticism and judgment	Hiding parts of yourself	Suppressing your feelings	Not trusting instincts	Perfectionism
I		I I I I	I	

People-pleasing	Not acting according to your values	Not speaking up for yourself	Not honoring your needs	Codependent relationships
I I II		I I I I	III	II

Next . . . do nothing. Seriously! Again, the point of our observations is not for us to be obsessed with how to FIX ourselves, but rather just to SEE ourselves and sit with what is true. There will be plenty of opportunity for action as we move forward, so exhale into any discomfort that may be coming up and melt into the present.

If you need to release discomfort, you can do some thinking or journaling and ask yourself:

- *What feelings are coming up for me right now?*
- *Why do I feel the way I do about my feelings?*
- *Am I more uncomfortable with the truth I see now or the self-judgment I feel about the truth?*
- *Are the feelings I am feeling my own, or are they the influence of others? (For example, do you hear your mother's voice in your head or a former partner's?)*

SELF-ABANDONMENT IS A LIFETIME PRACTICE

Becoming a chronic self-abandoner happens over time. Although we may start out a novice, after years of practice we can find ourselves standing on the podium, winning the gold medal in the Self-Abandonment Olympics. (You know, like Yours Truly did after moving cross-country for a married man. #Winning.)

The big question is, Why do we self-abandon? Where do these patterns come from?

I'll give you the most real answer I can: I don't know. First, I don't know you personally. Second, I'm not a therapist. That being said, this is a *great* question to bring to a therapy professional you are working with. You might ask, "I'm realizing that I have a pattern of self-abandonment, especially with not honoring my needs. Can we explore where that comes from in my past?"

Here is what I *do* know—at some point in your life, you learned that the best way to protect yourself and have one of your (totally normal) needs met was to self-abandon in some way. Prevailing wisdom suggests this probably started in your childhood as a learned behavior. Something you did in order to feel safe and loved and to get feedback that was valuable to you to feel "okay" in the moment. When you had an emotional or physical need that someone (a likely source was your parents) didn't—or couldn't—meet for you, you learned tactics that helped make things feel smoother and more stable by yourself. Sometimes you were aware of what you were doing when you did it and it was a conscious choice, a conscious mechanism for survival. Sometimes it's probable that you did these things without even realizing you were doing them.

Even if the things we've done were dysfunctional, they "worked" in some capacity because they helped to meet our immediate needs, so we kept doing them; they became patterns. It is important to remember that once patterns become familiar to us, we keep turning to them again and again, long after the initial circumstances have passed, because these actions feel familiar—and, as we all know, familiar stuff always feels comforting or reliable in some way.

We may start with small acts of self-abandonment, but as time goes by, the ways we self-abandon can become more and more insidious and destructive to our greater well-being. My earliest memories of self-abandoning are related to being a child with divorced parents and going ice-skating on Friday nights each week with my dad. There was an awareness that I had to "zip up" my feelings—not showing excitement either while waiting for him to pick me up or when I returned back home to my mother. The question "Did you have a good time with Dad?" was always met with a noninflammatory answer on my part, like "Fine." I started denied and downplayed my feelings early in order to make other people (in this case, my mother) more comfortable. I also tried to down-play and hide the anger I felt toward my father for, as I saw in my child eyes, "leaving me" and my parents' divorce. In doing this, I learned that if I could keep my feelings to myself and be "easy," then people I loved would be happy and not get angry at me; I did this all throughout my teens, and then denied and downplayed my emotions throughout the sex-ually coercive relationship I had with my boyfriend in college. I did it in all my relationships after that, and eventually, I did the same with Jake. By that time, I had spent so many years telling myself my feelings didn't matter that I was unable to really see how damaging these situations were to my well-being. I was numb to the impact of my own actions.

When I finally saw how often I'd self-abandoned in my life, I felt ashamed and embarrassed. I soon realized there was absolutely no reason for me to feel shame or to judge myself for doing the best I could at the time. Shame and embarrassment have no place in self-reflection, espe-cially if the strategies we use for self-abandonment are ones we originally created as children to help us feel safer. That being said, as adults look-ing to live a more self-loving and liberated life, we now have a chance to recognize how those old patterns of self-abandonment no longer serve us. And if we see that, we can work to do something different.

Living a Self-Loving Life is about learning to align your life to *your* personal values. This means you become the North Star of your life— guided by your values, your parameters, and your boundaries. As a result, you will naturally self-abandon less because you are shifting the focus from serving others to serving yourself.

Oftentimes, when we self-abandon, it is done for the benefit of others— to keep them happy or to serve them. When we do this, we are placing our happiness and our personal value system in the hands of another, giving that person the keys to the car and putting them in the driver's seat of our life.

Once we see the ways we have self-abandoned in the past (and, therefore, the ways we will likely do so again in the future if we don't make changes), the only way to stop the past from repeating itself is to create new patterns that are rooted in our self-love and that build our self-trust. When we start to utilize these new, more self-loving patterns, it's as if we are building a house from the foundation up—each choice we make that serves us is a brick that solidifies our building, making a strong, sturdy, and supportive house for us to live in.

OKAY, I GET IT; NOW WHAT?

If you want to stop self-abandoning, you need to focus on rebuilding trust in yourself. Sounds simple, right? Well, building self-trust is simple...It's just not easy.

You have actual basic needs that you deserve to have met as a human. Things like respect and to be valued by others and yourself. You have a need to see yourself, listen to yourself, and act accordingly based on your own best interest.

Here's the problem: Whether or not you realize it, chronic self-abandoning will convince you that your needs cannot or do not deserve to be met. This can turn into a self-fulfilling prophecy. Meaning the belief or expectation that you have about something that could possibly happen in the future actually manifests itself because you already held it to be true.[3] *You feel a certain way, which translates into actions and choices that have a specific outcome. But because you feel a certain way, the outcome you end up with is created around the actions and choices you make, which then make you feel a certain way. So, you take actions and make choices, influenced by the way you feel . . . and so on, and so on.* It's a cycle that has to be broken.

The only way to break your cycle is to prioritize yourself in ways you have not done before. In ways that are self-loving because they support you, take into account your needs, and provide ways for you to serve your needs. This is why moving away from self-abandoning is actually a return to yourself. It is about learning to listen to yourself and deciding that you value yourself enough to prioritize what you need. This is how you uncover your Ultimate You.

Use Your Tools!

The greatest part of all this is that you already have a starting point for what to do next. You have a tool in place you can begin using right now. There doesn't need to be any guesswork, because if you've been doing the practices in this book, you've already created your Self-Love To-Do List, and if you did it honestly, every single item on that Self-Love To-Do List is a way for you to start building trust with yourself.

Holy shitballs, I love it when things start to make sense and the gears click into place! You have a strategy. You know what to do next! Now you just need to get that shit done! The more you are committed to your Ultimate You, the more you'll stretch yourself, grow, and hit walls. Yes, there will always be challenges that test your patterns of self-abandonment—you can't stop them from happening, but you can get better at navigating them when they occur!

In order to illustrate what a shift away from self-abandoning toward building self-trust looks like, let's break down two clear examples. One is what it looks like when you are more committed to your own self-abandonment than you are to your growth—when you are stuck repeating your patterns. The other is what navigating a challenge looks like when you are willing to get uncomfortable and break the pattern, to let self-love be your North Star when building trust in yourself is your priority.

How Breaking the Self-Abandonment Cycle Allows You to Do Things Differently

On the left side is a real-world example of what your thought pattern can be like when you are caught in a cycle of self-abandonment. On the right is an example of what your thought pattern can be like when you break it.

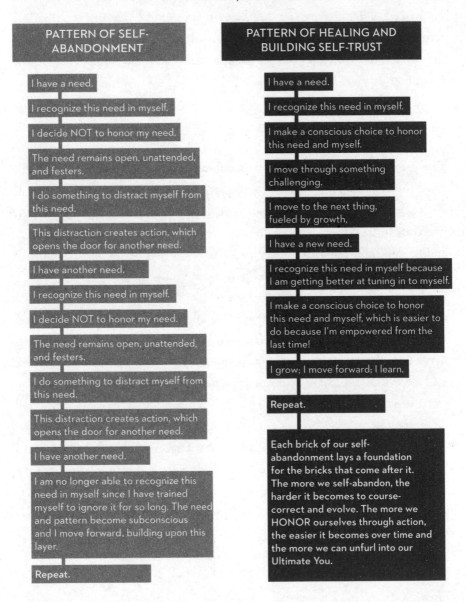

PATTERN OF SELF-ABANDONMENT

I have a need.

I recognize this need in myself.

I decide NOT to honor my need.

The need remains open, unattended, and festers.

I do something to distract myself from this need.

This distraction creates action, which opens the door for another need.

I have another need.

I recognize this need in myself.

I decide NOT to honor my need.

The need remains open, unattended, and festers.

I do something to distract myself from this need.

This distraction creates action, which opens the door for another need.

I have another need.

I am no longer able to recognize this need in myself since I have trained myself to ignore it for so long. The need and pattern become subconscious and I move forward, building upon this layer.

Repeat.

PATTERN OF HEALING AND BUILDING SELF-TRUST

I have a need.

I recognize this need in myself.

I make a conscious choice to honor this need and myself.

I move through something challenging.

I move to the next thing, fueled by growth,

I have a new need.

I recognize this need in myself because I am getting better at tuning in to myself.

I make a conscious choice to honor this need and myself, which is easier to do because I'm empowered from the last time!

I grow; I move forward; I learn.

Repeat.

Each brick of our self-abandonment lays a foundation for the bricks that come after it. The more we self-abandon, the harder it becomes to course-correct and evolve. The more we HONOR ourselves through action, the easier it becomes over time and the more we can unfurl into our Ultimate You.

In a pattern of self-abandonment, you keep yourself stuck in a dysfunctional spin-cycle. Even though the circumstances may change—the geography, romantic partners, or job title (or whatever it is) may be different—the pattern itself stays the same. It's why you may feel like you're no longer in charge of your own life path.

In a pattern of self-trust, you are continually learning and growing. You may make mistakes, but your mistakes are used to move you forward. You are continually checking in with yourself—you are listening to yourself and adjusting accordingly. You are strengthening your bond to yourself and learning to depend on yourself when it matters the most. You know that there may be some sort of higher power at work, but you know that you can count on yourself to show up for you. As a result, you are less anxious, more in control and in alignment, and more yourself.

Build Self-Trust with Small Choices Made Again and Again

When you created your Self-Love To-Do List, I stressed the importance of making the items on your list as specific and accessible as possible. The reason for this is that little decisions and actions may feel small, but each of them is a brick that is part of a bigger foundation. Some experts say we make 35,000 choices every day—roughly 2,000 an hour.[4] Wouldn't it be powerful if the majority of those choices were ones designed to help you be an absolute badass?

Not every one of these choices is earth-shattering. Some are benign—like the choice between buying single-ply or two-ply toilet paper. Other choices carry a little more weight, like *Do I really want this third drink? I know that tequila hits me hard and I'll need to get a ride home tonight because I won't be able to drive.* There are also choices that are a nuisance to make, but you make them anyway: *Ugh. I really want takeout, but my funds are low, and I have all those perfectly good leftovers in the fridge . . . Yup, I'll eat leftovers and stick to my budget; I can get takeout next week.* Then there are the choices that should be obvious, like hanging up the phone on the guy who regularly puts his penis inside of you but has the balls to call you "a six" and expect that you're still going to talk to him.

Here's the brilliant part. The more you practice making smaller decisions that serve you—the more you ask yourself what you want, what you need, and what is truly self-love for you—the stronger your muscle of self-trust becomes and the easier it is to do what is the best thing for you when the really hard decisions roll around and you are tested to your core. You will be so proficient with your own self-trust that even if you *really* want to do something else, you'll still pick yourself above everything else that demands your self-abandonment. You will be able to trust your judgment in the face of really hard shit.

SURVEYING THE SITE:
WHAT WE DUG UP IN THIS CHAPTER

Hopefully, this chapter opened the curtains to a dark room and let rays of sunshine warm the dusty corners of your self-worth. We introduced the concept of self-abandonment and went through lots of examples of what self-abandonment can look like in our daily lives. We talked about how, though familiar and possibly comforting, the things that we do when we self-abandon actually keep us from feeling what we truly want to feel in our lives. This chapter shared the importance of building trust with ourselves, and how self-abandoning erodes the trust we have in ourselves and what that diminishing can do to our ability to think for ourselves and make judgment calls that serve our self-interest over time. The key is to have a strong self-trust muscle that allows us to listen to ourselves, cultivates our confidence, and empowers us to do things that are good for us. Last, we compared two decision cycles—one where self-abandoning is our priority, and the other where self-trust navigates our decisions.

In this moment, I'm going to stand next to you and remind you that you aren't alone. I've shared some examples of self-abandonment from my past because I want you to know that to do those things is human. The desire to feel love and to feel like you matter can be a really strong one.

It would be easy for someone to judge me for the things I did when I was trying to give and receive love—in fact, you might have even cringed when you read about my relationships with Jake and George. That's okay.

In life, we have choices to judge others, and ourselves, or not. We can see our actions for what they were and simply that, or we can use them as weapons to wound. But you cannot grow from a place of hate. You don't have to like everything you've done in your past, but you *can* let it be just that—the past. And you can know, deep in your heart, that the painful experiences you've had may teach you valuable and important things that can change your life in beautiful ways you've never imagined.

In the next chapter, we're going to talk about courage, specifically the courage it takes to truly see what it is you long for. You may have spent a lifetime unable to see, drowned out by your desire to please other people. But you exist, and what it is you truly want matters. You just have to open your heart.

Chapter 9

WHAT DO YOU *REALLY* WANT?

The Courage to Listen to Your Heart and the Road Map It Creates

George arrives at my apartment and I wheel his rolling suitcase into my bedroom. While I'm fidgeting, he places his hands on my waist and leans in.

"You nervous?" he asks in the deep voice I've grown accustomed to on the other end of the phone. I nod, and then we're kissing, which feels comfortable and familiar and like an action with a purpose I can wrap my head around. This I understand. This has boundaries and rules and neat lines to color inside.

We do our usual dance. Sex. Drinks. More sex. Dirty jokes and catching up. Round three (yeehaw!), and then we both fall asleep. Easy-peasy. It isn't till the next morning that cracks start to appear. I offer him milk for his coffee only to learn he drinks it black. Then there is an awkward dance around who will shower first and what we'll do for the day, the answer to which turns out to be...nothing. We do nothing. The small talk fades away into silence, and I am left grasping for topics to discuss. This goes beyond the shtick I know. And, believe me, I know shtick.

George is asleep, snoring lightly. His head is flopped back; in his lap is a red bowl with straggling crumbs of Chex Mix. His left knee, in nylon Denver Bronco lounge pants, is touching my right thigh, the soft and worn nubby tie-dyed fabric of my pants faded thin.

This moment is so utterly normal that it terrifies me.

I had eagerly anticipated our time together this long weekend. We had scheduled a four-day trip...which would turn into ninety-six hours of me being totally, utterly out of my element as I wrestled with the presence of another human body in my living space and, even more terrifying, the realization that *I liked it*.

I've been single most of my entire adult life. So much that I feel like I've gotten good at being alone.

Sure, I've dated, and I've had one (totally dysfunctional long-term) relationship after the age of twenty-five. But neither the dating nor the relationship ever spilled out over the constraints of planned activities or specific and designated periods of time. I've never lived with a partner or cohabitated for any length of time, unlike the majority of my peers, who have long been shacked up.

If I were being honest, I might even admit that I was more used to dating someone "inaccessible" than someone who was fingertips away. I never balked at the idea of being with someone who traveled for a living or split their time with parental duties. Being with someone who was never around to make plans with (or even someone who bailed on plans in favor of something "more important last-minute") was my normal.

I've told myself that I like to be alone all the time.

I've told myself that relationships like this allowed me to remain "fiercely independent."

I've told myself I didn't actually want to do everyday, basic life shit with someone. One time, I dated a guy who, between kids' soccer practices and work and obligations, had only slivers of time to allot to his personal life. He told me, "If you're looking for a guy to sit on the couch and watch *American Idol* with you, that's not me." I thought that was cool. Who wanted to sit on the couch with someone watching TV anyway? That sounded boring as fuck.

At least that was what I told myself.

During our time of nothingness together, I've screwed up roast beef sandwiches by adding mayonnaise (which, apparently, George hates), and I've offered him grapes (which, apparently, he also hates), and now we are back on the couch. (We've been sleeping together for years; I should know these things about him, right?) George grabs the remote control and flips through the channels. I teeter precariously and uncomfortably on the couch, forcing my legs to "tuck under themselves" like I'm a Jane Austen heroine and not a three-hundred-plus-pound thirty-something pretzel with thighs and a stomach that thwart my desired pose. I want my assets presented properly, and I keep my eyes on George as I adjust to check and see if he's noticed. *He hasn't.* I wiggle my shirt down a little in the front . . . Still nothing. *He seems unfazed.* What do I do now? It is just as I am asking myself this question that I notice he has fallen asleep.

There's a knock at my door. I scamper up to answer (and, believe me, I do scamper just in case George magically opens his eyes, because I want him to see me looking agile and curvaceous, like a chunky gazelle).

My landlady has popped by to pick up a set of cookie sheets I borrowed. I tell her I have company, and she notices my silver ballet flats, which are lined up neatly next to George's large sneakers.

"Aw, look," she coos, "boy shoes, girl shoes . . ."

This hits me like a brick wall. The simple appearance of shoes, in perfect symmetry next to each other. His shoes, my shoes. My shoes . . . next to the shoes of another.

I've never seen them that way before. It looks foreign and funny but, at the same time, totally normal . . . My center shifts. *Why not my shoes?*

The silver ballet flats are girly and look slight compared to his big, rubbery sneakers. I like the stark difference between the two. As if our shoes existed to complement each other, to maneuver them into position and the natural order of life. The idea that one pair could belong to another. Make a home next to each other. It's so simple. *Maybe I want this . . . Do I want this? I think I do.*

A little truth bomb has been planted; soon, it will explode. I ask myself, *Why do I want this now when I've never wanted it before?* But I know that is a lie. If I'm really being honest with myself, I've *always* wanted this.

Walking back to the couch, I settle into position while George snores away, unaware of my burgeoning existential crisis. My mind veers back to a specific memory of when my dad would pick me up for our Friday night ice-skating dates after my parents' divorce. It was a neat few hours every week that we'd always finish off with a cup of cookies-and-cream ice cream from my favorite place. On the off chance I'd spend the night at my dad's apartment, I'd show up as Happy Sleepover Sarah with my Gap tote bag containing everything I'd need for the time away, including a toothbrush, pajamas, and a book. (I hated doing this. Did I mention I couldn't leave any of those things behind?)

I didn't know why I wasn't allowed to have this kind of time and space with my dad; I just knew it wasn't offered to me so, eventually, I stopped hoping for it. But I *did* want it. I knew I wasn't allowed to express this desire to my mom, who still carried a degree of resentment toward him after their split. And why would I reveal it to my dad? If he wanted to see me more, surely he would. I gather that was the moment I tucked my dream away of ever feeling safe and unguarded and completely at home with a male figure. There was no use in even wanting it, since I so clearly didn't deserve it . . . *And just like that, this lie became my truth.*

As one would expect, the relationship I had with my father would set the tone for all the relationships I would have with men as I grew up. Like many people naturally do when denied something they deeply desire, I eventually hardened to the idea of what it was I really wanted. I told myself I didn't want actual intimacy with a man. I learned to protect myself a little by self-abandoning, telling myself time and time again I didn't care about spending more time with my father; I didn't need it and I certainly didn't want it. As an adult, I repeated the pattern, self-abandoning time and time again, telling myself I didn't need a real "life" with a romantic partner. I saved myself the pain by never even allowing myself to think about it. Hardening your heart, over time, can easily turn into an allergy, and then resistance, and, ultimately, full-on denial. *Why would I ever want to sit on the couch with a guy and watch* American Idol? *Ugh, that's so fucking boring . . .*

I couldn't see that I was screaming for a man to prove me wrong, to heal the open wound from my childhood that had festered for so long. To show me I deserved life with someone! All I knew was that I was ending up in relationships with guys who perpetuated the pattern of inaccessibility. So, there you go. I was right! *I didn't deserve it or need it. I didn't even want it. Like with Jake. I let the armor of my heart crack open just a bit and dared to believe it was all possible for me—the life, the family, the shared space—and so I moved to Kentucky to claim it once and for all! And we know what happened there . . . See how good that fucking worked out, Sarah. That's what you get for even bothering to try.* So, I put the desire back on the highest shelf, until I saw those fucking shoes.

I wanted my shoes lined up next to someone else's. There you go. I said it. This crack in my wall was small but decisive; everything had changed.

THE IMPORTANCE OF OWNING THE THINGS YOU REALLY WANT

Do you know what you want in life? Maybe you absolutely know, or you kind of know, or you're like me—a real "denial pro"—and you have no idea just how deep the inability to be honest about the things you actually want runs through your veins. If you're "DP proficient" (that's "denial pro"; get your mind out of the gutter), it may be because allowing yourself to see what you want feels really hard. But that doesn't mean you shouldn't do it, or that it's not important. Au contraire, ma chérie, it is quite the opposite. What really matters is that you own what you want when you figure it out.

Until we acknowledge what it is we truly want, we cannot truly be fully ourselves; the depth to which we are willing to be honest with ourselves reflects the depth to which we can experience our own lives. Without owning the things we want, we can't follow our personal path of Soul Archaeology, which means our ability to uncover our really good, authentic nitty-gritty will be limited. I cannot stress to you the absolute beauty of a human who knows what it is they truly want and is unafraid to own it.

The decision to start living a Self-Loving Life will reveal all sorts of goodies—new feelings, new roadblocks, and new layers of you. Every time you brush aside a layer of dirt in your Soul Archaeology, you will see something you never saw before—strange and exotic artifacts and remains may start to poke through the freshly exposed dirt of your personal dig site. Some of these artifacts can be dreams and feelings you've buried away for safekeeping. And one of them might be a really big feeling, a thing that speaks to you, that is core to the fiber of who you are but, to this day, may still be untouched and undiscovered.

If you were an actual archaeologist, you wouldn't stop digging whenever you encountered a precious fragment of bone or a shard of pottery at a dig site. You'd cover the precious land with a tent and then turn all your energy into exploring what you've just found. You would look at it from every angle and try to understand it in order to get a complete picture of it. When, in the course of your life, you stumble upon the revelation of a thing you really want, you let that guide where you go next, where you dig next. What you find is your road map, and, by uncovering, listening, examining, and adjusting (again and again and again), you will move forward into a truer version of yourself.

In this chapter, we're putting a tent in place so you can safely move aside the fresh dirt to expose your discoveries. This will require courage, because what you're digging up are the kinds of wants you may keep tucked away because if you admit that you want them, you'll have to deal with how far away they may feel right now; the wants may feel so untouchable that it feels safer to pretend the feelings don't exist than to ever open the door and invite them in. It's safer to deny you have the feelings, because to do otherwise is simply too raw and unimaginable.

HOW TO FIGURE OUT WHAT YOU WANT

You may know what your heart wants as clearly as a lightning bolt shooting through the sky. But you may also not know, and that is okay too. You may also know but not be ready to admit it to yourself. This is going to sound a little tough—but it comes from love: If you can't be brave enough to name what you really want—even if only to yourself—it probably won't happen. How can you create what you cannot acknowledge? You cannot change patterns without acknowledging them, and you will only grow greater in proportion to how willing you are to dig deeper into the depths of yourself. In order to unfurl into your Ultimate You, you need to be willing to see all your parts as best as you can. This is especially true when it comes to what you truly want and hope for in your life. Having hope makes you vulnerable; making yourself vulnerable is like opening a door to your life where anything can *whoosh* in to fill the empty space—pain, joy, despair, anxiety, or even unconditional love. But unless you open the door to possibility, you'll never know.

This book makes the assumption that either you don't know what you want or you're not comfortable expressing what you want just yet. If you do know...Woo-hoo! You can jump into the following "Dig Deeper" section and get to work. If you're the former—keep reading. We'll get there together!

 ### DIG DEEPER AND CLAIM WHAT YOU WANT (IF YOU ALREADY KNOW!)

Instructions: Turn on Whitney Houston, get naked, light a candle, and jump up and down on one foot while asking the Great Goddess to come to you and deliver her messages through the container of interpretive dance as you loudly proclaim your deepest desires to the universe.

Kidding. If you are reading this, it's because you've got an answer to the question "What do I really want in my life I have yet to claim?" If so, let's get to it. Take a deep breath. Know you are safe. Ground your feet . . . and let it out.

In your journal, finish the following statements:

1. I really, truly, deeply want . . .
2. It scares me to own this because . . .

That's it.

You can also make a ritual of this! Find a box, basket, vase, or any sort of vessel that brings you some joy to look at. Keep a pad of paper or index cards nearby. Every time you acknowledge a deep desire, get it out of your head and onto a piece of paper—write it down! Then fold it up and put it in the container.

Release it! Let the container hold it safe. If you want, every now and then, you can open it up and read what you've written. Or you can simply let the truth live somewhere outside you, and give it space. A piece of paper won't judge you. It won't "tell" on you or laugh at you. It won't think you're silly. In this instance, paper does one thing—it receives. It shares the weight of knowing so you don't have to carry it all yourself.

If you don't know . . . you'll know when you catch yourself pretending things are okay.

"It's no big deal . . ."

"It's okay . . ."

"Don't worry about it—I'm fine . . ."

Do you ever catch yourself saying these things? If you do, these could be "tells" that you are denying yourself a level of truth. Tells are the evidence that can illuminate the discrepancy between what we believe we feel and what we *actually* feel like a bright neon sign.

When you say, "It's okay" or "I'm cool with the way this is," do you find yourself feeling dissatisfied or uneasy after? As if you've had to talk yourself into believing your own feelings? If so, we have ourselves a DP here, folks! (Remember . . . denial pro.) Or maybe you have a thought but quickly invalidate the thought right after. Or you think a thought and then find yourself scrambling for something to distract or anesthetize yourself from the emotional reaction your own thoughts are causing.

Our bodies are brilliant. Oftentimes, the body knows better than the conscious mind when things are really good for us and when they aren't. It knows when we are lying to ourselves. It shows us in different ways that we're going against our truth by turning our stomachs into knots, making our tempers short, or making us want to go to Target to spend $100 on scented candles when we don't even like scented candles but now own an entire collection of Blueberry Vanilla Sprinkle candles.

Sometimes, we are so used to feeling out of alignment that the unaligned feeling becomes our normal and we lose the ability to even listen to ourselves, let alone hear the messages when we're getting them. When denial starts to drown out who we really are, we stop being ourselves. The longer this goes on, the further away we get from authentic joy and the more we're likely to drown in ourselves. We can, however, catch ourselves in a moment of denial. In a millisecond, we can zoom out of our bodies and zip thirty thousand feet into the air to look down at ourselves, and we can see the things we are doing, and we can see how warped some of the things we are doing are, and that's when we go, *Whoa, am I really this person?*

The moments when I caught myself doing something that seemed so blaringly out of character with who I knew myself to be that I had no choice but to see that something was off, I was hurting, and these hurts were really flashes of clarity. Each hurt-flash offered me opportunities to course-correct, to read the data and to see the evidence staring me in the face—that my life was unaligned, and I was going in the wrong direction. Each was a chance to see how I was an example of self-abandonment in the living flesh. There were moments in the present when I had the choice to look the pain I was feeling in the eye so I could do something different, or I do something to avoid the hurt. Because my normal was to habitually, chronically, and effortlessly deny my feelings, I chose everyone and everything over myself and, in doing so, put myself emotionally in the path of an eighteen-wheeler barreling down a freeway to run me over time and time again. Tells can be your saving grace if you allow yourself to see them. I invite you to think about what your tells are, because if you flip them over, you'll uncover what it is you truly want. What you run from is oftentimes what you long for the most.

Like when I cried in the bathtub after Elvis's daughter had walked in, I was hiding how tired I was of having to be someone's dirty, hidden secret.

When I drank tequila on my closet floor, I was wrestling with how much I loved George, who didn't love me back the way I craved being loved.

When I caught myself driving to Jake's bar in the middle of the night to confront him, I was reacting to the anger I felt because of his years of lying that I'd dealt with and allowed to diminish my self-worth.

Or the morning after I slept with three different men in a twenty-four-hour period, when all I really wanted was to sleep with one special person who loved me and I was scared I'd never find him.

If you don't know ... you'll know when you dig into the space in between.

Another way to see what you really want is to pay attention to your runaway expectations. Meaning when you find yourself with expectations that aren't met, or things that don't happen according to "your plan," it helps to see what those expectations are and what that "plan" was. In seeing those, you can shine a light on what it is you are really longing for. Cultivating mindfulness is a good way to do this.

Mindfulness is the practice of looking at something and seeing it as it is, without commentary and without judgment. To practice mindfulness, start by thinking about something in your life that happened and left you feeling differently than you thought it would. For example, maybe you were fiending for a new, superexpensive designer bag and when you got it and brought it home, you felt empty. Or you thought you were super horny so you engaged in some casual sex, but when it was over, you felt like crying.

If there is a discrepancy between how you imagined something would feel (an event, an experience, a relationship, whatever) and how it actually impacted you, it could signal an area in which you are denying a want. This is where you shine a flashlight. That moment you were fiending the $900 aqua-blue Marc Jacobs bag and bought it, you might have really been craving social acceptance from others. The casual sex moment? Maybe you were just plain lonely and wanted some actual friends. Now, of course, it doesn't always have to be deep. Sometimes you just want to buy an expensive sexy bag, and sometimes you just want to have sex and that's okay too! But if you do things thinking they are going to make you feel a certain way, and you don't feel the way you thought you would afterward, there could be a reason why.

The space between your expectation and your reality is loaded with juicy data you can gain knowledge from if you hone your ability to ask yourself questions and give yourself truthful answers.

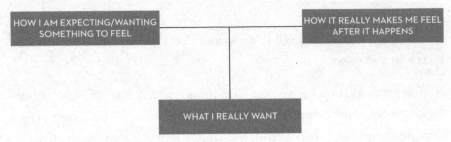

In order to navigate the space between the expectation and the reality, try asking yourself questions like this:

How was I hoping this would help me feel?
What was I feeling before I decided to take this action?
What was I doing right before I decided to take this action?
How did I feel right after?
What did I do right after?
Did the action I took make me feel better or worse?

In my life I have often craved physical intimacy, so I would initiate a connection with a partner or have an encounter of some kind that I hyped up as being fun and frisky and awesome but that, when over, would just leave me feeling blah. There was a gap between what I was hoping the experience would give me and how it actually made me feel. Eventually, I started to ask myself, *What am I really wanting here? Because obviously I'm not just looking to get off.* Then I asked myself the following questions:

How was I hoping this would help me feel? Sexy, important, alive.
What was I feeling before I decided to hook up? Lonely.
What was I doing right before I decided to take this action? Sitting on the couch and texting a guy who wasn't answering me back.

How did I feel right after? Eh. Nothing really.

What did I do right after? Took a shower, ate something, and went to bed, checking my texts every few minutes.

Eventually I would see a pattern—that I craved physical intimacy when I was feeling stressed out, bored, or lonely. Every time I felt like I wasn't connected to myself or to others, I would turn to sex to help me feel like I mattered. When you look at it through this lens, it's easy to see that my real desire was to feel actual connection—to another human but, more importantly, also to myself. Both of these things I had denied mattered to me for so long, and I had spent a lifetime self-abandoning in order to avoid feeling hurt. Keep your ears open for the whispers of your behaviors when they happen, because the sounds they make are louder than you can imagine.

ALLOWING FOR MY WANTS

"How about one-eyed Jacks?" George offered the next morning, standing in front of the open fridge. I sat at the counter as he piled a plate with toasted bread he'd filled with gooey-egg centers.

The night before, after the landlady left, I was lying down with my hair messy on top of my head, and my untethered boobs falling under my armpits. George and I were seven episodes into an *Archer* binge on Netflix, and in between laughter we took turns nodding off to sleep. With my head on his chest, I eschewed arching my back like a plump Grecian goddess in favor of a leg-drape that was considerably less attractive but far more comfortable. It was life in an unscripted form.

There was no engaging conversation or canned recitation of reliable jokes—there was intermittent snoring on the couch. When it seemed late enough, I nudged him gently and, in my softest voice, I prodded, "Hey, let's go to bed; c'mon." In bed I made a brief home in the hollow crook of his arm before he told me he could only sleep on his side. I kissed his shoulder and he turned over and moments later was snoring. Our feet, diagonally angled toward each other, touched under the covers.

I drove him to the airport a few days later; when we parted, I clung a bit tighter than I probably should have and hoped he didn't notice. I reminded myself it wasn't him that I was clinging to but this *thing, this truth that I'd decided he represented*...I got back into my car to avoid lingering longer or showing more than the prescribed level of emotion our relationship allowed for. I was anxious to let go of the presence of him. The flutter of little chin hairs from his electric razor sprinkled in the bathroom sink. The scent of cologne mixed with deodorant. The big, dark sneakers pushed against the wall parallel to my shoes. These were the things I wished for...These things that I'd never allowed myself or experienced in the past. There were little marks of his presence everywhere, and yet the more potent remains were far from tangible because they were inside me.

Later that night I attempted one-eyed Jacks for dinner, but I was clumsy as I struggled to re-create what I felt while watching him prepare my meal—that surge of intimacy and life. The egg slipped from my fingers and erupted in a yellowy splat on the floor. I pushed the dog away as I dropped to my knees to clean it up. I wondered when I'd feel that again, and the vulnerability started to creep in, so I focused on the dishes.

I realized that I was ready for more. "More" is imperfect. It's mundane and unscripted. But as I thought of the soft swish of George's nylon pants as he walked down my hallway, it also seemed like *me*. It seemed like what I wanted and what I was designed for. That kind of natural dance between two people—I was made for that. And as I got ready for bed, peeling off layers of clothing and folding and storing them away, I slipped off my shoes and lined them up, neat but unaccompanied. I stared at them, sitting in perfect symmetry with themselves. They were alone for now...but hopefully, not for long. Soon, there'd be "boy shoes and girl shoes" again. But the next time, I'd be ready for them—and it was on me to make sure.

But then I realized the only problem was I had literally no idea what to do with my newfound knowledge. I scrambled for some history in my mind, trying to remember a time when I felt what I thought I wanted to feel in the future, but there was nothing to grab on to. All I knew was what I *didn't* want. I didn't want to scamper on the surface; I wanted depth. The little details. I no longer wanted my relationships to exist in segregated chunks of time. And the chance to achieve that was my responsibility.

If I didn't want to live a shallow life full of shallow connections, I couldn't offer shallow versions of myself. I had to see myself as a whole. I had to offer all of me or offer nothing. I didn't know what that looked like, but I knew what it didn't look like. *It didn't look like shtick.* Or a slew of first dates but no second or third ones. It wasn't the same body-con dress with Spanx on underneath, showing off my ass and my boobs. It wasn't carefully curated Sarah or Answering-the-Door-in-a-Cute-Outfit Sarah, complete with a glass of whiskey and mascara that never smudges.

This was about me, not them. If I changed how I saw myself and how I OFFERED myself to people, the relationships would change automatically because they HAD to. If I wanted things to change, I had to do things differently.

DIG SITE: GET HELP!

This is your reminder that one of the most empowering things you can do when you see a truth in yourself is to better understand it. You may not be able to do that alone and that is perfectly okay. Find a trained and licensed therapist or counselor who can help you look at your history and figure out why you have the feelings you have, and why you've created the patterns you've created. Patterns start somewhere. They are learned, and the only way to change them is to see them as clearly as you can, without judgment or shame. If you've discovered a "want" for yourself in this chapter, and you want to learn more about where it comes from... advocate for yourself! When you talk to a new professional (or if you are currently working with someone), you can say, "I want to experience _____ in my life and it's something I don't understand. Will you help me?"

Adjusting Forward ... Backward

If you are feeling stuck, oftentimes if you listen to what you *don't* want, you'll know what to do next to move forward.

We talked about this a few chapters ago. You don't have to stress over finding the perfect magic solution for figuring out what you want. All you have to know is what's NOT the solution and start there.

Realizing that I wanted more depth in my emotional relationships was the fuel I needed to see that I was the only common thread in every relationship I'd had that didn't get me what I'd wanted. Sure, it would be easy to blame the guys—they took the bait, right? And sometimes they were assholes, for sure. But my perception of myself shaped how I came to the dating table. I limited myself, and because of that, I entered into relationships where I could safely "chunk myself" to my heart's delight.

Do the things I did make me a bad person? Of course not. This was all I knew. I learned how to compartmentalize myself from the time I was little, so I kept doing it; it became ingrained in me. I don't blame the men I dated, and I don't blame myself. But I did have to make a conscious choice to do something differently so that I could experience a different outcome once I saw the truth. Without judgment, or shame, I moved forward.

While I didn't yet know how to develop more intimacy in my relationships (it would take me a few more years of Soul Archaeology to realize that I first needed to cultivate intimacy within myself), I knew what was keeping me from it, at least with a surface level of understanding. So, I used that as a jumping-off point. The first thing I did, based on the data I learned from acknowledging my wants, was to stop dating—the way I'd been approaching it wasn't working for me, so I needed to get some space between myself and my patterns. I knew I would be uncomfortable, but I also knew if I didn't do something different, things would never change.

To create change, I deleted all the dating apps from my phone. I went through my phone and deleted the phone number of every man I'd had some sort of a casual relationship with over the years. I even deleted Jake's phone number from my phone—tearfully, and carefully, but I did it.

I didn't know what would work, but I knew what wouldn't and I was confident that by not repeating my patterns, I would experience something new. And I did. I encountered anxiety and self-doubt and sexual frustration, loneliness and fear of the unknown and unfamiliar. But I also started the process of seeing myself more deeply than ever before.

Because I brushed off a layer of the stuff that was keeping me from unfurling into my Ultimate You, it made room for me to see new things beneath it. I then examined what I found on the newly revealed layer and brushed the surface off once again. And then I examined again. And brushed off again. Eliminating casual dating from my life changed more than just sexual logistics. Ceasing to fill my time with surface-level relationships left me with the raw space and room to examine myself without the dirt and distraction that kept me clouded. By following this path, I would uncover a deep desire and readiness for more intimate relationships. In honoring this desire, I would change the trajectory of my life.

Fast-Forward

I am getting dressed for my first date with Man Candy. It's my first date in a long time, the first since I marked four years of commitment to living a Self-Loving Life. After I'd parted with George, everything about me had seemed to fall away to make room for a major rebuild.

Man Candy and I had met online, and when we chatted, I avoided the stock flirty jokes and sarcastic quips that used my femininity as a chess piece and, instead, I asked (and answered) questions with sincerity. I made a conscious choice to be very clear about who I was and what I knew I wanted in life. I told him I was open and ready for a serious relationship. I told him I was uncertain if traditional monogamy was right for me. I told him I sang in the car with the windows rolled down, lacked subtlety, and had a habit of telling inappropriate jokes at inappropriate times. I could recite lines from *The Hunt for Red October* and I liked coloring books and I hated cheese. And he still asked me out. Here I was on my way to show up for him, but really I was on the way to show up for myself.

I look at myself in the mirror—this is not the first-date outfit of my past—tight dresses flaunting my assets before 10:00 a.m. I'm wearing fitted jeans with a small rip at the knee, a casual wine-colored swingy top that skims my curves but does not place them on a billboard. I have a cardigan on and a pair of ballet flats and, wrapped around my neck, a breezy scarf in a bright color. *I look like Sarah. Just Sarah.* Nothing put on. Nothing fancy. Just a woman wearing some jeans and looking cute going to meet a guy, with no end game in sight other than to be present in that moment. Even if this date ended up being appalling, trying something new like this would still help me learn something useful about myself for myself, and as long as that happened, I was serving myself well.

I fluff my hair in the mirror and take a deep breath. This is me, no fancy gimmicks. This Sarah might not know all of herself, but she *knew just enough*, and the stuff she knew, she knew very well. The stuff she didn't know so well, she wasn't scared to uncover—some of it, she was even excited to reveal. As I'm picking up my bag to head down the stairs and leave, I think about all the uncharted territory ahead of me—there is so much I don't know about myself. But if Man Candy is a good fit for me—which has yet to be determined—we will pitch a tent to cover my exposed dirt and uncover the new things right alongside each other.

DIG DEEPER:
How to Adjust

You've started digging. Now, you get to adjust your actions and idea of what self-love will mean for you based on what you've uncovered at your dig site. This practice will help you get clarity and be SPECIFIC about what adjustments you can make to your daily life that will move you through Soul Archaeology.

As with many of the exercises we've done so far, to get clarity, we're going to work backward. We'll start with what we know to be true and use that as data.

1. Pick one thing that you really want in your life. Claim it. Write it down.
2. Being compassionate and honest, ask yourself, *What am I currently doing in this area to shape how I experience this want?* Write out the answer. Get specific.

3. Identify what it is you can STOP doing (this is usually going to be related to what you currently do). You may not like what you write here. That's okay. If you find yourself getting stuck, consider that what you can stop doing is one of the things you just identified in the second step.

4. As an option, you can take this one step further and identify a pro-active action that you can take to course-correct. This will mostly be doing the opposite of what you just expressed. You may even want to refer to your original Self-Love To-Do List. Are there any overlaps here between what's on your list and the "course-correcting action" you just identified? If so, yay! If not, consider adding this action item to your Self-Love To-Do List so that it stays top of mind.

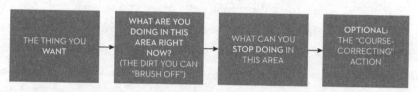

Determining what you can STOP doing is an act of self-love, because it serves your Ultimate You—the version of you that listens and honors herself, acknowledging what scares her yet making a conscious choice to prioritize her truest self regardless. Whether or not you are able to determine a "course-correcting action" at this point doesn't matter. What matters is that you start by removing obstacles and then begin to cultivate faith in the process and journey that comes next. By eliminating something from your life, you will automatically make space for what is next to eventually reveal itself.

Here is an example of what this exercise can look like:

1. **What is the thing that I want?** A real relationship that has intimacy and also involves casual, day-to-day life, where I can actually "know" someone and "be known" by them.

2. **What am I doing in this area right now?** Casually dating and hooking up a lot. Talking to guys on the surface and hoping it turns into more.

3. **What can I STOP doing in this area?** I can stop casually dating and hooking up. I can take a break from talking to guys online.

4. **What is a "course-correcting" action I can take?** Delete dating apps. Delete old texts and remove numbers from my phone of people I may be tempted to flirt with when I'm feeling lonely.

Breaking my own cycle by giving up casual sex was enough to move me into my next layer of Soul Archaeology. By removing the energy, busyness, and actions that defined my casual dating patterns, I left space for something else to grow in their place.

If you are deeply committed to repeating your patterns, there will never be room for anything else to grow or take its place. Like uncluttering a closet, you have to remove what no longer fits you and clear it out to make room for what does!

SURVEYING THE SITE:
WHAT WE DUG UP IN THIS CHAPTER

In this chapter, we opened a huge door to your heart. If you are going to live a Self-Loving Life, you have to honor what you really want, and if your life is going to be liberated, you must know what you need to feel free from in order to thrive. Even the stuff that you want so badly it scares the shit out of you is necessary to honor. If you have spent a life-time ignoring what it is you want—if you have been told it is something you don't deserve, or you have been made to feel that hiding this desire was the best way for you to stay "safe" in your everyday life—it may be nearly impossible to embrace the possibility that comes with saying, "I deserve what I want." You may not even be able to fathom what your life could be like if you allowed your "wants" to be true and seen and part of who you are. That's okay. This is big stuff.

This chapter is also a reminder that not doing things is just as impor-tant as doing them, and finding the courage to remove things from your life can oftentimes be what you need most in order to keep growing and unfurling into your Ultimate You. As I've mentioned, we don't have to have a clear vision of what the road looks like in front of us in order to travel and grow. Instead, we start with the data we know to be true right now and we use that as our guide map.

Sometimes in life we create solutions to meet our needs in the pres-ent tense that don't work for us in the long run. As we grow and change, and life changes with us, the same solutions that initially made us feel better may be the exact things that are keeping us from our Ultimate You! This is why we have to get very clear about both what it is we want and what it is we believe about who we are. We'll be talking about that next.

Chapter 10

THE MOVIE IN YOUR MIND

The Core Wound at the Heart of It All

We tell ourselves stories about who we are and how we relate to the world around us. Sometimes these stories are awesome and empowering. And sometimes they are not.

These stories play constantly in the back of our minds, like movies. They influence how we treat ourselves and how we show up in our lives and relationships. People have all sorts of movie stories:

- *Everyone I love leaves me.*
- *If I tell people what I really think, they won't like me.*
- *Nobody will ever want me because of my fat body.*
- *In order for me to get love, I have to trade sex.*
- *I don't deserve to make money.*
- *Only stupid women rely on men.*

You name it, people think it. And, believe me, there is no correlation between how "smart" someone is and how virulent their movie can be.

Some of us have several stories, or movies, that play in the multiplexes of our minds all at the same time. In Theater One could be a blockbuster called *I Don't Deserve Love Because I'm Ugly.* Theater Two features a flick called *You'll Never Be as Good as Your Sister.* Theater Three is showing a lesser-known indie flick called *I Always Get Shit on, So Why Bother?*

These stories are powerful. But it doesn't actually matter if our movie plotlines are true or not; as long as we *believe* they are true, they *have the impact of* truth. More often than not, our movies are NOT true, but we have watched them for so long and they have become so much a part of our lives that we can't imagine a different way of thinking. This is how our movies become powerful. We blindly base our lives around these ideas, and in turn, they shape everything we do and experience. For the most part, we never question them, so we are always under their control. For example, if you think everyone you love will leave you, then you will probably bring this truth into every relationship you have.

In short, our movies are so powerful that understanding them is the only way to break their control over us. My movies have led me to repeat scenarios in my romantic relationships. Ever the seeker of that burst of self-acceptance that came when a man I was into deemed me worthy, it was never enough for me to have one blockbuster experience. I had to go back a second time and then back again and again to repeat the storyline I learned in the first movie, perfected in the movie sequel, and have subsequently mastered in all movies since. Spread out over the course of my dating life, this pattern has made for one hell of a film franchise!

Sales Guy was a key character in my franchise. He lived in San Diego and spent his days doing high-powered sales things while wearing Brooks Brothers shirts and Patagonia vests. Our meet-cute is not so cute, as it happens on a dating app only a few weeks before I move to San Francisco, and, though we've never met IRL, I think about him *all* the time. I move to San Francisco for work and my life is miserable, but talking to him daily seems to make it more bearable. He calls me by my last name, "Sapora," and when he says it, it is teasing and loving at the same time. Our connection is palpable; we seem totally in sync.

It's a short flight between us, so I am always asking him if we can make plans. A weekend here? Something there? But the answer is always "No." This confounds me, but I stay my course. I keep sending sexy photos. I try all my best material, but he always turns me down. I ask him why. He says he is giving me all he can give, and all he *wants* to give, but I am committed. I am a walking Sales Pitch for Sarah, and I will close this sale.

Eventually, I take matters into my own hands. I lie to him and tell him I'll be in San Diego for work and ask him to meet for lunch. If he isn't going to come to me, I will go to him and be my most irresistible, and we will bang and it will be everything I need it to be and more, and then everything will work out perfectly.

He answers the door and is skinnier than I imagine him being. His apartment is (freakishly) clean. I stand in a series of poses that I design to feign my indifference, but my heart is bursting through my chest and I'm waiting for him to kiss me. I'm waiting for him to do *something* and instead he does nothing, so we go for drinks.

Back at his apartment later, we are sitting on his couch, and I am thinking, *Okay, NOW it's going to happen.* But, instead, I end up rubbing his head for half an hour before I ask him, "Why haven't you kissed me yet?" And he gets weird and can't give me an answer, and later, when I get in the car to leave, I feel so ashamed. I stop at the gas station and get two Twix bars, which I eat as I cry and drive home, wondering the whole time what I did wrong.

You would think that experience would be suitable evidence for me to stop talking to him. It is not. Even when I move back to LA and he moves from San Diego to LA and we get closer than ever, we never meet up. But we are still talking, all the time. One day on the phone he casually tells me he loves me. I ask him why we can't be together, then. "Stop campaigning, Sapora, just BE. I already know you're awesome; you don't need to keep telling me!" he says. But if I'm so awesome, why aren't we together? Clearly, I need to be MORE AWESOME. I come up with a (clearly) awesome idea and invite him over to my apartment for hot dogs and sex. Why I think this magic combo is a good idea, I don't know. But we have sex (it's terrible), and we go out for hot dogs (which are also terrible, especially after the terrible sex), and then the conversation after is terrible and awkward and so is our goodbye, which might be the most terrible part of all of it.

Once again you would think that would be suitable evidence for me to stop talking to him…It is not. A year later we meet one more time for lunch—I wear a low-cut blue dress that shows my breasts off from behind the bowl of ramen I am erotically eating, if one can erotically eat ramen. After, we go for a walk and pass his new apartment. I ask to use the restroom, and he gets weird and can't give me an answer and won't let me in the house. That's when it hits me that he must have a girlfriend, and they must live together, and they have probably been together this whole time. I drive home in silence, wondering what about me isn't good enough that, yet again, he isn't picking me. *I wonder what it is about me . . .*

Why do I keep coming back for more when I keep getting shut out? I feel compulsively driven to try to find the answers so that I can just wrap my head around a truth I already feel like I know. I start to go a little mad. I send strings of texts asking for answers, thinking I sound strong and assertive, but my texts go unanswered. I demand to know why I wasn't treated better and ask him why he wouldn't be honest with me. The lack of answers hurts for a good long while. And then I just move on. If I can't find any logical reason my relationship with Sales Guy couldn't get off the ground, the only reason I have to cling to is the only one that could possibly make sense: that I could never, and would never, be enough.

DIG DEEPER:
Recognize the Movie in Your Mind

This is your invitation to recognize what the movies are that play in your mind.

Before you start, take a few deep breaths. Put your hand on your heart—feel it beating? I promise that whatever you are feeling now is okay. If doing this feels overwhelming, that's okay too. Now, take some time and answer the following questions in your journal:

1. What is the main movie that plays in your mind about who you are? What is its plotline?
2. What messages does this movie tell you about who you are and how you relate to others around you?
3. Can you remember the first time you "learned" this "truth" about yourself? If so, who did you learn it from and what was the situation in which you were taught?

4. Are there secondary movies that play in your mind? If so...what are they? Where did you "learn" them and when?

5. This next question might feel harder to answer. But you can do it.

List all the situations (or at least as many as you can identify) where your movie has replayed itself. If this number is too many to count—what are the major instances where you can see that your movie defined a relationship, a choice, or a specific moment in your life?

HOW A MOVIE BEGINS

Of all the movies that play in your mind, one probably stands out the most. It hurts the most. It may even be like a tree, planted at the center, from which smaller movies and stories grow. This story that goes the deepest can be thought of as your core pain or core wound.

There are variations of this term and idea used in psychology, but they all mean the same thing. They explain how one thing we believe about ourselves can color our personality and also how we believe the world sees us. Psychologist Stephen Wolinsky calls this our False Core.[1]

Wolinsky suggests that the False Core is something determined early on in our childhood, a time when we are learning key things about ourselves and emotional security. How we see ourselves, and how we believe the world sees us, is our "False Self." This False Self part of us will, therefore, spend its entire life compensating for the false conclusions it believes are real. For example, my False Core told me I didn't deserve a healthy relationship with a guy, so I spent almost my whole life believing this and compensating for it.

I've heard it said that our core wound is formed when our suppressed pain and emotions become internalized into our identity and sense of self. It's also been suggested that our core wound motivates the part of our energy that compels us subconsciously to create and attract painful experiences that feed the wound.[2] Our core wound becomes such a big piece of how we see ourselves that it creates our lives for us; based on our search for evidence that our wound is the truth, our core wound becomes a self-fulfilling prophecy.

We must remember that our core wound is the center of all our other wounds. It goes the deepest and spreads the widest. We can dance around all the other shit that impacts us, but at the end of the day—this is our Alamo. To overcome it and work through it may be the hardest work we will ever do in our Soul Archaeology.

To fully understand where my movie begins and to show you exactly what I mean when I explain that our core wounds travel with us until we address them, we have to go back to the night my parents told me they were splitting up. I was seven years old, and we were sitting in the living room on the Chinese brocade couch that my mother always said she hated.

"Sarah," my father said quietly and with a metered tone, "your mother and I have something to tell you—"

"No, we don't," my mother said, cutting him off. "I don't have something to say; *you do.*"

What he said after that, I can't remember. I don't think I even understood it. But I knew the words scared me. I sat on my mother's lap and put my head against her turquoise-colored T-shirt and cried, leaving small wet marks on the fabric. Later that night in bed, I slept with my head at the wrong end because it felt like everything was turned upside down and that was how my seven-year-old brain made sense of everything it had learned.

I don't remember my parents telling me when my father would be moving out, but I do know he moved his stuff out of the apartment while I was at home. There were no expectations set or explanations given for where my dad would be living or how often I would see him. There were a lot of unknowns... But what I could count on was my dad taking me ice-skating on Friday nights. I've shared earlier that this was the time in my life when I learned to downplay my feelings for the comfort and benefit of my parents—telling neither one of them how I truly felt about them or the other in order to keep things smooth and peaceful for myself. This was how I "learned" a (fake) truth—that by self-abandoning, I would keep my parents happy, and if they were happy, they would give me the reassurance that I needed to know they loved me. I practiced this every Friday night with my dad, and I lived it every day with a mother who subconsciously wanted me to be as angry at my father for leaving as she was.

My dad had a series of apartments, none of which I ever remember seeing. It wasn't until he and my (soon to be) stepmother moved into an apartment on the Upper West Side that I felt welcomed into the places my father lived—and even then, it felt conditional. Subconsciously, I became a hunter, looking for evidence that my existence mattered to him, and I got very used to feeling like I didn't deserve space in his life. Without a bedroom to call my own in my father's apartment, without stuffed animals or a dresser full of clothes or anything left behind that would prove I existed with any feeling of permanence—I zeroed in on photos as being my sign of success. On the rare occasion I was allowed a sleepover, I'd pad barefoot through the apartment late at night, after everyone else was asleep, and count the number of photos with me in them and compare them to the number of photos with other people in them. The more photos I was in, the better, right? If comparing the number of photos I was in was how I gauged my level of importance in my dad's eyes, then in my mind I thought I was on the losing end. There could only be one reason why—I wasn't good enough.

I gave myself answers to all the questions I had about why things were the way they were between my parents and myself in general because none were provided. In the head of a child, and then a preteen searching for acceptance, and then a teenager looking to be loved, the only assumption I could make was that there just wasn't room for me. I was optional, like a seasonal decoration that could come and go. I wasn't enough to be displayed year-round.

My father and I have wonderful memories between us; he was and is a loving man. What laid the foundation for my core wound was a perfect storm of well-intentioned dysfunctionality. There was a pair of divorced parents who thought that the best way to keep me happy was to tell me as little as possible about what was going on—which ultimately would only leave me scrambling and confused, when as a child what I really needed the most was consistency and answers I could depend on. My father thought he was doing the best thing by letting my mother call the shots, all the while having a pretty reserved style of showing love in general. My well-intentioned but overbearing mother had lots of anger about the divorce and, along with my dad, unknowingly made a bunch of bad calls regarding our family dynamics. My father says less and gives more space. My mother says more and gives less space. Both of them loved me in their own unique way, which wasn't necessarily a way I could understand. Combined, all of this created an uncertain child who felt that she didn't belong and was fixated on earning approval. It never felt safe for me to fully express my feelings or ask questions. Nobody imagined I might have anger or fear, or that I might feel caught between two adults I loved, whose approval I craved. As a result, I created a story whose plotline was that the reason things were the way they were was because of me and my shortcomings. This was, of course, wrong. But feelings don't care about the truth; they feed on whatever scares us the most. Your movie doesn't have to be correct or based in any truth—when you feel it, it feels real as hell.

All I wanted as a child—all I ever wanted—was to feel like I was loved and cherished, to feel like I had a home with my father. I believed, to my core, that the reason I didn't was because I was not enough. I played that plotline throughout my entire life with every single personal relationship I had with a man, in the movie I wrote about a woman who believed she'd never be enough. No matter how much I said I wanted things to be different, no matter how much I cried and said I hated it, it was the only truth I knew, and I brought it to life.

Your Movie Is a Self-Fulfilling Prophecy That Will Run on Autopilot

I can't tell you when your movie started. What I can do is give you a safe place to begin to open your eyes to seeing your own story so you can reveal just how much it has shaped you. Unless you are able to see your story clearly, you cannot rewrite it to create a new story that serves you.

More than likely, you learned your movie between the ages of four and eleven. This is when kids learn the most about their value and are the most influenced by those around them. Research shows that by age five, children already have some sense of who they are.[3] Psychology 101 rather obviously explains that adult figures in a child's life are the most influential in shaping self-esteem.

For this conversation, let's operate under the assumption that your parents were well-intentioned humans of reasonable and sound mind. Statistically, your parents (or any adults that were responsible for your upbringing) were probably decent people who were just doing the best they could at the time. Perhaps this assumption is false, and your parents were ill-intentioned (though I truly hope not), but if so, the origin of your movie is probably easier to identify. Whatever the case, it is important to remember that even with the best of intentions, parents are human, and therefore innately imperfect themselves. Your parents had their own movies, which inspired their relationship with you and influenced you on a regular basis, colored with their own humanity and flawed upbringing... Because of this, you learned your truth from a potentially unreliable narrator. Basically, you learned shit from your parents, who were shaped by the shit they learned from their parents and life, who were shaped by the shit they learned from life and their parents, and on and on. So, the shit you learned probably has very little to do with you and your worth and everything to do with the people who taught you, their life experiences, and how they felt about their worth. The shit we learn has the power to shape every single thing in our lives, and when that shit is painful, the impact on us can be pervasive and deep.

You would think we'd automatically run from and do our best to avoid painful things, right?

Actually, we do the opposite. We are innately drawn to re-creating the experiences that hurt us, because those experiences are familiar to us. The more deeply those hurt feelings are ingrained in us, the more powerful pull they have. We repeat what we learned as children because, as counselor and psychotherapist Sharon Martin says, "beliefs, coping skills, and behavior patterns that we learned in childhood become deeply entrenched because we learned them when we were vulnerable, and our brains weren't fully developed. And after years of using them, they are hard to change."[4] We re-create the dynamics that hurt us unconsciously so that we can try to fix them and "master them" and get them right. Martin says, "When we recreate dysfunctional relationship patterns from our past, we're unconsciously trying to re-do these experiences, so we can feel in control, so we can fix what we couldn't fix as children. We think (again, this is mostly unconscious) that this time if we can be lovable or perfect, we won't make the same mistakes and thus avoid the abuse or rejection that we suffered as children."[5]

Think honestly about your interpersonal relationships for a minute. Do you feel like you continually end up in the same situations? Maybe you constantly find yourself working for domineering, female bosses. Do you regularly learn your partners have cheated on you? Are you always attracted to romantic partners who ghost you? Or do you feel like all your relationships are the equivalent of "same cowboy boots, different cowboy" again and again?

Whatever it is, if the same things keep happening in your relationships on repeat, there are reasons why. One of them is because the movie in your mind is running the show. It will continue to do this until you make it stop. We may want something so bad it hurts, but that one thing is what exists on the other side of our core wounds. We have to overcome our core wounds in order to pass through the hurt to find something more self-loving.

If you find yourself in a capsized boat, safety rules advise you to put your life jacket on and minimize movements to stay afloat. Don't flail; the harder you flail about, the more danger you pose to yourself and to others. What you have to do is remain calm to assess the situation. To think, *Okay, I am floating, this is where the shore is, this is where people are, this is how my body feels, and this is the situation.* Only in doing this can you calmly strategize a way to safety. Sometimes, it's the same for our movies. The more we flail around trying desperately to avoid the same painful experiences again and again, the more we increase our chances of tiring out, running out of oxygen, and sinking. The more our arms and legs kick and spasm to avoid sinking, the more likely we are to sink. In an effort to avoid our movies, we can oftentimes make things even worse, even harder. We can repeat them, add to the pain, and exacerbate our open wounds. It is only when we can slow down enough to SEE the truth, to assess the situation, that we can find ways to heal through it. We may feel like we are doing everything humanly possible to avoid the experiences we have as a result of our movie playing on autopilot—but unless we can see how our story stops us from true change, and unless we can focus on the movie itself and not the effects of it, we will never reach the other side.

DIG SITE: TRAUMA AND YOUR MOVIE

You don't need to have experienced deep "trauma" in order to have created a movie in your mind. But a movie, and your core wound, does require some kind of pain. (The American Psychological Association defines "trauma" as "an emotional response to a terrible event."[6] It helps to remember this when you look back at your pain and experience a rush to demonize it or label it so you can better distance yourself from it.) That being said, some people really experience trauma. Hard, hard stuff.

I had a privileged childhood. I was hugged. I wasn't abused. In truth, the pain I felt as a kid—compared to others—was pretty mild even though it was real. It's important for me to acknowledge that some people experience brutal stuff and that is the root of their movie and core wounds, things like sexual abuse, violence, real poverty... There are so many awful things that can happen to a person. It can be really hard, or nearly impossible, for someone who's endured so much to work through the movies in their mind. We all have backstories. Different brain chemistry. Different mental health profiles. All of those things must be considered when we explore the ideas expressed in this chapter.

Remember that pain is not a competition. Your reactions to experiences are fully allowed, and they are real to you.

I invite you to put your life, your pain, and your journey into perspective and to honor it for exactly what it is at the same time.

MY MOVIE TAKES OVER

I am in a dark place when I meet George. I am living in San Francisco and feeling trapped in a series of choices I don't realize are bad when I make them; I am looking for a particular kind of distraction. When we match online, I tell him I need curtains hung in my bedroom, and he offers to help. The first time we meet, he shows up with a three-foot level and hangs my curtains with the obsessiveness of an engineer, and we have sex.

In the beginning, we share just enough about ourselves to fit neatly inside the metal-fence guideposts of emotional boundaries that each of us establishes right away. Neither of us wants anything complicated but mutual trust is essential. We sleep together regularly. We have sex in the full daylight, which says a lot for me, as I am existing in a really fat body that I kind of hate, and he makes me feel alive.

One year later, the guideposts of our relationship have moved. We are getting increasingly closer. And, although he says he does not want to be in a relationship with me—or anyone—his actions seem to indicate otherwise. Because I like him, I choose to follow his actions instead of listening to his words. I tell him I'm fine with things being just the way they are even though I don't understand what that is and it bugs me. We talk every day. We share more. Then he visits and I see our shoes lined up next to each other, our boy shoes and girl shoes. At some point, we begin talking every day, all day long. He sends selfies from the road when traveling for work, and we create our own personal language of dirty jokes. We admit we love each other. We ask ourselves if we should be together. He says he can't give me what I want right now but he can give me something else. He wants to give something to me. *He cares. He thinks about me. He wants to try.* "Okay, let's do it," he says, sounding confident enough for us both. When he shows up at my doorstep a week later, I feel something I haven't felt in ages—possibility. *I belong to something. I belong to someone. I have a place—there is space for me.*

The possibility lasts moments. As quickly as he opens the door for me to love him, he closes it. On the same trip that promised the delightful reunion of a rom-com movie, he tells me he just wants to be friends. No obligations. I want to ask him what happened. But I don't. He says he wants what he wants. I can accept this, or not. So, of course, I accept it. What else would I do? I don't want him to go away. And with this decision, I once again cast myself as the star of my own dysfunctional movie.

My relationship with George represents years of the highest of highs peppered with the lowest of lows, gravitationally pulled forward by my desires (thanks, vagina) and a compulsive need for his positive affirmation, however sporadic it is. Time goes by. I wait for what feels like the inevitable evolution of our coupledom, but it never comes. I wait. I adjust myself to be a mirror of what he says he wants and needs.

When things are good, I feel whole. Vibrant and cherished. I am none of those things without him, of course, but when we are together, I am the delightfully perfect leading lady inside a romantic comedy. Like the time he sends a ticket for a plane that leaves in three hours with a text telling me to hurry up and pack a bag. I rush to the airport, tingling. I run through the airport like the perfect movie heroines do. I catch myself thinking, *Holy shit, this is my life; this is really happening!* I'm convinced I know what real love must feel like and all the nights of uncertainty spent questioning myself and my sanity and my feelings were TOTALLY WORTH IT BECAUSE THIS IS EVERYTHING AND MORE! When he opens his hotel room door, he takes me in his arms as the music swells to a crescendo in the soundtrack of my heart while I thank whatever higher power I'm capable of believing in for bringing such a man into my life. *I* get to be next to him. Not someone better. Me! But that's only when it's good... When it's bad, it's a mess. I cry at random moments. I am clumsy and messy. I drink tequila alone for the first time in my life to numb the pain, from a bottle George picked out for me. I lie on the floor of my closet holding the bottle—only three shots in and I curl up into the fetal position and cry, big loud tears, releasing all this energy and fear. I get lost in my confusion and all the questions I want to ask him but will never have the courage to. Like what's the deal between him and the girl who he says he's just crashing with? Is this whose perfume he bought on the cruise that time? He insists they are just friends. *But, then again, he insists that* we *are just friends.* I teeter constantly on the edge, scrambling to understand what is real and what isn't. Is it "Sarah, I want us to be special; you need to understand, I will always come back to you; you are who will survive; it's you and me"? Or is it "I don't have time for this; I can't deal with you right now"? I have so many questions without answers that I find myself crouching on the floor of my shower, praying to a God I have yet to believe in to help me, *just please help me and guide me through this,* because I am in over my head and I cannot find a way out, and it is consuming me.

When George finally settles into a new apartment in a nearby state, the apartment is full of pieces of him I've never seen before. There is no sign of my existence . . . but there are pieces of George all over my house; his picture in a frame, his favorite Coors Banquet in the fridge. I count all the photos I see—pictures of him as an Eagle Scout, and pictures from his travels, one of him standing smiling in front of the Guinness factory in Ireland. I wonder what woman took that picture. I wonder what she had that I don't. There are at least a dozen photos, and none of them include me. These don't seem like very good odds. Suddenly I am a girl again. Padding barefoot down my father's hallway, counting the photos.

Understanding How Your Movie Impacts You

While science can't tell us how many thoughts we have every day, we can tell how many times our thoughts transition and, from this, we can surmise. Every day we have more than six thousand "thought worms" that transition us between individual thoughts.[7] Our thoughts are in the driver's seat of our lives. What we think evolves into what we believe, and what we believe translates into actions, and these actions create our lives. We are one continuous loop of thoughts, beliefs, and actions.

The direction of the loop can go both ways. Our thoughts can shape our beliefs, which shape our actions. Just the same, we can experience actions that mold our beliefs and, ultimately, break apart into individual thoughts.

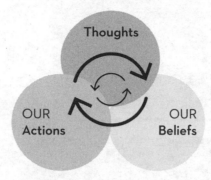

What matters here is that *our thoughts matter*. You already know this. What you may not already know is that you are not even aware of all the things you are thinking when you are thinking them. Sigmund Freud, the founder of psychoanalytic theory, suggested that we have not just one whole mind, but three layers in our minds, and in turn, we have three levels of thinking: conscious, subconscious, and unconscious. Our conscious thoughts are the ones we can call upon with clarity—they are accessible to us. Our subconscious thoughts live just beneath the surface of our recall, but when we are introduced to them, they make sense and feel familiar. And then there are our unconscious thoughts. Those live deep down, and accessing them is really, really hard.

It might help to think about this like an iceberg.

This is where things start getting sticky. Science tells us that only 5 to 10 percent of our thoughts are conscious. This means that 90 to 95 percent of the things we think are in our subconscious or unconscious— if you're keeping track, that means of six thousand thoughts a day, only six hundred of 'em are conscious ones.[8] So the overwhelming majority of thoughts you have every day—the same thoughts that guide your beliefs and shape your actions and, in turn, create your life—are ones you aren't even choosing or super aware of, or even slightly aware of at all.

This means you probably have no idea just how wide and deep the movie in your mind actually goes into your thinking. How much space it takes from a volume perspective, and just how ingrained in your behaviors it truly is.

CONSCIOUS MIND OF FULLY VISIBLE THOUGHTS
The thoughts we are aware of having when we have them. They are above the surface of the water and are the tip of the iceberg.

SUBCONSCIOUS MIND OF PARTIALLY VISIBLE THOUGHTS
The thoughts we are unaware we are having when we have them. BUT, if our attention is brought to them, they can usually be identified. Our subconscious is often on autopilot and based on years of internalized data. These thoughts are below the surface of the water, but are not lost to the depths of the sea.

UNCONSCIOUS MIND OF NOT VISIBLE THOUGHTS
These are thoughts and feelings totally outside of our awareness. These are deep below the surface and cannot be seen.

You Can Rewrite Your Movie

I don't want you to lie to yourself. I'm also not suggesting that you pretend things that aren't real are real. And, for the love of everything, I don't want you to ever feel like you need to deny that painful things have happened to you. What I do want you to do is to feel empowered to write a version of your movie that works for you. I invite you to make that version more important than the one you've been playing in your head for years.

Doing this, of course, won't turn back time. It is an exercise in training your subconscious mind to work for you and not against you. But a note here: Let's get real and clarify that every single thing in life that happens to you is not the result of your own doing. So much stuff is totally out of your control—it's liberating to really understand that. Your mental and chemical makeup are also out of your control. You cannot think your way into erasing pain that has hurt you throughout your life, nor should you. But what you can do is try to find ways to support yourself with thoughts that nurture you instead of hold you back.

We've already established that we have conscious and subconscious mind levels and that each has different capabilities. According to experts, one of the primary functions of the subconscious mind is to "follow the instructions of the conscious mind, and it does this by proving that whatever the conscious mind believes, is true. In other words, the job of the subconscious mind is to prove that the conscious mind is always right."[9] In light of this, if what your conscious mind focuses on is a destructive movie in your mind, your subconscious will work hard to be destructive. If what your mind focuses on is a movie that supports you, your subconscious will work hard to be supportive. The opportunity on the table is for you to rewrite your movie so that you can be the boss of the story that plays in your mind.

Dr. Catherine Collautt specializes in paradigm shifts in self-development; she describes this process of interacting with your subconscious as "gaining mastery" of it. "Mastery," she explains, "involves taking up our position of power in relation to our subconscious, not by trying to outdo it or by doing without it; but by realizing it's *our job* to clean up the programming and directions we have (wittingly or unwittingly) given our blessed processing powerhouse."[10] Collautt explains that the process of gaining "mastery" can be compared to a workplace situation, where we are the CEO and president, and our subconscious is our loyal employee. We want our employee to work for us, to assure our success and productivity. Unfortunately, we gave our subconscious an assignment a long time ago—so long we can hardly remember—that our best employee has been working to complete. While the assignment made sense at the time, it no longer does, but our subconscious has been committed to it ever since!

It's our job to get ahold of this employee, set them straight, and make sure the employee has the new and updated assignment that works for us and not against us. As a child CEO, I told my subconscious employee to people-please in order to keep my mom and dad happy. The dedicated subconscious employee in me ran with that direction for years, unsupervised, until I realized that the job it successfully did for me when I was a child didn't work for me as an adult. To gain mastery of my subconscious means to rein it in and give it a new task—to help stop using people-pleasing as a way to keep people happy!

I don't know *how* our brain chemistry actually makes this shit work, but I know that it does. So, if you are willing to believe that you can *feel* something different in your life... it's time to get (re)writing. Through the help of a great therapist, I did work to rewrite my movie. She helped me to recognize that the self-preservation techniques I created as a child were not my fault, but a natural response to my natural needs. She asked me, "What do you think would have happened if your parents had explained things to you differently, so you could have understood it better?" What would have happened if my parents had explained their divorce, the back-and-forth, and the lack of home I felt with my dad? I would have known it wasn't my fault. And if it wasn't my fault, I wouldn't have spent a lifetime believing I wasn't good enough. And then everything would have been different...

Through our work I am able to envision a childhood where I had answers and reassurance. I am able to see a parallel version of my life where my father and I have conversations that make me feel seen and understood. I imagine all of this in detail. I say the words as if they had actually been spoken—what I would have needed to express and what I would have needed to hear. In gestalt therapy this is known as "chair work," where you bring role-play into previous situations to reimagine them for the benefit of healing and growth. It is in this practice that I find freedom from this poisonous, old movie. It is what helps me to decide that I will rewrite the script and consciously choose to live the rest of my life with a new plotline—I do not need to erase what happened in my past; I just have to make room for the alternative version of my life to exist and grow from there.

By rewriting our movie, we are creating a new story for our conscious minds to wrap around. We put ourselves in the driver's seat and create conditions around which we determine our worth and value. We take the story back from other people; we stop allowing other people—with their flaws and their pain and their subconscious agendas—to make decisions for us. We decide how we want to feel, and that is epically powerful because whatever our conscious mind decides to believe, our subconscious mind will work to prove it right. So, it's important that what you focus on works *for* you, and not against you. In the end, this is what living a Self-Loving Life is all about.

DIG DEEPER:
Rewrite Your Movie

This practice walks you through a visualization to help you rewrite your own movie. It is important to know that there are professionals who can help you do this on a deep soul level—you may even find that an intervention like EFT (emotional freedom technique) done with a trained guide can help you work through trauma, depression, and pain. For now, start here.

1. **Identify the "core" of your movie by answering the question "Where did my movie come from?"** This is the heart of your story. When you identify this, get as specific as possible. Was there one moment you can remember that launched this movie for you? Or a "type" of interaction that has happened again and again? Trace the story back as far as you can. If you have not already written this out as clearly and as detailed as you can, do so now.

2. **Think about how this moment would have needed to be different in order for you to receive more loving and supportive information from the parties involved.** Would a conversation need to have happened? An interaction or experience? In your journal, finish this statement: *"In order for me to feel differently about _____, this would have needed to happen..."*

3. **Create this moment.** This moment didn't happen in real life, but you can create it in your head. Get as detailed as you can and walk through

the interaction or experience exactly as it would have needed to happen in order to liberate you. Journal it out and use details—details are data! Who would be involved in this experience other than you? What would they say? How would they act? Where would this moment have taken place? What would you have said? What did it smell like? What were you wearing? What were they wearing? For me, for example, this means going beyond saying, "I'm no longer going to be the girl who never got a bedroom in her dad's house—from now on, I am treating myself as if I did," and, instead, re-creating what that bedroom would have looked like. How it would have felt. What posters were on the wall. What the conversation would have been like with my father and what he would have said that would have made me feel like I was enough. The more details you can visualize, the more liberating your thoughts can be.

4. Ask yourself, *How would THIS movie have changed things for me if I believed it instead?* Again, this is not about living in denial of where you have been and what you have done in your life up to now. This is about seeing the extent to which your "old movie" impacted your life so you can, in the same breath, see how a more loving movie can empower you moving forward. How would the information and assurance you receive in your new movie have impacted your life? Think about the alternative reality, the parallel version of your lived life. What would have happened in your life had you been empowered and not held back by your movie?

5. Give yourself permission to believe. Yes, you are crafting your own reality. You are allowed to believe what you need to believe in order to be able to feel as powerful and whole and awesome as you really are. You must make the choice to support yourself time and time again until it becomes natural for you. Say to yourself, *I know this is not what truly happened, but this is what I truly need in order to know that I am enough. And knowing that I am enough is more important to me. I am the source of my knowing. I CAN be the source of my enough-ness.* Be willing to believe that you are the person your new, loving movie has created.

6. Commit to your story. Time and time again. Repeat it. Write it out. Print it out. Email it to yourself. Reinforce it. Let it simmer in your brain. Make friends with it. Get jiggy with it. What matters is that you understand how to love yourself and foster your Ultimate You.

SURVEYING THE SITE:
WHAT WE DUG UP IN THIS CHAPTER

This chapter—this entire section—addresses new layers of feelings you may encounter in your journey while living a Self-Loving Life. This book, like your path of Soul Archaeology, works in an order. At the beginning, we laid a foundation by establishing some ground rules for Soul Archaeology. Like "There is no perfection, only the messy-beautifulness of you working to be greater every day." We established how insidious the "Before-and-After" diet culture–based nature of personal growth can be. And we talked about the importance of including body liberation as YOU define it in your process of liberation.

In the second part, we created LIFELOVE for us. We got empowered to claim who we want to be in our lives and acquired a practical tool to help us start creating change. Our Self-Love To-Do List is a vibrant, organic, and powerful tool that can help us to understand what we can do to start showing up for ourselves in the present. It takes "self-love" from flying around all loose and wild in the ether and grounds it in shit we can do *right now* to start feeling less pain and more joy in life.

Here, we embraced the sticky, ooey, gooey feelings that start to come to the surface when we use our Self-Love To-Do Lists and prioritize our growth over our comfort. The truth is that we are in the driver's seat of our own growth. It's on us, and until we start to get comfortable with ALL of our shit, we can't pour love into ourselves fully and thoroughly to honor exactly who we are. The same things we are ashamed of or scared of are the same things that deserve our love. The parts of us we have kept hidden or tucked away are the ones most deserving of the warm, radiant sunlight of our own self-acceptance.

So much of life is ultimately out of our control. But our shit? It is ours to own, to control, and to love into. We've been trained to think that the easier life feels, the better it is. Feeling at ease is great—to be in flow with who we are feels awesome and absolutely makes our lives easier. But there is a difference between experiencing the ease of living in alignment and living comfortably in the cover of our denial. Short-term coping mechanisms and familiar yet dysfunctional solutions to getting our needs met in the present often require us to forfeit the truth. And what is true will always find a way to find the light. It is up to us to decide if we will let it shine or not.

IV

LET GO TO LET LOVE

Saying Goodbye to Expectations, Other
People's Shit, and Your Own Damn Shame

Chapter 11

SURRENDER

The Most Intangible, Frustrating-Yet-Necessary Part of It All

I am sitting on the toilet in George's bathroom with what feels like lightning running through my body. Our relationship (or whatever it is) is crumbling, like my teeth do when they crumble out of my mouth sometimes in my dreams. I can't do anything about it. It's over. For the last few days, we've been mutually skirting the neon pink elephant that seems to fill every room of his apartment. My temper is sharp, and I've been holding back tears the entire day. The pressure building up in my mind and my body has made my movements fraught and tight. I am so tightly wound that when I lean forward to wipe my tush, I "stumble" and take the hard plastic toilet seat with me, making an audible crack as it breaks away from the plastic bolts holding it in place. *I broke the man's toilet seat.* My tears burst forth, having been held back behind a measured, counterfeit smile for days. (At least the sound is hidden by the merciful white noise of the fart fan.) This is one of the single lowest moments of my entire life.

I could feel this moment arriving from a mile away. Not the whole "breaking the toilet seat" thing, but this awful, deteriorating situation I was finding myself in with the guy I loved and was sure was meant to be the One. I could tell something was different between us, but I couldn't put my finger on what it was. He had changed—it was a subtle change, but loud. And then there was me, and my thoughts, and where I was in my life. I was a few years into my Soul Archaeology journey by then and seeing things with more clarity than ever before. Some of the new things I saw, I liked. But some of the things I saw, I fucking hated, because they weren't what I thought I wanted, especially the reality that my time with George was coming to an end. Because I could tell, I could finally see, that the one thing I truly, madly, deeply wanted was the one thing he would never want to, or be able to, give me—healthy intimacy in a present, on-the-ground relationship. It was a nagging reality I'd just as soon have ignored. *How lucky am I that the one person I love is the one person I have to learn how to walk away from?*

It was clear he'd already moved on and I was hanging on for dear life to something I never had to begin with. We were supposed to grow old together in a sea of dirty jokes and karaoke versions of "Islands in the Stream." But now, there was nothing. As I'm sitting on the floor of his apartment, sorting books and avoiding eye contact, I know it's time for me to say the things I have been avoiding saying but need to say if I'm ever going to release myself from him.

"You changed the rules on me," I say quietly. "You told me to trust you. You told me you would tell me if things were ever different, but they changed, and you didn't tell me. Somewhere along the line you stopped wanting to be with me—"

"I don't want to be with anyone. It's not you; I don't want anything with anyone—"

"Fine, I get it; that's not what I mean. I know, fuck, I know . . . something changed. You changed your mind and you didn't tell me." I take a deep breath. "I wish you would have told me. Because I was still *there* . . ."

He is beyond silent. I have no idea what the look on his face is. I can feel tears choke up in me a bit, but the weird thing is, I'm not self-conscious about what I know I'm going to say next. It's just the truth. The sooner I own it, the sooner I can move forward. "I thought you were my person. And, like, I know that there's no such thing as just one person for us, but if you'd asked me up till recently before all this shit got weird, I would have said that *you are my person*." I wipe a single tear that is threatening to fall. "And it'll be okay; I'll be fine but, like...I wish you would have told me."

He takes it in, barely responds. I wish he would hug me or hold me and tell me everything is going to be okay. I wish he would say that he'll always care. I wish he would tell me that he'll always be in my life. I wish a lot...but later in bed that night, even though there are two of us under the covers, I can tell it's just me alone and I have to move on.

THE SURRENDERING IS NOT NUT MILK

Surrendering always sounded like bullshit to me. Like the kind of thing that women in LA do who wear T-shirts bearing the slogan "spiritual gangster" while proudly talking about the non-GMO nut milk they made from scratch that day in the sun-sprinkled kitchen of their Silver Lake apartment. Well, I drink Diet Coke, and just thinking of the phrase "nut milk" makes me want to laugh like a thirteen-year-old who hears a good joke about ballsacks. So, surely, "surrendering" was not something that would ever, could ever, be a part of my life. And yet, learning how to do just that would be one of the most crucial things I'd ever wrap my literal brain around. You hear a lot about the concept of "surrender" in the world of personal growth. Spiritual teachers, especially, like to use this word. "Surrender...," they say in wispy tones. "Surrender..." As if Surrender is actually the name of a good witch who floats into town and waves her glitter wand in your face and *poof* makes life suddenly better. Yet, for all my sarcasm, there is absolute truth to the necessary practice of surrendering. (*You still lose me on the homemade nut milk, though.*)

I'm making these jokes intentionally. Because, in all of our Soul Archaeology, there may be no single part that sounds as nebulous, maddening, and mind-numbing as the concept of surrendering. So, let's embrace how silly this may feel, and then look it in the eye and make peace with it. I want you to be able to soften into your life, into possibility, and into feeling more peaceful than you'd ever imagined possible. I want you to swim in the direction of the river, not fight against it. If you can do this, you will save yourself a colossal amount of anxiety and, ultimately, pain.

It's time to . . . *surrender*. Shall we? (*She says with long flowing hair, sparkling kaftan, and glass of nut milk in hand.*)

What Does It Mean to Surrender?

As you move along the path in your Soul Archaeology, you are going to start noticing more and more when things don't go "your way." You have your SLTDL, your plans, and your ideas about how you are going to show up in the world and what things are going to be like when you do. This is all normal. But shit is not always going to play out according to whatever plan you feel like you've made. More than likely, it won't. In fact, some people say that the more we try to make our plans, the more the universe laughs in our face. (There's a Yiddish expression for this: "Der mensch tracht, un gott lacht." It means, "Man plans, and God laughs.") It may even seem like the harder you dedicate yourself to the work, the more things don't go according to plan. This can make you want to throw in the towel and give a big "What the fuck, Universe? I'm doing all the stuff you want me to do. Can you cut me a break?"

This is where surrendering comes in. The more you fight this what-the-fuck-ed-ness feeling, the more things can feel like they are falling apart. The more likely you are to morph into an avalanche of control freak hurling down a snowy mountain, decimating all the trees and hikers in sight. Logic ceases to exist. Reason feels like it no longer makes sense. You find yourself wanting to bite the heads off of people you normally love.

When we "surrender," we stop trying to control everything. We "let go" of what is "supposed" to happen and soften into the present of what *is* happening. This might be mildly obnoxious to hear—believe me, I know—but there's no way around it. Let's look at it this way: Imagine you are on a river, floating along peacefully in a boat. Suddenly, the weather turns, and the water starts to get choppy. You're bouncing around. You kind of want to barf, and then the water gets angry and dark. Surrendering is not saying, "Oh well, this water is rough, so I'll jump overboard and die because I give up," and abandoning both the boat and your life. It is also not saying, "This water is rough and choppy, and it is MY JOB TO MAKE IT CALM!" and then spending all your precious energy trying to calm the water, which would be virtually impossible because we can't control nature. Surrender looks more like acknowledging, "Oh shit, this water is choppy but I know I will be safe, so let me use the tools I have to make this boat ride feel better till the weather calms down," and then proceeding to take out a Swiss Army knife and a pack of Mentos and turning into MacGyver, and making the ride as smooth as possible with a roll of duct tape.

What "Surrendering" Is Not	What "Surrendering" Is
Giving up.	Staying committed to your Ultimate You but understanding the journey of unfurling may look and feel different than you thought it would.
Fake / toxic positivity.	Acknowledging shit fucking sucks while also knowing that things can totally suck all around you but that you can still be totally okay. Understanding that sucky things don't happen because you aren't worthy or lovable—they are just part of life.
Not caring.	Allowing whatever sadness or discomfort you feel over things that didn't turn out the way you wanted. Letting yourself mourn the loss of whatever it was you thought you needed or wanted—and then looking with honesty and compassion at why you felt like you needed this thing. Becoming an objective person looking at your life with as much clarity as you can.
Turning off your feelings.	Understanding that feelings are human and a part of life, even the icky ones. Having faith that you can "ride" the wave of your feelings through the intensity to the other side.

The Art of Fighting FOR Your Life, Not Against It

I've mentioned that our aim is not to "fight against" life. What does that look like in practice? Because, honestly, the idea of "fighting against life" sounds esoteric and beyond real-life application.

Deciding not to "fight against your life" isn't just "going with the flow." When we "go with the flow," we cope with adversity by accepting our lot and letting shit that's destined to happen go ahead and happen without trying to change it—we're letting the current sweep us along.

But it is... being proactive in shaping our lives but flexible as to what life looks like, and not fixated on or obsessed with achieving a specific outcome or end result.

Deciding not to "fight against your life" is not the same as "giving no shits." It is not about pretending you don't care or denying you have feelings or purposefully deciding that the feelings you have don't matter.

But it is... being more mindful of what you feel and how much energy you give to different feelings so that you can focus more on possibility than perceived defeat.

Deciding not to "fight against your life" is not "giving up." We don't throw our hands in the air, say "Fuck it," and walk away. We don't stop showing up for ourselves and others while feeling hopeless and defeated.

But it is... being more strategic and intentional about what you care about. It is asking yourself, *What can I be responsible for in this situation and what is not mine to carry?* and making a conscious choice to direct your energy into the things you can control.

Deciding not to "fight against your life" isn't giving away personal agency. It doesn't mean other people are in charge of your life experiences. You do not absolve yourself of accountability and responsibility.

But it is... taking accountability and responsibility for our feelings and experiences. When someone does something we don't want them to do, or something happens we don't want to happen and we spend a ton of energy trying to change someone else's mind or the situation, we are spending precious energy reacting to other people, their values, and their decisions. Time and energy are our currency! The alternative would be to allow others their experiences, to allow life to play out, but to keep returning to our values as the North Star.

Here are two examples in a life setting:

Fighting Against a Situation	Surrendering to a Situation
The person you've been dating ghosts, and you text every hour on the hour. You ask why and beg for another chance. You lash out and then apologize, all the while spinning yourself into an emotional tizzy and feeling a little out of control. You drink to make the hurt go away—it doesn't go away.	The person you've been dating ghosts, so you send a short, simple email expressing curiosity and inviting a conversation at some point. You feel hurt and call a friend to vent and express how crappy it feels. Then you remind yourself that someone doing something shitty is not a reflection of you and make a note to remove their contact information from your phone.
You forgot your twenty-five-year reunion is coming up, and you "feel fat" these days, so you crash-diet because you really need to look great, and that expensive juice cleanse is totally going to help you lose fifteen pounds in two weeks. You overdraft your bank account to buy something new to impress people.	You forgot your twenty-five-year reunion is coming up, and you "feel fat" these days. But rather than freak out, you realize everyone else will probably be equally nervous and the best thing you can do right now is be confident in your skin, so you schedule a blowout, buy a new lipstick, and chill the fuck out.

HOW TO FALL

In the morning, when I leave George's post-toilet-breaking, I drive away quietly. The road between Phoenix and Las Vegas is 302 miles—I spend the time alternating between ugly crying to a carefully curated Spotify playlist and questioning all my life choices. *I don't want to let go. This was not how it was supposed to be.* The cacti and shrubs zip by me out the windows, keeping pace with my thoughts.

I keep asking myself, *What is it exactly I'm so scared of? What do I think losing him will mean for me in my life?* I've spent so much time and so much energy painting red flags white and trying to wedge square pegs into round holes. *Why am I holding on so hard to the idea of this one man and I having our happily-ever-after that I've been willing to live a roller coaster of highs and lows just to keep him around? Why am I willing to pay for moments of sexy, total belonging with moments of total self-doubt and total, utter worthless confusion that leave me uttering "I know I'm not crazy" again and again?*

By the time I crest the hill on the 93 entering Henderson on that long stretch from the Hoover Dam to the city, the sunset is a kaleidoscope of pink and orange and blue and purple, and I pull the car over to stop and take it all in. I see the truth now. I have been holding on so tight that I haven't allowed myself to see the depth of possibility that could exist on the other side of letting go. Like dangling off a cliff, trying so hard not to fall I've been unable to see a tropical lagoon below me full of the most beautiful water. Yes, if I let go, I'll feel the fear of the fall and the sting of the landing, but once that happens, who knows what beauty I might find. I just have to be willing to feel the sting of the fall—*I just have to learn how to fall.*

"The fall" is the empty space between when we let go and when we land in what comes next. It's a time of uncertainty and it can cause panic. The fall is totally unavoidable, but you can learn to strengthen your self-love muscles and get better at it when it happens. What will emerge will be an ability to gracefully mourn the outcomes you intended and your expectations in order to make room for something else to grow in their place.

Getting better at falling is about two things: your mindset and your tool set. For now, we'll talk about the first. Our aim is to shift our thinking so we can get comfortable with uncertainty, which includes allowing ourselves to get familiar with the idea that, at the end of the day, no matter what we want or intend to happen, how things play out will be out of our control. In order to navigate this uncertainty, there are three shifts I'd like to share with you.

Mindset Shift One: Mind Your Own Beeswax

"Mind your own business." You've probably heard people say that before. Getting into someone else's business isn't usually that self-loving—unless, for example, you're keeping someone out of danger. While it may feel gratifying in the moment to dig up the goodies, in the long run, spending time obsessing about other people's shit isn't usually in our best interest.

The spiritual teacher and author Byron Katie has a wonderful idea that is so simple, to fully accept it is to be rocked to your core. Katie believes "there are only three kinds of business in the universe: mine, yours, and God's." More than that, she believes we increase our chances of feeling pain and anxiety in life when we linger outside of our own business and start hanging out in other people's business and God's business. "Reality is God," she says. "Whose business is it if I am feeling happy or sad? My business. Whose business is it if you are feeling happy or sad? Your business. Whose business is the weather? God's business. (Anything that's out of my control, your control, and everyone else's control—I call that God's business.) Much of our stress comes from mentally living out of our own business."[1]

When we catch ourselves being absorbed by something that is someone else's business, it gives us the chance to learn how to say, *That is not my business. That is someone else's responsibility. I acknowledge that this makes me feel [insert feelings here] and those feelings are fine to have. But I can honor those feelings and then bring the focus back to me.*

Think about it this way: Minding your own business + surrendering = a self-loving way to handle a crappy situation. Deciding to keep your focus on YOUR business doesn't mean you aren't allowed to be hurt or bothered by someone else's business or God's business. Of course not! You are allowed to be hurt, angry, pissed, whatever . . . all while remembering what is (and what isn't) yours to obsess over. Here are a few examples of what a mindshift into surrendering can look like:

My Business	Someone Else's Business	God's Business	How I WANTED to Feel in the Moment	How I Can Shift My Mindset
How I feel about George.	George deciding he doesn't want to be my partner anymore.	The faulty fasteners on the toilet that made it so easy for me to break the seat off.	"I am pathetic and feel defeated. I'm embarrassed."	"Yup. I'm embarrassed. This toilet seat sucks. George sucks. Everything sucks. I can't control any of that, so let's have a good cry and plan how to leave early so I can process this suckage alone peacefully."
Deciding you want to consciously lower your body weight as part of a plan to increase mobility.	The person who says that your desire to lose weight makes you a bad, fatphobic person.	The broken ankle you got when stumbling out of a bus, which made it hard for you to work out, causing you to take a step back from physical activity for a while, which resulted in some weight gain.	"I'm fat and nobody will ever want me. I'm a failure. What's the use of trying when nothing I do makes a difference anyway?"	"Yup. This blows. But plans get derailed sometimes and it's not because I'm a bad person. It just is. The most self-loving thing I can do right now is some stretching or swimming—the only one who has to understand my journey is me!"
How you drive.	The lady who cut you off in the parking lot because she was on her cell phone.	The big pothole you swerved into in order to avoid hitting the lady who cut you off because she was on her phone.	"Mother @#$%&!) stupid *****, you suck! @#$%&!) everything and @#$%&!) everyone."	"Mother @#$%&!) stupid *****, you suck! @#$%&!) everything and @#$%&!) everyone . . ." (Breathing deeply.) "Let's deal with this. Shit happens."

DIG DEEPER:
Mindshift—the Business and the Surrender

We've just covered a mindshift strategy you can use to help in surrendering through a tough moment. With this exercise, you're going to recall a moment from your past, deconstruct it a bit, and reimagine it.

Step One: Think about a moment in your life when you were holding on really tight.

You were on the edge of that cliff. You could not and would not let go. In your journal, recall the experience and write it out. Make sure to get detailed and specific here. Ask yourself the following questions:

1. At that time, what was I afraid to let go of?
2. What did I think would happen if I let go? What was I trying to avoid?

Step Two: Identify the business.

Looking back at the situation with both honesty and lots of self-compassion, do you feel as if you were seeing what happened in this situation as your business, someone else's business, or God's business? In your journal, fill in the following blanks:

1. "At that time, I thought _____ was my business."
2. "Seeing this as my business made me feel _____."

Step Three: Back in business.

If you made this situation that wasn't your business to carry *yours*, whose business was it *really*? Let's take a step back and put it into perspective. In your journal, flesh out the following:

1. "I can see now that _____ was really _____ business."
2. "Understanding that this was not my business could have allowed me to see _____ instead."

Step Four: Reclaiming and letting go.

It's time to reimagine how the situation could have played out differently had you approached it with a surrender mindset. What's done is done. While this cannot change the past, it may help you find more peace in the present. Walking through our history in an objective and compassionate manner is a great way to learn from our past.

In your journal, flesh out a conversation you might have had with yourself and (if applicable) the other person involved in this situation. What would you have needed to hear in order to make peace with this situation? What would you have needed to say to them? For them to say to you? What would have needed to happen for you to understand? It's okay if this feels silly—it's allowed. What matters here is that you open your mind to accept a different version of the situation. So, you allow yourself to see that another version is possible and you are deserving of softer, more peaceful outcomes. You are deserving of surrender.

Mindset Shift Two: Decide the World Is Good

I'm not going to spew fake happy bullshit here; a lot of things that happen in the world are terrible. A lot of bad situations are created and maintained by people who are malcontent and some who are just along for the ride. There is no denying any of this. That being said, you get to decide if the world, people, the universe, or God (or whatever higher power you believe in) is benevolent or malevolent. Is a greater power at work to create good or is this greater power innately cruel in its purpose?

People often chime in here to say, "Everything always happens for a reason" and that even the worst suffering and the most terrible of terrible things have a purpose in life. I don't necessarily agree with that. When a young child develops a terminal disease, for example, we shouldn't be forced to feel as if there's a greater reason for this with a happy ending. We don't have to find a bigger reason for something like that happening that helps us to make sense of it. The truth is that bad things are just a part of life.

Some come to this conversation with the idea that we can be one of two things—either consciously free and empowered or living as victims. You've probably heard someone say something like "Don't be such a victim." While they are (possibly) acting like a bit of an asshole when they say this, what they (probably) intend to say is "Don't act like life is out to get you." This is the idea of victim consciousness—when one approaches life through the lens that all things are being done *to* them for a reason, and that reason is usually because someone, or everyone, is out to get them. To believe that is, quite literally, to believe that the world is ill intentioned. (This can be really hard, especially when we know that there are some systems in life that are flawed and do discriminate against certain people!)

The alternative to having a victim mentality is to live a conscious life. To live life not in reaction to things around us, but proactively. This doesn't mean that we have *full control* over how we experience the things that happened to us—for extreme example, a Jewish person in Auschwitz was not responsible for their experience; an enslaved African would not have been able to take responsibility to create feelings of freedom in their own life. While many people have been able to take their power back after experiencing extreme trauma, there are a lot of people who will not and maybe cannot do the same, even after experiences that are far less extreme. Their circumstances in life prevent it, or perhaps their ability to react is skewed by the biology of their brain. We can't say that it's fully, totally possible for all people to walk around fully, totally conscious in life—all people can and will achieve this to different degrees—to say otherwise simply lacks empathy and awareness of institutional injustices.

What's important here is the idea that we have a degree of choice as to how we want to view the world. We get to decide: Do we want to believe that the universe has our best intentions in mind? Or is it out to get us? The answer doesn't change what has happened, but it does mean that we might feel more softly when future suffering does occur. The mindshift to believing the world is good can help us ease the fall of surrendering.

Mindset Shift Three: Emotions vs. Feelings

When you are surrendering, you are allowing yourself to exist. You're not frantically grasping at the past in order to make sense of the present. There is no writing the script for your future so that you can feel more assured in the moment. There is just making a home in the current state of your existence and the feelings you are having right now. There is awareness between what things are and what they are not, and these two truths live in mutual respect of each other. The trick is this: knowing that your icky feelings can exist in the same space as your peace. Your discomfort can share a home with confidence. You can, simultaneously, experience painful and uncomfortable things while feeling totally and utterly safe exactly as you are.

"Awakening is not a process of building ourselves up but a process of letting go," Pema Chödrön writes. "It's a process of relaxing in the middle—the paradoxical, ambiguous middle, full of potential, full of new ways of thinking and seeing—with absolutely no money-back guarantee of what will happen next."[2] Could you experience every day knowing that there was no money-back guarantee for any of the things in your life? Would that horrify you or liberate you? Maybe a bit of both?

If we find it hard to surrender, we want to understand why we are holding on so tightly. We want to awaken into this answer and not sleepwalk through our own shit. To do this, we need to learn to differentiate between our actual feelings and the feelings we have about our feelings. Those are two different things. One is "feelings," and the other "emotion."

Emotions are sensations we experience in our bodies. Feelings are the thoughts we have about our emotions when we have them. Both of these data sets are equally important, but they tell us different things about our state of being. Our emotions tell us the truth about the present moment, whereas feelings are colored by our subconscious, which takes into account both our interpretation of the past and our expectations for the future. It's important to understand that emotions are usually pretty reliable, but our feelings are not nearly as reliable—they are what pops up from our subconscious mind when our emotions ring the doorbell.

Here is why this matters: In between the emotion and the feeling is a whole lot of truth about what is real and what isn't. When we have a "moment" and do the work *in that moment* to separate our emotions from our feelings (to see our emotions and feelings as an objective observer would and not as a quasi-middle-aged woman freaking the fuck out), we will be able to more accurately see what in the situation is ours to take ownership of and what is ours to release because it is not true or not ours to carry. When we can off-load the shit from our backs that isn't real, we can make a choice that is self-loving and will help move us forward to our Ultimate You. Remember...we cannot stop hard feelings from happening—but we can learn how to navigate them.

After George and I broke up, I thought about having sex with him all the time. I also felt mad at myself for wanting to sleep with him. How could I still be fantasizing about this person who I knew wasn't good for me? I felt like I was betraying myself, but in the same breath, I wanted him to do any number of mind-numbingly dirty things to me. The two sets of data I had were my emotions and my feelings. My emotions of lust and desire were raw and desperate and totally normal. My feelings of shame and embarrassment were colored because of how I thought I should feel about my (totally natural) emotions. Experience told me that my desire for George was bad because I was hurt that he had rejected me and yet, I still wanted him. I thought, *What woman wants a man who rejects her?* I was angry at myself.

From an objective viewpoint, the desire I felt for my former partner was deeply human. He had been my sexual partner for years, so residual lusty emotions were totes normal. Add to that all the other emotions I was experiencing in life that magnified my desire—like loneliness—and what was happening was perfectly human. I had every right to own them in my body! But the self-judgment, the narrative I created based on how I felt? This was not mine to carry. And the more I held on to it, the worse I would feel and the harder time I would have of surrendering.

RELAXING IN THE MIDDLE
(AKA SNAPPLE IN THE PARKING LOT)

When relationships end in the movies, they usually go straight from utter heartbreak into a movie montage of scenes that show our plucky heroine learning how to conquer life again. One day there is a breakup and the next day, she is running on the treadmill and losing weight or getting a new hairdo that will, inevitably, make her unrecognizable to the person who broke her heart. This signals to us (and her) that she is victorious. She has let go.

In reality, the process of letting go—regardless of if what we're letting go is a relationship or another challenging situation—is a path some people take rapidly, while others take longer. (There is no set timetable for our ability to surrender!) The general journey can start off painfully, still gripping tightly to what we don't want to accept, then move into the "falling" phase, where one releases what was without the assurance of what comes next, and then move into the landing phase. It's only when we land that we can move forward into what's next. For me, it took around seven months to go of my relationship from letting go, to falling, to landing in the crystal clear water below, ready to move forward with my life. For me, some of it looked like this:

- Crying. All the time. At everything. Any and every random act could bring forth a seemingly endless well of tears and snot bubbling out of my nostrils, which would result in a huge headache, which made me want to curl up into a ball and hide away in the darkness forever, while playing the aptly named "Oh Shit" playlist I created on Spotify (this is absolutely true).
- Engaging in what can only be defined as both delicious and deeply painful emotional self-flagellation that comes from listening to Fleetwood Mac's "Silver Springs" on repeat nonstop.
- Deciding I needed a Diet Peach Snapple in the middle of the day and going to CVS for said beverage without a bra on and then sitting in the car while (you know it) crying and listening to Fleetwood Mac's "Silver Springs" yet again.

I found my "falling period" to be sticky and transformative. I downsized everything I could in my life to help keep things as calm as possible while I accepted the loss of the man I loved and, even more, while I mourned the death of my big dream about what our life could have been. I also spent a lot of time reminding myself that, even though I had no idea what was coming next, I was actually totally okay. I was feeling. I wasn't hiding my pain. I had all my basic needs covered. Shit hurt but, really . . . I was doing pretty good. In doing this, I made a home for myself in the sticky middle phase of my letting go. Doing this gave me the room to walk through my hard feelings, stop escaping my pain, and do the really deep soul work that helped me see my life with objectivity, accountability, and compassion.

After years of Soul Archaeology, I am now able to use a bunch of tools that keep me from reaching the levels of desperation I felt in the past when hurt. Then, pain prompted me to do all I could to anesthetize my hurt, potentially endangering me emotionally and physically. These days,

I feel hurt without it owning me. I am able to actively talk through what I am experiencing when I am experiencing it rather than getting swept away by it. I may feel huge tsunamis of sadness, but I know my feet are planted firmly on the ground. The wave can come, but I remain standing and self-loving.

IF SANDCASTLES WASH AWAY, WHY BOTHER BUILDING THEM AT ALL?

If you like checklists and clarity, having someone say, "Stop fighting and embrace the present of what is without caring about what happens next" can feel patronizing and maddening. What's the point of doing anything if you aren't going to care about the end result? Does the end result even matter at all if you're trying to live in the present? What the fuckity fuck?

The point of doing things is the doing of them itself. To approach our lives with the mindset of surrendering is to understand that we don't learn lessons from the achievement of a specific end goal, but from what we do along the way. If we focus on the process and not the end result, each experience will teach us what we need in order to grow and move to the next level.

It's the process that teaches us how to grow, not the "getting" that happens at the end. We grow when we are figuring things out and working through them. We develop our strengths and resilience when we consciously choose to do hard things, or when we are forced to work through hard stuff.

It's not that I don't want you to care about what happens in your life—I do! But I am suggesting that you leave room for life to reveal itself through process, rather than fixating on specific outcomes. This practice of nonattachment is the core of Buddhist philosophy; I am hopeful that hearing it explained through my stories will help it feel more tangible and accessible.

"We are like children building a sandcastle," Pema Chödrön says. "We embellish it with beautiful shells, bits of driftwood, and pieces of colored glass. The castle is ours, off limits to others. We're willing to attack if others threaten to hurt it. Yet despite all our attachment, we know that the tide will inevitably come in and sweep the sandcastle away. The trick is to enjoy it fully but without clinging, and when the time comes, let it dissolve back into the sea."[3]

If embracing building a sandcastle without reassurance that it won't fall apart sounds impossible, try to soften into the uncertainty of what could happen to it instead. Maybe you will build a sandcastle and it will remain untouched for eternity! Maybe you will build it and Sam Elliott will happen upon it and decide that the spot where the castle stands, of all places, is perfect for a shrine in his name to be erected, so therefore you must destroy your castle to make room for his monument and be forced to build another, even greater one in a different place! You never know. And that is why "success" isn't found in a guaranteed outcome, but in the processes we undertake every day.

I ached for resolution to wrap a bow around my relationship with George and gift me peace, but I never experienced it. I just learned to allow the fear and loneliness I felt about losing him to wash over me. One day, my feelings stopped being so hot and desperate and, instead, started to cool off. I let his sandcastle wash away as it needed to during that chapter of my life.

On the other side of my annihilation was clarity. This clarity allowed me to learn all the stuff I've shared in recent chapters, like my core wound and the movies in my mind. Surrendering allowed me to feel sturdier. The more confident I felt in my ability to land safely in the water below me, the deeper the roots of my own self-esteem tree grew—and the more I learned to trust myself. The more I learned peace.

SURVEYING THE SITE:
WHAT WE DUG UP IN THIS CHAPTER

Section 4 is about self-love in the real world. What happens when the shit hits the fan and when we have to do our work against the odds and in the face of challenges that happen every day. If we know that so much of life is out of our control, it would be foolish to enter into our Soul

Archaeology without a strategy to deal with things that throw us off or don't go our way! Because of that, we focused this chapter on the perhaps strange idea of "surrendering."

We started by acknowledging how bizarre a concept surrendering is—how foreign it feels and yet how it can be essential in our living a Self-Loving Life. In its essence, to surrender is to let go of our expectations and to not fight against reality. It means to soften into the present, all the while remaining aware of what is actually ours to own and be accountable for, and what we have the opportunity to release.

We then reviewed three mindset shifts we can make that can help us to surrender: to understand what in a situation is really our "business" and what is not ours to own; to decide whether we want to believe the world around us is good or malevolent; and, finally, to understand the difference between our emotions and our feelings—to know that when we experience something, we oftentimes experience both an emotion, which is a natural reaction, and feelings, which are our own personal editorial commentary about the emotional experience we're having. These feelings are based less on logic and more on our subconscious and our history.

We introduced the idea of "relaxing into the middle" between discomfort and resolution. This is a space where we know something hurts but we don't yet have the solution for how to resolve the pain—instead, we must just make a home in experiencing it as it is. Last, we answered a simple but deeply powerful question: Why should we even work to aspire and create a vision for our lives if we have so little control of anything? The point is the doing itself. We learn from experience, not from arriving upon a set destination. As frustrating as this idea can sound, understanding it allows us to be more present in our lives. And when we are able to be more present, we can stay more self-loving. And when we do that? We grow. And we move through our Soul Archaeology to connect with a more empowered, more truthful, and more liberated version of ourselves.

Chapter 12

OTHER PEOPLE'S SHIT

How to Stay Self-Loving When Other People Make It Hard

It **doesn't matter** how often you meditate or how many green smoothies you drink or how big the stack of chakra-aligning crystals is on your wrist. Your self-love means squat until you learn how to take it out of your personal bubble and into the everyday world. Maybe that's harsh, but none of us operate in a vacuum. We all interact with other people for large parts of every day. Some of us interact with a lot of people all day long, every day. Some interactions will be utter perfection. Some will be a horror and test every ounce of our sanity. Regardless, we get to learn how to maintain our commitment to ourselves in tangible, practical ways, all the while being tested by the things around us. Because if we allow every disturbance or pothole in the road to derail us, we'll spend more time reacting to our lives than living them.

Of all the chapters in this book, this will be the most straightforward. We don't need poetics here, nor do we need vulnerable stories to connect with each other. It's a simple fact: We all find ourselves tested by people. And when we're tested, in a millisecond, all of the hard work we've done on ourselves can fly right out the front door.

It's not unusual to pick up a book on personal growth and encounter advice that is based around how to avoid stressful situations entirely. I can never get my head around that, because stressful situations aren't always about us and it's important to know how to deal with stress when it rears its head;

the more you commit to your growth and actually start making changes, the more your life in the present will shake up. Your values may change, your perception of self may change, and your relationships will change. It's almost naive to think that we, ourselves, can control the wake of our growth to a limited, wave-free radius. We can only do so much to mitigate painful and frustrating situations in life. But what we *can* do is prepare for them so that when they happen, we can handle them as smoothly as possible.

In an ideal situation, we create a world for ourselves that exists in such perfect alignment that there is never even the possibility of feeling stress or discord—stress can occur, but we would float delicately above it. And, yes, it is 100 percent true that when we start swimming in the direction of our life-stream current, challenges *will* feel easier because we are more settled, more comfortable, and more agile in our ability to let pain pass through us with ease.

When you start doing things differently and challenging both yourself and others through your actions, you're going to meet resistance from yourself and from others. You may find yourself more acutely aware of things that bother you or hurt you. You may have less tolerance than you did before. All of these can actually be signs indicating that you're growing—that life is shifting, and you are shifting alongside it.

In this chapter we'll discuss tangible tactics for navigating sticky situations. We're also going to be reviewing some tools, including mental (and physical) check-ins that you can call upon when needed. This, combined with the mindset work we previously talked about, will help you navigate some of the unexpected. Let's do this!

BREATHE, BECAUSE SECONDS CAN MAKE ALL THE DIFFERENCE

When I was studying to become a Kundalini yoga teacher, there was one woman in class who really got under my skin. At that time, I didn't have many tools in my Self-Love Tool Kit, so our interactions drilled deep into my inner sanctum. Throat-punching this woman, as I often wanted to do, would not have been a wise way to handle the dysfunctional situation for a variety of reasons. But outside of throat-punching, there were many other ways to handle our relationship that, although less violent, would have been equally reactive and unhealthy for me because some form of self-abandonment would have been at the heart of each of them. I never learned to handle our unpleasant dynamic in a peaceful way. Instead, I allowed her to get under my skin from the first week of class to the twenty-fourth. In doing so, I allowed her to steal my precious energy—reacting to her sapped my resources, which would have been much better off spent nurturing my own hurt, and handling the things that were really impacting my ability to live a Self-Loving Life.

In your life, this person could be anyone or anything. A difficult boss, an ex-partner, a judgmental parent, a traffic jam. Anything that elicits intense negative emotions—from the smallest annoyance to the deepest of pain—can be viewed through a lens as being either something that helps you to grow or something that keeps you stuck in place.

Think about all the things in life that really get you going. The situations and the people. The conversations and the experiences. Each and every one of these moments that awaken intense emotions is an opportunity for you, in the moment, to make decisions that either support you or serve as a way to self-abandon. These moments are unavoidable, so it's best to look them in the eye and deal with them as practically as you can.

When you're experiencing stimulation and your emotions get activated and you feel yourself wanting to retaliate in some way, mere seconds can make the difference between self-abandoning and staying self-loving. In those seconds, will you have your own back or drop your own hand? The hope is that you can give yourself a few moments between the emotional recognition of a disturbance and the processing, and then again take time before you react to the stimuli. As much as we'd like to, we can't control the things that happen around us, so the next-best thing is to strengthen the muscle of connection we have to ourselves, so that we can do our best to remain in the driver's seat and stay as self-loving as possible. The easiest way to do this is to breathe.

In order to become a certified Kundalini yoga teacher with the Kundalini Research Institute, I had to experience White Tantric yoga. On paper, this is described as "a day of meditation, exaltation, and transformation." In real life, it's a room of all-white-wearing devout Kundalini yogis who partner up in pairs, sitting in lines knee-to-knee and face-to-face, doing a series of sixty-two-minute meditations all…day…long. Meditating silently for sixty-two minutes multiple times in one day is equal parts terrifying and beautiful. There is no place your vulnerability can run. There is only YOU. It was during this time I learned that if I can breathe through something, I can sit through anything. Pain can come, but if I can find even a few moments of stillness and breath in a situation, I can make my way through to the other side. I can feel liberated from things that scare me. The emotions will still be there, but they have less control over me because I can find my breath, connect to it, and control its pace and its depth. How I experience my breath is a reflection of how I experience my life. When I have the ability to breathe deeply, I can be deeply present. When I am anxious or afraid, breathing rapidly and sucking in air, I am in survival mode and my body is activated by fear.

There is a reason for this: "With each breath, millions of sensory receptors in the respiratory system send signals via the vagus nerve to the brainstem. Fast breathing pings the brain at a higher rate, triggering it to activate the sympathetic nervous system, turning up stress hormones, heart rate, blood pressure, muscle tension, sweat production, and anxiety. On the other hand, slowing your breathing induces the parasympathetic response, dialing down all of the above as it turns up relaxation, calm, and mental clarity."[1] The more time I spent as a yoga student studying pranayama (the yogic practice of breath work designed to connect the body to its breath and, therefore, the body to its life force), the more I felt how deep the connection between my breath and my state of being was.

By manipulating our breath in different ways, we can influence ourselves both physiologically (by stimulating our parasympathetic nervous system) and psychologically (by using breath to direct our attention where we want it to go). In a moment of stress, precious seconds give us time to observe our reaction and choose a response that serves us. The more space we can give ourselves, the more likely we will be to stay self-loving in our reactions.

I have created several video tutorials showing you how to do a few powerful breath techniques for use in your everyday life. You can find them on my website at SarahSapora.com/Soul. Watch, learn, and breathe along!

ACTING PROACTIVELY VS. ACTING REACTIVELY—IT MAKES ALL THE DIFFERENCE

Sometimes our choices are clear:

- Do we choose to be vulnerable or defensive?
- Do we decide the world around us is loving or cruel?
- Do we want to see ourselves as the victim of something or as someone having an experience within a greater context?
- When given the choice, do we self-abandon or stay self-loving?
- When upset, do we want to react to other people and put them in charge of our experiences, or do we want to do our best to shape our experiences ourselves?

Merriam-Webster's Collegiate Dictionary defines the word "reactive" as "readily responsive to a stimulus; occurring as a result of stress or emotional upset."[2] It defines "proactive" as "acting in anticipation of future problems, needs, or changes; relating to, caused by, or being interference between previous learning and the recall or performance of later learning."[3] The difference between the two may not sound like a big deal, but when it comes to creating a Self-Loving Life, it can mean everything.

A reactive response to an emotional experience . . .	A proactive response to an emotional experience . . .
Reacts to the past. It brings the past into the present. It means when we react, we are focused, either consciously or subconsciously, on our previous experiences, which can be either negative or positive.	Focuses on what happens before an experience occurs. It is a way to keep our attention on what is next and our eyes focused on what is constructive and moves us forward.

A reactive response to an emotional experience . . .	A proactive response to an emotional experience . . .
Problem-solves on the spot, which may become harder when your emotions are activated and overloaded.	Solves something before it becomes a problem. This means you can apply logic and reason in advance, making it easier to react in the moment because, when in a bind, your job is to recall and take action and not solution-find from scratch.
Forces you to be creative on the fly. Which could be awesome or absolutely terrible.	Relies on prepared strategy, which can be awesome or terrible.
Is oftentimes unintentional.	Is intention-driven.
May often result in the perpetuation of self-abandonment.	Offers you a tool to help move away from self-abandonment.
Is data and a learning opportunity, regardless of outcome.	Is data and a learning opportunity, regardless of outcome.
Puts the locus of control outside your agency, in someone or something else. It means you are reacting to someone else's values, priorities, challenges, and needs.	Helps you keep your internal locus of control. This means you can take ownership over your actions based on your values, priorities, challenges, and needs.
Puts someone else in the driver's seat of how you experience life!	Puts you back in the driver's seat of how you experience life!

AVOID THE STRUGGLE AND PLAN AHEAD

My father used to tell me that we don't get health insurance and pay a fortune each month for the times that we don't need it. Rather, we get it for that one time we don't *expect* to need it. It's the same for what we're talking about here—we don't spend time when we're calm and focused thinking about how to be more self-loving sometime in the future when everything feels awesome and easy. We think about it so that when things get hard, we have a go-to plan top of mind that we can simply reach for.

You practice self-love so that you'll be able to call upon it when the shit hits the fan. You don't work out your self-love muscles once—you work them out again and again and again. For example, maybe you struggle to separate your work life and personal life, so one of the items on your

SLTDL might be a tool to help you do just that. In this case one of your tools might be a two-minute ritual where, when you get home every day, you take off your shoes and grab a notebook or pad left near the door, and write down all the things in your head about work on a piece of paper so you can get the thoughts to stop spinning in circles, but also so you can remember them in the morning and pick up where you left off. In doing this, you help free your head up to be mindful and present when you're at home with family. This is a proactive tool. You do it every day for months while life is swimming along fine. One day, your boss is really acting fucked and your partner is sick, and you are hating life more than ever before and all you want to do is walk in the door and rip your bra off and lie on the couch... but you do your ritual anyway. Because you know it helps and you didn't even have to stretch hard to remember to do it, because it's become part of your natural life already. That is when the tool really becomes a life-changer!

We spend time deconstructing the ways adversity can show up in our lives so we can better handle it when we come face-to-face with it.

Assembling Your Tool Kit

Man Candy has worked as a general contractor. He can fix anything. Judging by the pile of tools he keeps in his work truck, he probably has any tool he could possibly need for any situation. Right now, you and I are going to gather a whole bunch of tools you can store away for when you need them the most. We're going to create a Self-Love Tool Kit full of self-love tools that have your Ultimate You at the heart of them.

You already have some useful tools in your kit—the proactive tools that we created earlier in the book—your feeling word, your power statement, and your Self-Love To-Do List. Here you'll acquire the reactive tools for your kit. These are the tools you can reach for when prompted by outside forces or whenever you feel yourself reacting to challenging stuff happening around you.

Questions to Fill Your Reactive Tool Kit

Right now you'll create a proactive plan for reactive situations. To do this exercise, I suggest you keep your journal on hand and a timer to help you stay focused. Give yourself two or three minutes to freewrite an answer for each question. For a completed example, visit my website at SarahSapora.com/Soul.

1. How would you describe yourself when you are feeling content and good? *For example, what is your breathing like? Describe your emotions. What do you feel in your body?*
2. What do you have to do, every day, in order to feel content and good? *Make a list.*
3. What could you do to feel good if you needed an extra boost to get there? *Make a list. These are things you can do but they don't need to happen every day.*
4. What in life activates you? *Make a list.*
5. What does it feel like for you when you are activated? *Describe your emotions. What do you feel in your body?*
6. How do you know when things are about to get worse for you? *Are there any signs that indicate your state is about to worsen?*
7. When you are activated, what are things you can do to feel better and improve your condition? *Make a list.*

Your aim is to make these lists as detailed and specific as you can! When you are done, it may be helpful to make copies of the list you came up with in question #7 and combine it with your Self-Love To Do List, and put a copy in all the places you might be when distress hits—on your phone, in your bedside drawer, on your desk, and so on. Whenever you get activated, you can refer to your full Self-Love To Do List with these tools added and pick the tools that are the most relevant and accessible to you to intervene on your behalf.

Four-Step Awareness Check-In

This simple practice is good when you need to come back to yourself and your surroundings when you feel that you've fallen away. This check-in can be done anywhere at any time as long as you can focus—in the restroom at work, sitting in a parked car, et cetera.

- **Step One: Awareness check.** Notice what is around you. Where are you? What is happening in your presence? Observe and make a mental list. Get as specific as you can.
- **Step Two: Body check.** What is your body feeling right now? Scan your body from the top of your head to your fingertips and toes. Travel along, stopping at different parts along the way, noticing as you go. Observe and make a mental list. Get as specific as you can.
- **Step Three: Feelings check.** What emotions are you experiencing? What feelings are generated as a result of those emotions? Remember not to judge yourself for anything; your job is simply to get specific and observe.
- **Step Four: Breath check.** What is your breathing like? This is a great chance to center your breath and pace if you need to realign.

OTHER PEOPLE HAVE SHIT . . . AND YOU DON'T NEED TO UNDERSTAND IT

As it usually goes with these things, there was another, earlier draft of this book. Before it grew and evolved into what it is today, I'd basically written a rambling memoir told in chronological order. You've read a bunch about George so far in this book, and there's a reason why (because our relationship was a major catalyst for my Soul Archaeology); and, in truth, you probably wouldn't be reading this book right now if it wasn't for him and what we shared. But there was a ton more about him in the first draft. Pages and pages. But they weren't pages and pages about us or me, but pages and pages spent trying to understand him. Trying to decode his words. Analyzing him so I could better understand myself because I needed to understand *why* he did all the things he did to me. In some way, I think I believed that understanding his shit and why he didn't want to be my partner was necessary in order for me to move on. It was...a lot. It was also really unhealthy of me. The truth is, you don't need to understand someone else in order to understand yourself. And while, yes, it can be helpful in the context of relationships to understand each other, this one fact has become really clear to me since then: Other people's shit is *their* shit. The more time you spend trying to decode their shit, the more you are trying to—in some way—control them and the situation. It just is. You can't control them. The only thing that you can really do is focus on yourself.

I get that sometimes we really, really want to know. We want to know why our parents did what they did, or our bosses, or ex-partners, or friends—so much so that the desire to know consumes us. Maybe because the more we feel like we understand what makes someone else seemingly fucked up, the less we believe we have to think about ourselves. Except we are all fucked up in our own ways. In order to stay self-loving when other people's shit starts to show up at your door, you have a choice to make. You can decide how much of their shit you want to let impact your life. This is what boundaries are for.

Boundaries mean you can love someone but still want to put distance between you, them, and their shit. You can accept them, accept their shit, and still not want it in your life. Boundaries help us to know understanding them is not more important than understanding ourselves. Understanding someone else's shit does not buy our freedom. It is not a magical key that unlocks our ability to surrender. That lies only within us and is granted by us and us alone.

SURVEYING THE SITE: WHAT WE DUG UP IN THIS CHAPTER

Our friend Pema Chödrön writes, "Instead of asking ourselves, 'How can I find security and happiness?' we could ask ourselves, 'Can I touch the center of my pain? Can I sit with suffering, both yours and mine, without trying to make it go away? Can I stay present to the ache of loss or disgrace—disappointment in all its many forms—and let it open me?' "[4] While these words may seem dramatic—not everything in life is as acute as suffering, loss, disgrace, and disappointment—we can take a step back from the sentiments and extrapolate the big idea, that our aim in life shouldn't be to rush toward resolution but rather to find safe ways to be present in our lives. In order to be present and navigate things safely, we need to have tools.

There are lots of tools that do a nifty job of helping us escape discomfort! Some of them are maladaptive and feel great in the moment but, in the long run, hurt us even more. You probably know some of yours. Whatever they are, these tools can be super powerful at helping us deal with life as it orbits around us, but they aren't necessarily rooted in our greatest, best interest. Together, in this book, we've explored how to stay committed to self-love when the rubber hits the road of our journey, and when we drive into some big-ass potholes along the way. We have created a Self-Love Tool Kit to tap into when life makes it hard to stay committed to our growth—when people piss us off, or the news of the day becomes too much, or our boss nags us (again), or we find ourselves wanting to pull the hair out of our heads or scream at the top of our lungs for any reason. (To think we can avoid these things by consciously creating our own perfect reality is toxic positivity and spiritual bypassing.)

We walked through the difference between proactive and reactive actions and created a reactive to-do list. We worked to understand the role our breath plays in navigating sticky emotions and covered how to use a quick awareness check-in when feeling overwhelmed or when we need to connect to ourselves.

These tools are offered to help you walk through totally natural, totally human, and totally unavoidable moments in life that are out of your control.

Chapter 13

FORGIVING YOURSELF

Yes, You Have to Do It

I **have been ashamed** of many things in life. About how I treated my body and who I gave access to it. How I used my body to get the instant gratification that I felt would validate me. I've been ashamed of my weight. I've been ashamed for thinking I was lucky to have people who wanted to associate with me or touch me and the wrinkly, lumpy bumps of my body.

I've been ashamed of the people I've unintentionally hurt. Of the nice guys I mocked because I couldn't accept their kindness. The thank-you notes that I never sent to people who were generous to me.

I've been ashamed to be unmarried and childless, without a family of my own. For having not given my parents a grandchild.

Mostly, I've been ashamed of myself for just being myself. I felt that all of me was broken and, in some way, wrong. And I carried the shame for a long time. Some of it I could see clearly; some was obscured. The shame stacked up on my shoulders, pressing down until all that was left was a woman who had no idea how hurt and worn down she was by the self-judgment she didn't even know she carried. By that time, I was tired of feeling like a walking highlight reel of things I felt certain I was not. I had a general, low-level angst buzzing constantly in the background—a feeling I constantly had something to preemptively apologize for when walking into every situation and every relationship in my life.

That was then. I no longer carry any of this shame. In order to do that, I had to offer myself forgiveness.

When you ask yourself, *Is there anything I'm ashamed of in my life?* what comes up for you? Maybe you don't have anything from your past that you feel ashamed of—but, if that's the case, it's unlikely much else in this book has spoken to you. Or it could be that you don't want to answer the question, because although there's stuff that has weighed you down, you've never associated the word "shame" with it, because really, you think, it wasn't even *that big of a deal* compared to what you know other people have gone through. If that's the case, I want you to understand that shame is not a competition; other people's experiences do not invalidate your own.

The places where you feel shame are also places where there's a great opportunity for you to grow and lean into vulnerability. Wherever you have walled up to protect yourself are the same places you have a chance to soften and invite others (and yourself) in to rest. When you are able to look mindfully at the things that make you feel the most broken, you can birth great courage—if the greatest sources of our suffering are the lies we tell ourselves about how unworthy we are for the things we feel we've done,[1] the greatest fountains of joy can be the ability to alleviate our own burdens by putting down the weight of self-judgment.

THE STORY OF MY SELF-FORGIVENESS

Of all the things I have carried shame for, there is one that stands out the most. This was the time I erased myself in order to try to save a man I loved from himself.

After Jake and I broke up in 2009, he started using cocaine and Xanax. One day he called and said he was in a hotel using; he'd spent the night hallucinating. "You're gonna die," I told him. "You need help."

"Come and get me?" he asked. So I did.

I put him in detox. And when that finished, he spent days in my apartment, shaking and sweating in the guest room while I worked on getting him into a residential rehab facility. Juggling logistics, I found myself caught between my desire to help the man I'd loved and an awareness that I was the hidden ex-mistress now trying to save the day. When I called his insurance company, they wouldn't talk to me, because I didn't have the right last name. I wasn't the wife; I was nobody...*But he needed me.* I called again, and this time used the name that wasn't mine, the last name I wanted for so long. It rolled off my tongue so easily it scared me. Sarah was nobody, but *this* woman had a use.

I erased myself so I could love someone and be who he needed me to be. I couldn't do that as Sarah—Sarah didn't exist, because she was never allowed into his life to begin with, and I had to admit that some of that was my fault because I stayed. I walked through the promises I made to myself because I couldn't stand the idea of losing what I thought we *could* have. The years I spent nights crying alone. Pretending my feelings didn't matter so I could hang on to hope.

Eventually, I would leave Louisville and attempt to move on. Eventually, Jake would succumb to his addiction and die of an overdose. Even before he passed, I was incapable of understanding the depth of pain I felt toward him and myself for my own self-betrayal. To compensate, I was aggressive in every bucket of my life, numbing with surface-level sex and doing everything I could to show everyone just how okay I was. Except it would be years before I'd be okay again.

When I look back on this time, I realize that I thought I'd spent years mourning Jake but what I really mourned was the pain of recognizing my own choices. Accepting that I was deserving of forgiveness felt almost as crippling as the things I thought I did wrong in the first place. How was I deserving of anything that could be considered self-loving after treating myself with a lack of respect that felt hard to swallow?

I know now that I was only doing the best I could. Sometimes our blind hope and misplaced optimism lead us down a bumpy road. Sometimes, in an effort to make sense of a shitty situation, we end up taking ownership of things that aren't ours to own. I am deserving of self-compassion. I am allowed to let it go. I am allowed to forgive myself. I do not need to be redeemed.

THE WHY, WHEN, AND WHAT OF
SELF-FORGIVENESS

On a physical level, self-forgiveness does many things for us. Biophysically, higher levels of self-forgiveness are related to our well-being; forgiveness in the general sense is good for the body. One study monitored participants' blood pressure, heart rate, facial muscle tension, and sweat gland activity while they thought of someone who had hurt or mistreated them. Sure enough, "when people recalled a grudge, their physical arousal soared. Their blood pressure and heart rate increased, and they sweated more. Ruminating about their grudges was stressful, and subjects found the rumination unpleasant. It made them feel angry, sad, anxious, and less in control."[2] The *Journal of the American College of Cardiology* even reports that "anger and hostility are linked to a higher risk of heart disease, and poorer outcomes for people with existing heart disease."[3] Forgiveness of any kind, whether toward others or ourselves, is physically good for us.

On an emotional level, self-forgiveness is directly linked to the strength of our self-esteem; a reduction in anxiety, neuroticism, and depression; and improved productivity. It also reduces self-punishing patterns like self-criticism, self-destruction, and negative self-talk. There are studies that show a direct correlation between high levels of shame and a lack of self-forgiveness and the development of eating disorders and sexual disorders; studies also suggest that self-forgiveness is a necessary part of eating disorder recovery.[4] If we are able to forgive ourselves for the things we feel shame over, we can improve our quality of life, feel happier, create more joy, and live more deeply connected to ourselves in a loving way.

As you put space between your actions and reactions and learn to stay self-loving in the face of challenge, as you learn to use the self-love tools you've created for yourself and use your new Self-Love To-Do List, you may start to see yourself differently. You may start to look at your whole life differently. And you may start to uncover some things that make you feel pretty bad—some may be things that you did; some may be things that other people did. There may even be something you accepted as fact or thought was "no big deal" that now, all of a sudden, seems like a big, huge mountain. Staring at these big things may cause some proportional discomfort. It can feel like weight you are holding across your shoulders, pressing you into the ground and rendering you immobile. If you want to live a Self-Loving Life, you need to put this weight down, because the only way to really feel liberated in life is to untether yourself from the things that keep you in place.

Brené Brown expresses that the depth to which we feel shame is parallel to the height at which we can experience our own beauty. If we remove our ability to acknowledge shame, we also remove our own ability to experience our own beauty, our *greatness*. "When we numb the dark, we also numb the light," she writes.[5] *Oof.*

Our darkness and our lightness are intrinsically connected to each other. There can be no faith without challenge, no light without shadow. We cannot unfurl into our true Ultimate You if we avoid the dark parts inside us that shame holds captive and uses as a weapon against our own self-love. Empowerment requires us to look at the difficult shit. "Forgiveness is not forgetting or walking away from accountability or condoning a hurtful act, it's the process of taking back and healing our lives so we can truly live," says Brown.[6]

Understanding the (Important) Difference Between Shame, Guilt, and Embarrassment

So, you feel something shitty...but you don't know what it is? Let's take this apart. Shame is the feeling that you, as a whole, are wrong. It is not to be confused with guilt, which relies on the self-judgment that you have done something specifically wrong. While judgment is specific, shame owns you entirely. When you feel shame, you are unable to separate yourself from the perception of your actions. Your feelings about what you believe you've done, or who you feel you are, cover you like a blanket. Sometimes the blanket is light. Sometimes it is heavy, keeping you stuck in place, whether or not you realize it.

Shame is not the same as guilt, nor is it the same as feeling embarrassed. Shame tells us we have fallen short of a society-wide moral standard; guilt tells us we have fallen short of our own standards. We have done something that isn't good, that is out of character with who we believe we are. Embarrassment, on the other hand, is a feeling of discomfort that some piece of ourselves is about to be (or we might be) threatened and that other people will witness this—or know about it in some way—and this revelation will change how people feel about us or impact the image of ourselves we want to present to other people.[7] To be clear:

Shame tells us:	Guilt tells us:	Embarrassment tells us:
I am bad.	Something I did was bad.	I'm uncomfortable because someone is seeing this thing that is going to make them think I'm bad.

This may sound like semantics, but the distinctions are important, because science tells us all three of these things—shame, guilt, and embarrassment—are caused by different chemical reactions in our bodies and brains. For the purposes of this book, I specifically focus on the idea of feeling shame—that something in us makes us feel unlovable and bad. But if you feel like you relate to the other two feelings more, there are a ton of resources you can explore to dig deeper.

When to Self-Forgive

Soul Archaeology tells us that we grow one layer at a time. With each layer that is uncovered, new things are revealed to us as we see ourselves with fresh eyes made wise from the learning. The same idea applies to our own ability to see the things in life for which we may subconsciously be needing our own self-forgiveness.

I had already been committed to my Soul Archaeology for over a year before I was capable of seeing that the relationship I'd had with a college boyfriend, who I'd dismissed as "being mean sometimes," was actually coercively abusive. I had the realization in the bath one day. "That wasn't right," I said out loud to nobody but myself. "Is this even possible?"

I sat asking myself questions for so long my fingers started to prune in the water. It was like a lightning bolt had illuminated my core. Once I saw it, I could not unsee it—everything changed. *Is it possible that was sexual abuse?* I asked myself. Sexual abuse was violent, though, and he wasn't violent with me—he didn't hit me or anything—he just got me to do stuff I didn't want to do by pushing or begging or making me feel small for not wanting to play along. That wasn't abusive; he just didn't respect me, right? I already knew the answer. I just couldn't understand why it had taken me so long to see it. And that made me really mad at myself.

That's not love. That wasn't right. I started to cry. *The fight he picked with me when I didn't want to have sex with his friend. Those times I said no when I didn't want to do the things he pushed me to do but did them anyway. I always said it after the act. I had felt so dirty. I hated what he made me do and he liked it. Why? That is not respect. That is not love.*

All these years I'd been saying he was just an ass, but no, it was a lot more than that—it was wrong. Nineteen years of denying myself anger, somehow believing that I deserved the things that happened. I deserved it because I didn't speak up for myself the right way, loud enough. I deserved it because I erased my voice so often, I stopped trying to have a voice in general.

I wish I could tell you that the realization I had been in an abusive relationship in my younger years liberated me right there on the spot. It didn't. For a while, the seeing made me mad for not having had the strength to walk away. I had to sit with that truth for a while, and work my way through it, before I realized that I was deserving of self-forgiveness. I did not need to feel shame. I was not morally wrong or broken because of what had happened to me.

It took four years to get from the lightning bolt to the self-forgiveness I deserved and never should have believed was needed in the first place. I say this to help you understand that the process of self-forgiveness is not always fast. It happens when it happens, and sometimes it happens slowly. You see the opportunities for self-forgiveness when you see them, and not any sooner, and that is okay.

You will actively seek self-forgiveness when you can no longer stand not to, when the pain of where you are hurts more than the fear of what might happen if you did something different. When you realize your survival depends on doing hard things. This is when you will finally embrace the idea that nobody is going to change the course of your life but you.

We Block Self-Forgiveness Because . . .

If I had to pick one word to sum up how I handled painful shit in my life, it would be "disconnection." I unknowingly used all the tools in my (disordered) tool kit to separate myself from the shame I experienced as a result of my relationship choices. I used food to numb out. I kept secrets from my friends, withdrawing because I didn't want them to know the truth. I suppressed my needs and pleased and pleased all day, every day, clinging to the reactions I got in return as if it were the currency I owed some cosmic landlord to take up space in this world. Ultimately, I blocked my ability to soften and forgive. Doing so kept me at war with myself in ways I couldn't possibly understand. When we are at war, we cannot possibly be self-loving, because we are so busy fighting ourselves.

"As long as you keep secrets and suppress information, you are fundamentally at war with yourself . . . The critical issue is allowing yourself to know what you know. That takes an enormous amount of courage," explains psychologist Bessel van der Kolk in his classic book *The Body Keeps the Score*.[8] So why do we block ourselves from the release that comes from self-forgiveness? The idea that we cockblock our own self-love, that we unknowingly can very frequently be the one who gets in the way of our living a Self-Loving Life, is a recurring theme in this book. Self-forgiveness is no exception to this—research tells us there are a few specific ways and reasons we block our willingness and ability to self-forgive.

We block self-forgiveness because ... biology isn't always on our side. Some people (literally) have an easier time working through self-forgiveness than others thanks to human biology. The regulatory mode theory of goal-pursuit, formulated by E. Tory Higgins, tells us that people approach "goal directed behavior" shaped with two different styles of thinking: assessment and locomotion.[9] Assessment thought drives people to process a lot of different types of information, as much as one can absorb and (sometimes) stew over, analysis-paralysis style; this kind of thinking wants us to get shit done *the right way.* The locomotive thought process drives us to assess things quickly and make decisions that move us forward as rapidly and efficiently as possible; this thinking is focused on getting shit done ASAP and moving on. Everyone possesses both types of thought-processing skills, but we all vary in what degree we have each. When it comes to our ability to self-forgive, studies show that people who are higher in assessment functions have a harder time forgiving themselves—they may get caught in the process, tangled in the details, and spend more energy evaluating the past than they do creating change itself. Those high in locomotion functions, however, may have more of a drive to move forward, move on, and get to the other side than they do to evaluate their past.

We block self-forgiveness because ... we disconnect. Dr. Judith Jordan, director of the Jean Baker Miller Training Institute at the Stone Center, Wellesley College, defines "shame" as "a felt sense of unworthiness to be in connection, a deep sense of unlovability, with the ongoing awareness of how very much one wants to connect with others." Because of this, when we experience something we feel shame about, our response can be to pull away and disconnect, both from other people and from ourselves. We do this as a way to protect ourselves against the experiences of our pain and the terrible feelings that come with it—in particular, feeling devalued or disempowered. Work done at the Stone Center reveals that there are three major ways we do this: We move away from our shame, we move toward our shame, or we move against it. Jordan calls these "strategies of disconnection."[10]

When we move away from shame, we . . .	isolate ourselves, make our situations secret, and don't talk about the thing we feel ashamed of.
When we move toward shame, we . . .	people-please as a way to avoid feeling.
When we move against shame, we . . .	(literally) fight back with aggression, doing something hurtful or painful as retaliation.

These are also referred to as "shame shields." We think doing these things will make our lives better, safer, and easier, but what they really do is put big walls up between the things we fear and the things we desire the most—real human connection that accepts us for who we are, exactly as we are. When we utilize these strategies of disconnection, we get further and further away from our Ultimate You and our ability to live a Self-Loving Life.

We block self-forgiveness because . . . we believe, without our shame-identity, we're nothing. I don't have any smart scientific research to support this, just my own deeply lived experiences. Sometimes we're so attached to the idea of who our shame makes us that we are scared to get rid of the shame because without it, we don't know who we would be. Our pain, although born from dysfunction, gives us an identity. This identity shapes the movies in our minds, and soon, we've crafted our whole sense of self around the wake of our shame. Sometimes we perpetuate dysfunction because it feels familiar and it's what we know and, even though it hurts, it's more reassuring than the nothingness that comes with redefining ourselves.

DIG SITE: DO I HAVE TO FORGIVE OTHER PEOPLE TOO?

It is a commonly held belief that offering someone forgiveness for the wrongs they have done you is healthy. For the most part, it is. Forgiving someone can allow us not to fixate, and negative fixation can absolutely be a key to healing through something. But there are some instances when self-forgiveness can actually be *unhelpful*. Some experts say that for victims of sexual assault, "taking responsibility and encouraging self-forgiveness could actually compound harmful feelings of self-blame."[11] The same goes for offering forgiveness to someone who continues to harm another person and does not accept that their actions are harmful, like in a case of domestic abuse. In this case, withholding forgiveness may keep a dangerous person out of someone's life and remove their risk for being hurt again. Remember that forgiving others is something we do for ourselves and not the other person. Forgiveness itself does not require or demand reconciliation. It may exist by itself, without another relational step to follow it up.

HOW TO FORGIVE YOURSELF IN FOUR (OR SO) STEPS

While spurts of self-forgiveness may happen like lightning bolts, illuminating your painful past, on the whole it is not a light switch one turns on and off. Self-forgiveness is something you cultivate over time with landmarks along the way. I can tell you that much of the early work I did around self-forgiveness happened without my realization; situations naturally presented themselves as opportunities to grow, and when they came up, I worked with them the best I could in the moment with the tools I had.

I'm going to make a crass joke now—are you ready? Self-forgiveness is not a game of "just the tip." It is not something you can half commit to—you must open your heart fully and dive in. You also can't fool yourself into thinking you're ready to go all the way before you're ready to. If you are really asking yourself the hard questions and answering them as honestly as you can, you'll know when the time is right for self-forgiveness. Self-forgiveness is sticky; it can feel like pulling on a piece of yarn in a knit sweater—the more you pull on a loose stitch, the more the sweater unravels, until a big tangle of yarn wraps around your feet and threatens to topple you over.

To gracefully make your way through the process of self-forgiveness without wanting to rub carbohydrates all over your face and dive head-first into a sea of Diet Coke (maybe that's just me?), try to approach it with these four (or so) steps. To go deeper, visit my website, SarahSapora.com/Soul.

Step One: Be curious when something feels "off." Listen to yourself if something feels off. When feelings you don't like start to bubble to the surface, you can choose to be curious about them rather than scared. (Remember, the idea of "starting where it hurts" can lead you down a beautiful path of discovery!)

When we are curious, we have an eager thirst for knowledge that can serve as an "engine for growth."[12] With this curiosity, however, can come anxiety and uncertainty—what if we discover something that makes us feel even more broken than we may have felt before we started digging? This is when we can remind ourselves that the reason we go through Soul Archaeology is not to be perfect or to "get it right," but to find a more meaningful way to live.

In this moment of curiosity-spawned fear, we have a choice: Live on the defensive or live with vulnerability. We can push away the potential for growth and stay safely guarded in our (possibly dysfunctional) present, or we can soften into the discovery and learn how to use what we find to strengthen our lives and our connection to our Ultimate You.

Step Two: Be willing to explore. Explorers discover new lands and new places, regardless of fear, because they feel driven to explore and uncover great things. When we explore ourselves, regardless of fear, we can also uncover great things. How much more might we embrace the process of our own self-forgiveness if we knew that whatever we found along the way could be marked by wonder and revelation and not regret and remorse?

While curiosity is focused on observation and acknowledgment, exploration is about understanding. Rather than saying, "What happened here?" we are saying, "Am I ready to understand *why* this happened? Am I ready for what the understanding will bring into my life?" This is when you are likely to think, *I'm sick and tired of being sick and tired.* When we are no longer being pushed by pain but are being pulled forward by hope we are ready for what's next.[13]

Step Three: See, feel, and foster self-compassion. I say this with nothing but love: If you are not willing to be uncompromising in your ability to have self-compassion, there's (almost) no point in digging into the hard stuff of your Soul Archaeology. Self-compassion is nonnegotiable when it comes to living a Self-Loving Life. You cannot grow or create change in life from a place of self-hate. We can truly create lifelong change only from a place of radical self-love, which includes compassion for ourselves exactly as we are. Although it may feel hard to practice self-compassion, you can think of it like a muscle. Just like self-love, you can sort of suck at doing it in the beginning but keep practicing and, in time, grow stronger and more agile in your ability to tap into it.

Dr. Kristin Neff is the queen of self-compassion, which she defines as the ability to be kind to ourselves when we fall short because this is an inevitable part of life.[14] Suffering and failing are (literally) part of the human experience—none of us have the exclusive rights to the idea of "fucking up," because all people are imperfect. We have an ability to be mindful of our imperfections without "overidentifying" with them, which is to say, we can acknowledge our perceived flaws without allowing them to define or own us.

Step Four: Surrender. And then surrender again. Self-forgiveness has no defined road map. It is going to look different for everyone, and it must be entered into without an expectation as to what the end result will be. It is the process that unlocks our liberation, not the neat little bow we tie on at the end. As we explored in chapter 11, there's no set practice for surrendering, which is what makes it such a hard idea for us logic-driven folks. In the case of surrendering for self-forgiveness, it may help to think of surrendering as a "deepening" into ourselves. We feel acceptance for what is and what has happened, and we soften into it. It goes from being a hundred-pound weight we're shouldering to a hanging bubble in the air nearby as we strengthen our connection to self.

This is also when we can find more meaning in the suffering we have experienced in the past by letting it be a gateway to finding community in the present. We can let the pain be a path to connect to others through empathy and grace, by sharing the journey with vulnerability. In doing so, we may find release from the "emotional prison" of "unforgiveness, bitterness, resentment and anger," says Dr. Philip Sutton.[15] It's time for you to cultivate a more meaningful relationship with the things you were once ashamed of.

THE LETTER OF MY SELF-FORGIVENESS

When I finally came to accept that self-forgiveness was my only path to moving forward in a healthy way, I confronted feelings of brokenness that made me want to cocoon myself in oversized sweatshirts and squirrel away from everyone and everything. I believed I was untrustworthy. Undeserving. I felt bitterness for myself because I had seen the pattern of self-betrayal I had come to understand had shaped me. All the times I felt "no" in my heart but said "yes" had bled past the boundary of my romantic relationships into every bucket of my life, all the things I did while searching for acceptance...I realized in one moment that either I could let the past keep hurting me or I could make room for something else. But in order to do that, I had to write it all down.

I sat at my desk and opened my laptop and made a conscious decision to offer myself the peace I deserved by writing letters of forgiveness to people who would never read them. *Dear Dad. Dear College Boyfriend. Dear Jake. Dear George.* I said the things I needed to say and twisted the pressure valve of my pain to release the steam. I exhaled into the long-awaited release that I didn't even realize I'd been denying myself all along. In doing this, I released the stranglehold these relationships had held on me for all these years.

Then it was time for me to reckon with myself. I was the last stronghold in this battle for my self-worth.

"Dear Sarah," I began. "I forgive you for all the times you wanted to send thank-you cards but never got around to doing it. I forgive you for abandoning your body. I forgive you for not treating it better when treating it better would have been easier for you than it is now. I forgive you for every time you have looked at yourself and hated what you saw. I forgive you for every time you rationalized the idea that you weren't beautiful. I forgive you for all the casual sex you had when you were lonely, all the times you tried to manipulate nice guys with sex because you couldn't wrap your head around the idea that someone nice would be interested in you."

There was no secret in my heart I did not type out. All of the things that had haunted me and convinced me that I was tainted and unlovable. Every time I secretly hoped for more from a man but recast myself into a role they would find useful so they had a reason to want me. The icky way that College Boyfriend made me feel when we sat around a kitchen table with his friends and he put a finger in the strap of my tank top and said, "Isn't my girlfriend hot?"

I forgave myself for wanting my love for George to be real. It wasn't him I forgave but myself, for putting my worth in his hands and refusing to let go. And for how ashamed I felt that I allowed myself to be excited about loving someone who, so clearly, didn't want to love me back.

"I forgive you for letting hope blind you, Sarah," I wrote when I thought of Jake.

By the time I finished, pages and pages of my regrets and contritions had been released from my heart. I ended with "I forgive you for holding on to your hurt. I forgive you for creating stories about what you are capable of based on the lies your hurt told you. I forgive you that it has taken you this long to forgive yourself." And then I signed it like a letter: "Love, Sarah." I closed the computer. I wiped the tears from my eyes. And I moved on.

 DIG DEEPER:
Writing Your Own Letter of Self-Forgiveness

There is no master plan with this activity, no magic script. Only a chance for you, too, to release and move forward. I do not need to know your pain to know that you are worthy of release from it. And so, I invite you to do the thing that may feel so terribly difficult. I invite you to forgive yourself for whatever thing you feel called to forgive—small, large, or in between. If it has scared you, it has held you back. And you, my love, deserve to be released into your full glory. You deserve your Ultimate You. Self-loving. Liberated. And alive.

Find a safe and quiet place—preferably in your home or a space that you can control. (Unless you fancy a potentially big, ugly snot-filled cry inside a coffee shop, surrounded by madeleine cookies and iced lattes. That's okay too.)

You are going to want something to write with. If you can manage an old-school pen and paper, I suggest that. Writing this way will force your mind to slow down for the thoughts to make it from your brain to your fingers to execute each stroke of the pen. If that doesn't feel accessible, use a computer.

Before you begin, take a few deep breaths. You may even want to refer to chapter 12 and do a four-step awareness check to help you connect to your surroundings, your body, your feelings, and your breath. This is a wonderful time to remind yourself that you are safe. Emotionally and physically. You are totally okay right now. And any fear and nerves you have—or anxiety that is coming up—are just feelings. Remember, you can do hard things and you are incredibly capable of sitting through hard feelings. You don't need to run and hide. Instead, you get to open your eyes.

Beginning at the top on a blank page, simply start a letter to yourself. "Dear [your name]," you can begin. You don't need any special prompt or permission here. All you need is willingness. Then write, "I forgive you for . . ."

Let it flow. I encourage you to be as detailed as you can be. Specificity will set you free, and remember, there is nobody who needs to read this but you! The paper does not judge you. Your pen does not judge you. All the elements are coming together in this moment to help you welcome in the peace that you deserve.

How will you know when you are done? Whenever you feel it. If you need to pause, take a minute to breathe, but do not stop until you feel you have finished. When you are done, put the note away. Step away. Shake your body out if you need to. If you are feeling clogged and heavy, you can take a shower and let the water run down your body to give you new life. Go for a walk. Turn on music and dance. Eat a cookie (and make sure it is delicious), and if you feel like you want a drink, pick something nonalcoholic and intentionally stay sober. (Again, no judgment here—keeping a clear mind will help you stay present to what you are feeling and help you not numb out to escape.) Or, if you want, you can take a nap. Go to sleep. Whatever you need to do to feel as if you are moving forward, I invite you to do.

Will this activity "fix" everything? Of course not. You are not broken; you do not need to be fixed. But this activity is a chance for you to start ushering in a new way of thinking about yourself. A way that is self-loving and defined by you, and not by the experiences from the past that have held you back.

SURVEYING THE SITE:
WHAT WE DUG UP IN THIS CHAPTER

In this chapter shit got real as we explored the idea of self-forgiveness. We began by talking about shame in general. What it feels like, how it can impact your life, and how it can weigh you down. We also got really clear about a simple and totally necessary truth—the things you feel ashamed of in your past are not reasons for you to feel or believe you are broken. More so, the places that we feel the darkest are our greatest opportunities for growth. The darkness and lightness inside us all are connected, and we must be able to acknowledge both in order to feel aligned.

We explored the physical and emotional impact that carrying shame can have on our bodies and our minds. Emotionally, shame and a lack of self-forgiveness are linked to so many things, like self-esteem, anxiety, and depression—not to mention how they impact our self-punishing patterns! We clarified that this chapter, most importantly, is not forcing us to forgive others, but to do the work to forgive ourselves.

We discussed the difference between shame, guilt, and embarrassment—these are three emotions that are often confused with one another. Next, we covered three of the most common ways we block our own self-forgiveness. We can disconnect, hold on because we don't know what else to hold on to other than the shame-story we create, and even have biology to consider as some people (truly) have a physically easier time moving through self-forgiveness than others.

After that, I shared how we can start to forgive ourselves in four steps. We must be curious when something feels off, be willing to explore what we feel and see, foster lots of self-compassion for ourselves, and surrender. We went into detail to better understand self-compassion, and how this ability to recognize our flawed humanity is deeply important.

There may come a time in your Soul Archaeology when you cannot go any deeper unless you unshackle yourself from your perceived mistakes from the past. We cannot ignore what hurts us deeply and expect to keep growing into our Ultimate You. Growth requires honesty, vulnerability, willingness, and lots of self-compassion, all of which we will come face-to-face with when addressing our own shame.

If we allow the shame of who we have been in the past to color our lives in the present, it is impossible to have a future that includes our Ultimate You. Without self-forgiveness, we cannot put down the stories that do not serve us in order to create new ones that do serve us. To be self-loving means we are choosing not to feel shame and, instead, to view ourselves as messy-beautiful humans who have had human experiences. To be liberated means that we do not define our sense of self by our perceived "broken parts" and by experiences that others shaped, but instead define ourselves proactively by how we see ourselves and the values that guide how we want to shape our lives.

Chapter 14

THE SHIFT

The Inevitable Changes That Come with Your Evolution

On the morning of my forty-first birthday, I wake up in a hotel room alone. The blackout curtains are drawn in the room, which is splattered with minimalist decor that screams, "You paid way too much for this room, sucker," but I kind of like it anyway. The sheets of my king-sized bed are cool to the touch and the comforter is lofty; I nest inside the blankets, lying in the darkness and quiet.

I have no plans today. Nothing special to mark the day. There is nothing but me and the realization that, for the first time in my entire life, my sense of self comes from nobody but myself. Not my friends. Not my mother. Not my father. Not the people who follow me on social media, and not a partner. *Just me.*

This was a year that things in my life fell apart so they could come back together. Separating from George and surrendering to change has set off a chain of dominoes—one thing after another has tipped over and evolved, each one triggering the next. The logistics of my life feel chaotic, and yet I have never felt more at home in myself than I do right now. This is literally, and most certainly, 100 percent the way it needs to be.

My carefully made plans have crumbled.

Some relationships have fallen away, and some have risen under me.

My work, in many ways, is unraveling right before my eyes.

Things have gone wrong and I feel revealed—as if I am standing on nothing. I feel like an island. I think of what a mentor said to me on the phone a few weeks earlier. "Sarah," she said softly, "the moment you feel like an island is really when the universe has you in the palm of its hand, giving you a safe place to stand while everything else around you falls away."

In the last few months, one thing has become crystal clear to me—I created my entire life based around a "truth" that is no longer true. I wrapped my entire sense of self around the idea that I could not be lovable and could never, ever be enough. This idea was insidious, and it touched every single thing I did. It shaped how I treated my body. It told me to put everyone and everything before me. It impacted my work, and it made my work my life. How I treated money. When I say everything, I really do mean *everything*. Because my subconscious believed I could never be enough, my conscious mind made a task of collecting all the evidence I would need to prove myself right. I made it my job to be useful and pleasing to other people, regardless of if I was useful and pleasing to myself, because without being useful and pleasing to other people I thought I would have no value and no reason for them to want me around.

Because I have learned this truth and seen its impact on my life, it has become clear that in order to keep growing, my life must evolve as well. I must leap into an unknown—I don't have a strong base of healthy behaviors and boundaries set in place, and I don't have the relationships and work structures set up to support me. I have to leap and make changes without knowing what will happen next, and have faith that answers will be revealed as I go.

I know now I have value simply because I exist. I do not need to be a reflection of other people—I exist to be fully myself. I am not built brick-by-brick of proof collected for other people to examine. My self-worth is mine to shape, and nobody else's. I am living a beautiful blank slate—and although the idea of building myself from the ground up with my new sense of self is a bit scary, it is also incredibly liberating.

For the first time, my greatest job in life is simply to be myself. To be as vibrant and truthful a Sarah as I can. And that is fucking amazing.

When the status quo no longer applies, things have to change. There must be, as I've learned, a death of *what was* before there can be a rebirth of *what will be*.

AN ANNIHILATION TO REBUILD

There may come a point in your Soul Archaeology when you feel as if you are falling apart to come together again. You can think of yourself like a snake shedding skin. It takes time for this shedding to occur, and while it does, it can be itchy and uncomfortable. After? Relief and renewal.

In spiritual communities, many people refer to this process of falling apart to come together as a "dark night of the soul." I like this expression because it paints a clear picture of the experience. It's reassuring, because we can count on the rising light of a new sun to illuminate the dark of night every morning—this always happens.

Michael Beckwith, spiritual teacher and founder of the Agape International Spiritual Center, talks about it like this: "The dark night of the soul is a profound movement in consciousness that unravels the entanglements of ego, metaphorically bringing us to our knees by taking us through a seeming disintegration so that we may reintegrate at a higher level of consciousness. If we surrender and give our consent to it, we receive the dark night's gracious fists. If we reject it, we miss its contribution to our evolutionary progress for, as Jung points out 'The birth of the Self is always a defeat for the ego.'"[1]

Let's break that down because, honestly, that sounds like a lot of spiritual word salad. During this period, you come face-to-face with the reality that what has served you in the past no longer serves you now. Your identity has shifted—you know who you have previously been is no longer you, but you don't yet have any idea of who you are emerging into. You feel like you have nothing to grab on to. You are trapped in the raw in-between of having let go without having yet created a new handhold. You have yet to become who you are becoming, but you no longer are who you once were. With this feeling comes a complete loss of identity. You feel untethered. You can experience fear and disconnect. You are in the dark, in your own soul. And yet you must make it through this period in order to emerge into the light. In order to feel renewal and relief.

Let Your Self-Love To-Do List Be Your Guide

We've established that a key to living a Self-Loving Life is the ability to utilize the tools you have at your disposal when you need them the most. When you feel your life starting to shift out from under you, when a "dark night" threatens to take over, you may be tempted to dissolve alongside it. This is when your commitment to yourself must be rock solid. Do not. Give up. On yourself. When the going gets tough, the tough get self-loving! The way to do this is by using the tools you have to serve the vision of your Ultimate You.

At this point in your journey, you have many tools at your fingertips. This well-stocked tool kit allows you to walk forward confidently into shit that feels confusing without a marker to orient your next step because that point of orientation will be inside you. When you can depend and count on yourself, you don't need to know what's next in order to feel safe. You can feel scared of what lies ahead of you and feel secure at the exact same time because you have your own back!

To create your own calm within the chaos, you'll want to refer to your Self-Love To-Do List and the initial nugget/power statement you created back in chapter 6. Because this was something you created to help you understand how you want to feel in life—this nugget and the action items that stem from it are 100 percent in service of you! By doing the things on your SLTDL when you need guidance the most, you can stay connected to the process and stay connected to yourself, without knowing what the end result will be. Just in the doing itself you will create what is next. Surrender + action = woo-hoo, bitch, you got this!

"If this experience were to last forever," Michael Beckwith asks, "what quality would have to emerge for me to have peace of mind?"[2] That one thing you would need in order for you to remain true to your Ultimate You is the one quality you cultivate. For this chapter, you let the rest of the shit fall away—it isn't important right now. Your biggest priority is that one quality you need in order to stay compassionate and self-loving for you. The great thing is, you don't need to scramble to figure out what that is! You've already done the work. You already have the answer—it's right at your fingertips.

Ask yourself, *What is the most self-loving thing I can do right now for myself?* Don't freak out to find the answers—just go back to your Self-Love To-Do List and focus on what's there. Small actions. Small changes. Small services of you every day. If something isn't on your list and isn't an absolute necessity, let it go—you will deal with it when you are ready. For now, you are the priority, and prioritizing what to spend your bandwidth on during this period of transition is your greatest act of self-love. Lean on what you know. Don't worry about what's coming around the bend. Just what is in front of you right now. That's it.

For me, I made it through my "shifting phase" by leaning into the quality of love. It was my ability to allow love *from myself for myself* and love from others that I called upon when I felt my world was falling apart.

WHAT THE SHIFT LOOKS LIKE

You've learned enough about yourself to understand that the ways you did certain things in the past no longer seem to work for you, but you haven't yet figured out new ways to do the same things in ways that will work. Welcome to the wonky phase of discovery and testing things out!

If your identity has been built on the foundation of a core wound that you now know isn't real (remember, from chapter 10), the whole nucleus of your identity is going to shift. All of this may leave you saying, "WTF, am I crazy right now?" You aren't. You're waking up to the discrepancy between where you've been and where you're going—to the reality that you don't have a new foundation to stand on, or a history of healthful patterns to rely on. In response to this, you may experience some of the following:

- You may have no idea WTF is going on, but you can feel in your soul that something is up.
- Purging, cleaning out, and sorting through stuff might feel really gratifying.

- You may reevaluate your coping mechanisms without any prompting.
- Your relationships may feel like they have to change. You may want to get closer to some people and put distance between yourself and others.
- You may feel a surge of vulnerability and the desire to "show up as yourself or not show up at all."
- Things you used to enjoy may no longer feel enjoyable.
- Stuff that used to feel important may now feel less important.
- People may get upset at you for doing things that feel natural to you.
- You may feel like turning to yourself for the answers when you used to look to other people for them.
- You may sense a general friction within your life but not be able to pinpoint why or what.
- You may feel compelled to "scale down" your life and adopt a "less is more" approach.
- Boundaries may start to sound really appealing, but when you do start to test them out, you may worry you're being "bitchy" or difficult.
- You may have less energy for some things that you used to devote a lot of bandwidth to.

Here are three things that will definitely happen:

1. **If you regularly self-abandoned in order to please people in relationships, someone will absolutely react unfavorably when you stop.** If this person expresses frustration, lashes out, punishes you, or is at all disparaging because of your newly found strength, this relationship is not healthy for you. People with whom you are truly aligned will not require you to diminish or abandon yourself for their comfort or in exchange for their approval or affection.
2. **You will feel called to start establishing boundaries.** It will feel really scary at first, and even setting the slightest boundary may be impossible. When you do it, you may think you're being "bitchy" or mean. You aren't being either. You are just so out of practice that

even the slightest assertion feels huge. Remember that boundaries are road maps directing other people how to show up in your life. The boundaries say, "This is how I need to be loved if I'm going to show up for you" and are more like carefully articulated instructions than demands. At the same time, you may feel hyperaware in your desire to set boundaries, which can also be a defense mechanism. You get to figure out what course of action is the most self-loving for you and what serves your Ultimate You the best!

3. **You're going to feel really out of practice at doing things that are self-loving for you.** Keep doing them anyway. It will get easier the more you do it. The more you practice recognizing what you need, the easier it will be to recognize what you don't need. The more you prioritize yourself, the easier it will become. Self-love is a muscle; it will build over time. Eventually, the process of "asking and answering" you do with yourself will become second nature to you. That is when you will naturally move into the next layer of your Soul Archaeology!

My Big Shift: Saying No

One big sign that I had shifted and grown was how differently I started showing up in my romantic relationships. Relationships started to become less about pleasing the men I wanted...*and more about pleasing me.*

The first time I consciously said "No" to a guy was with Sales Guy. I was forty years old. Driven by an intense run of self-discovery, I'd taken to reaching out to a slew of men I'd once dated in the hopes of uncovering more of my patterns—I knew seeing how my old stories had shaped my old patterns was the only way to create new stories and new patterns.

I sent him a text asking to chat and he replied a minute later.

Sales Guy: Absolutely! I figured you wouldn't want to talk to me because I was a complete tool before—I wasn't in a good place myself. I'm absolutely happy and grateful to connect tomorrow!

I felt a familiar leap of excitement in my chest. I started to text, almost as if on autopilot—*Don't worry about it, it's no big deal*—but I stopped myself. There was that self-abandoning, an opportunity in real time for me to downplay my hurt in order to reassure someone else that they were fine... *No, Sarah. We don't do that anymore. Your feelings matter too.* I paused a minute before replying.

Me: Great. You were a big tool. And it hurt me, a lot. That's in the past, so, let's be really honest with each other now.

Actually telling someone they had hurt me was a big step! I'd like to tell you that talking to Sales Guy the next day didn't light me up like a Christmas tree, but that would be lying, because it did. Even after our terrible, unhealthy interactions in the past, when we got on the phone, I fluttered inside like nothing dysfunctional had ever happened time and time again. He told me he was thrilled to hear from me. That he didn't want to reach out, because I was right, he had been terrible to me. We started to deconstruct things—who had been doing what, who felt what, and everything in between. In the end he apologized, and hearing him take responsibility for my hurt felt validating.

"You were right—you *did* deserve better." His voice softened. "But I always hoped we would talk again. I knew we weren't done."

After our conversation, I started to think about him more. Within a few days, we were back to texting all the time, talking on the phone, and I found myself excited (again) about the possibility of our meeting up. It took me a good few weeks to ask him if he had a girlfriend—maybe it was because I subconsciously knew that if he did, the version of Sarah I'd grown into wouldn't allow him into her life.

"Sales Guy," I ask in a calm voice, "are you in a relationship?" There is an eternity-like pause before the answer: *He is.* He tells me that it isn't working and that things will be over soon because he's ready to move on; he's really ready to move on... *Ding-dong!* I've heard this one before.

The movie in my mind clicks on. I am back where I have always been, on the precipice of screwing myself over. "Pick me, I'm awesome!" I'd scream, as I traded my dignity for scraps of attention.

Except, now I know this movie is not my Ultimate You. This is not self-loving. If I really want to feel differently, I have to do something different. Getting scraps from Sales Guy is NOT better than nothing. Something is not better than nothing if that something means I'm invisible, held away at arm's length.

I can show someone what I will and will not accept in my life and I can calmly, intentionally place boundaries that both protect me and show others how I want to be loved. My boundaries are an invitation for someone to meet me with the respect I deserve. Having boundaries is self-loving.

"I could really love you," I say with a soft and steady voice, "but I love me *more*." *Easy, Sarah, you can do this* . . . "I need to not do this with you while you are in a relationship. I will find a way to rationalize it and I'm done doing things like this." I tell him not to reach out to me until he's single and available—like, *really* available. I tell him not to push me, and to respect my ask. I tell him that's what I deserve.

When we get off the phone a few minutes later, I feel a twang of disappointment but, more than anything, I feel really proud of myself. Click on the movie in my mind . . . and click it off. I've rewritten my script. I have shifted. I have grown.

As you shift, life will give you opportunities to test your newfound growth and your new skills. Like Bambi walking on ice, you may approach this newness gingerly—it's scary trying to do things differently than you've done them before! But just because you haven't done something before doesn't mean you can't do it now. The older we get, the harder it feels to do things differently—it feels like more is at stake in our lives and, with each passing day, time weighs even more. There is something truly spectacular about a woman who liberates herself from former choices. This can happen at any age! When we do liberate ourselves, life suddenly becomes fresh and exciting at the same time. When you have been given an opportunity to slide back into an old pattern or build foundations for new ones and you pick the latter, growth becomes tangible.

Doing the Deep Soul Work in Real Time

You are made up of thirty-two trillion cells. Each cell contains a nucleus. Each nucleus stores the DNA that determines who you are and regulates how the cells function. Of these thirty-two trillion cells, there are roughly two hundred million different types, each of which does a different job. How well they perform these jobs is ultimately what shapes your overall health and well-being.

As a human with emotions, you have an emotional nucleus—a core and a center. This emotional nucleus stores data like your learned experiences and value systems—the things that help you discern what is "normal" for you, what is the status quo. Just like the human body has different types of cells that have different functions, we have different facets of our well-being that all have different functions. (We talked about these "buckets" in chapter 6.)

When our emotional nuclei are in alignment with our Ultimate You, the way we show up in life will also be in alignment with our Ultimate You. From this alignment, we are better able to discern what is good for us, what is not good for us, what we should do more of in life, and what we need to do less of. When our emotional nuclei are calibrated in ways that don't serve us (like when we see toxic behaviors as "normal" so we accept them from other people), it becomes almost impossible to live truly in alignment with our Ultimate You. No matter how righteous we perceive our actions to be, those actions still are not in service of our greater good—they will be in service of our off-center present. Here's the kicker—even out of alignment, our nuclei (and we) can still function. We will just function . . . dysfunctionally.

Through your process of Soul Archaeology, you begin to see which pieces of you are functioning in a healthful way and which are not. You may start to see how some of the pieces of your life support you and how some do not. You may see that your relationships are unaligned. You may not connect with work in the same way. Your spiritual beliefs may be out of whack. Whatever it is, it is important to understand that your whole life has been calibrated to serve the version of you that you have been up to this point. Your life has been set up to meet you where you have been—for your needs, your desires, your patterns, et cetera. If you want to create a new version of your life, you must set up your life to meet you where you are NOT now and where you want to go in the future. The you that you are unfurling into may have dramatically different needs, likes, and dislikes than who you have been in the past. You experience a discovery in your awareness of self that makes it really hard for you to live in the world the way you used to and not feel terrible discomfort. When your nuclei shift away from dysfunction, life must shift alongside it. In short... shit's gotta change, girl.

You will wonder if you are crazy. You may wonder if everyone else is crazy. You may feel like life is upside down and totally fucked. It might feel easier to put your feet into two bowls of chocolate pudding while trying to dance the Macarena. All of this is okay. In fact, it's pretty normal.

I don't have any science to support this shift. What I do have is a very simple truth—when you evolve, your world has to evolve alongside you. If it doesn't, you will probably feel at odds with all the things you used to find familiar. In order to move forward into something new, in order to experience your next chapter, what is not serving you in the current must crumble away.

MOVING THROUGH MY DARK SOUL

I didn't realize I was in the middle of my own "dark night of the soul" until it became impossible to ignore that everything I thought was supposed to be a certain way was playing out entirely different than planned. I found myself dominated by an overwhelming desire to remove anything that felt like "bullshit" from my life, even things that once made sense. Surface-level friendships, playing the social media game, brand deals that brought great money but made me feel like I was selling out, and a need to prove myself to industry gatekeepers—all of these things (and more) made me feel out of place in my own life. It started to become easy to see what things would help me grow and what would only hinder my need to show up authentically. But the biggest thing that clued me into my "dark night" had everything to do with the live event I'd been planning for that September.

I'd been running events for plus-size women for a few years. I'd stood onstage wearing denim and sequins, with hair extensions perfectly curled. I'd busted my ass to organize and execute every detail, and to secure brand sponsorships to bankroll the events. For a few years, powered by adrenaline, I'd secured tens of thousands of dollars. But by 2019, I was running on fumes. The work had taken a toll on my mental health...yet women were traveling across the country to be in a space I was creating.

I lost the desire to keep fighting to prove myself; I didn't want to push anymore. That's when it became clear that the way I'd been showing up for my work was no longer working for me. Life screamed at me, "This version of you that you thought was you is not you!" and all I could do was watch it all fall away and surrender.

The only way I could navigate the chaos was to keep asking myself, *What is the most loving way I can approach my life right now? What is the most loving thing I can do for myself?* Sometimes I knew the answers, and sometimes I did not. But I kept asking the questions regardless. I decided I could shape my life by opening my heart, but I couldn't control what happened and what was meant to be. When I turned forty-one alone in that hotel room, I realized the answers had been, and would always be, in my fully embracing myself in all of my wacky, vulnerable, and fierce glory.

Ultimately, the event I ran that year reflected my evolution. What emerged was an ability to create an experience that was more bare and vulnerable than ever before—and the attendees responded by opening their hearts in kind.

On the second day, I was standing on the stage barefoot when I reached the moment my old skin finished its uncomfortable shed. My tender, newer self fully took up its space for the first time. The weight of my self-judgment was cleared away. There were no sequins, no frills to cover up my perceived inadequacies—just me.

I remembered a quote I once read: "*Only to the extent* that we expose ourselves over and over to annihilation can that which is indestructible in us be found."[3] In that moment, I could see that all the work I'd done had helped me to find something indestructible within myself I never knew before—self-respect.

SURVEYING THE SITE:
WHAT WE DUG UP IN THIS CHAPTER

Especially as women, we so often find ourselves wondering, *Am I crazy? What's wrong with me?* when things feel out of balance. In many ways we are taught to erase our intuition and replace it with a quest for validation, to the point that we fail to see growth.

For me, romantic relationships with men serve as a great way to gauge my alignment with my Ultimate You. I can tell how connected I am to my Self-Loving Life by paying attention to my interactions with men I'm interested in. When I am out of alignment, my history of low self-esteem drives me to "fight" to prove my value to men who, for whatever reason, aren't showing up for me the way I want them to. I had a "normal," but that normal wasn't good for me, it didn't make me happy, and it didn't result in the kinds of relationships I wanted to have. My emotional nuclei were totally unaligned, but the push-and-pull dynamic felt familiar and, therefore, safe.

You will work out what your own best proving grounds are. There will be ways for you to practice doing things differently as well. Maybe, like me, it will be in your romantic relationships. Maybe it will be in your dynamic with your parents or your coworkers. Maybe your friends. What matters is that you seize the opportunities for growth when they present themselves.

You may have thought you had your shit together like a rock star—I know I did. But sometimes our sense of self has to fall apart a bit before it forges itself into something unstoppable. The shift from a dysfunctional life to a functional one can bring us to our knees, but on the other side of that destruction is rebirth. What you create in the place of the things that no longer serve you can be 100 percent aligned with your values, your Ultimate You, and your Self-Loving Life.

This chapter is meant to remind you that the best tool you can use when you feel like things are falling apart is your Self-Love To-Do List. Use it to stay guided and connected to what really matters to you—how you want to feel in your life and the small things you can do every day to create the feelings. Stay focused, keep the faith, and surrender.

To live a self-loving life means you are committed to the following:

1. Seeing your life with honesty and with an analytical yet compassionate eye.
2. Asking yourself, *What do I truly need right now in order to stay connected to my Ultimate You?*
3. Prioritizing these actions or thoughts above others.

We exercise all three of these muscles when moving through a transitional shift! To live a more liberated life is about untangling ourselves from the systems, relationships, thoughts, and actions that define us by someone else's needs, values, or expectations. To do this requires a shift away from dysfunction to self-loving functioning.

Chapter 15

THE END THAT ISN'T AN END

This book has no conclusive end. But there is a reason why! When you live a Self-Loving Life, the path itself is never ending. As long as you are alive, you can be on the path, committed to your Soul Archaeology, committed to your gloriously messy-beautiful self. You can always create something self-loving by utilizing the strategies I share here, because those practices have no expiration date—they can evolve right alongside you!

Maybe this whole "there's no end to this book" kind of thing will bother you. It might even piss you off. I'm okay with that. Perhaps you were expecting everything to be tied into a neat little bow so you could move on into the perfect After. This is the kind of thinking that most of us are comfortable with. But really, complete comfort is a bit overrated at times, don't you think? My hope is the fact that this book has no end liberates the shit out of you, because if this book does not have an end, then there is (quite literally) no pressure for you to show up fully transformed one day with all your ducks in a row, magically healed, magically happy, and living magically ever after! You have never been broken. You have never been too much. And you, in this exact moment you are reading this, have more power inside you to blossom than you ever could have imagined possible.

SELF-LOVE IS A SCRUNCHIE

The ideology of diet culture tricks us into believing that all things in life are a Before and an After waiting to happen—even if they have nothing to do with weight loss. This is a "straight-line" kind of thinking, in which there is a start, a middle, and an end. Before, we are broken and in desperate need of some kind of fixing. Then, we are "in progress," actively demonstrating a commitment to whatever it is we are committed to, and this commitment means we are more valuable than we were before we committed to commitment. Gold star for us! People give us more social credit now; they say, "Oh, awesome, keep up the great work!" and it gives us a serotonin hit that lets us know, man, we're kicking ass and taking names and people are really starting to see us now! And then we finish. Ta-da! We hit our goals. Everyone congratulates us. We congratulate ourselves! We feel valuable and empowered and on fire, bolstered by our own feelings of accomplishment and all the recognition coming from things outside of us.

Then life happens. We hit a setback. We start to slide backward. If it's the happiness we think will come at the other side of weight loss that we've been chasing, we gain some of the weight back and feel unhappy because of that. When we stop doing the things that were getting us all the pats on the back, whatever those things were, we start to feel progressively worse. Like we've failed. Nobody is cheering us on anymore. One setback leads to another, which leads to another...Before we know it, we feel worse than we did before we were a "Before" in the first place. There is absolutely nothing self-loving about this at all.

I challenge you to see yourself, instead, as a scrunchie. Yes, one of those velvet or satin floofy, poofy things you put in your hair. A scrunchie, unlike a straight line, has no "beginning" and no "end." It is a circle that dips and rises over and over again. Self-love is this scrunchie. Self-love, like this scrunchie, goes on and on.

Please refer to this very fancy graphic that is a rendering of something I drew in my mother's Brooklyn apartment the summer I found myself

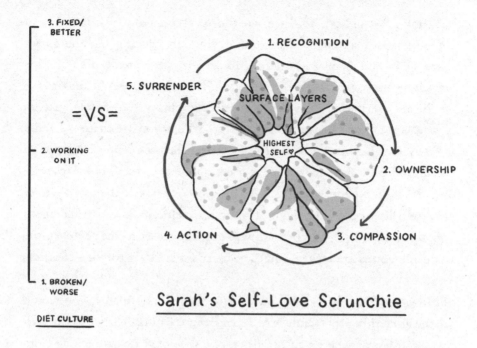

3. FIXED/
BETTER

=VS=

2. WORKING
ON IT

1. BROKEN/
WORSE

DIET CULTURE

5. SURRENDER

1. RECOGNITION

SURFACE LAYERS

HIGHEST
SELF♥

2. OWNERSHIP

4. ACTION

3. COMPASSION

Sarah's Self-Love Scrunchie

shifting out the wazoo. On the left is a straight line representing the "Before and After" mentality I desperately want you to move away from. At the bottom, where the line starts, we are broken. Halfway through, we're getting better as we work on ourselves. At the end is our finish line! We are fixed and better. And there is nothing after that. Nothing. Except, that's not fucking possible.

Have you ever noticed how fairy tales never reveal what happened after Cinderella's prince put that shoe on her foot, or after Beauty kissed the Beast and he became a hottie? It's because the "After" is oftentimes fraught with the intricacies of everyday life. Reality can dim the sparkle, and once the big "ta-da!" of anything has passed, we're left dealing with the mundane. The challenges. The blech. This, however, is a guaranteed part of life. So, rather than pretend that it doesn't exist, we get the opportunity to look for ways to lovingly embrace "the blech" as an inevitable part of our everyday process that does not indicate failure in any way, shape, or form. It just indicates...life.

In my drawing, you will see what looks like an amoeba. It is not an amoeba; it is a scrunchie. Notice that you can travel along the curvy shape again and again and again. This is what life is really like. This is what it means to live a Self-Loving Life. This is our Soul Archaeology.

You are a scrunchie. Maybe you are electric-pink velvet. Maybe you are black satin. Doesn't matter. What matters is that you see that scrunchies have layers. The top edge—the surface—and then the center bit, through which you pull your hair. This is a metaphor for your Soul Archaeology. When you begin your Soul Archaeology, you're at the top layers of your self-discovery—the edge of your scrunchie. The more and more you dig and grow, the deeper you will go. The closer to the center of the scrunchie you will journey, and the closer you will get to your Ultimate You.

Now, here's the kicker. If you were to slice the scrunchie, you would see the same thing the whole way down from the outside layer to the center, regardless of where you cut. (Picture a slice of the earth, seeing from the crust to the core.) Just the same, the stuff that is your shit to work through in life will be yours no matter how deep in the scrunchie you go. The hard things you encounter earlier in your Soul Archaeology will be the outer layers of the same things you will encounter later on in your journey. Lovingly put, your shit is your shit. It will always be your shit. When you start your Soul Archaeology, the shit you deal with will be the same kind of shit that you deal with as you progress, but (and this is a big but) you will hit it at different layers and more deeply and get more agile at working through the shit when you encounter it.

The point of all this is not to try to eliminate shit from your life—shit just is. The point is to be able to open your eyes to your shit and see it, understand it, stop fighting with it, and, ultimately, get better at navigating your shit so that the shit itself doesn't prevent you from living a liberated life on your terms.

In my life, feelings of unworthiness will always be my thing. Working through a sense of unworthiness was my thing at the start of my Soul Archaeology, and it is my thing now as I sit here writing this book, thinking, *Man, I hope I'm good enough for people to like this book and buy it!* I will experience and work through feelings of unworthiness my whole life as I move around the scrunchie, year after year, and that is okay. I should never feel ashamed that this is one of my things! *We all. Have. Shit.*

Diet culture thinking would have me saying to myself, *Man, Sarah, you did all that work and now your feelings of unworthiness are magically gone, and you are HEALED FOR GOOD!* Well, imagine how crappy I would feel if those feelings of unworthiness started to creep in again. Now, not only would I be dealing with the feelings of unworthiness, but I would also feel ashamed of the fact that I hadn't "gotten it right" the first time and embarrassed that I wasn't perfectly healed and still had more work to do until I was deemed perfect.

I will not tolerate this lack of self-acceptance any longer, for either myself or you. To live your life in a deeply self-loving way means you can have both radical self-acceptance and radical self-accountability. The two combine together to make a fierce yet vulnerable version of you that lives life in total alignment with her own values. Not dependent on others for validation or feedback, but able to rely on her own inner compass for navigation and assurance when she needs it the most.

Your Self-Love To-Do List and the Scrunchie

I will say this clearly and precisely: Your Self-Love To-Do List is what helps you live the scrunchie life and avoid the Before-and-After. The process of asking the hard questions, regularly evaluating how your Ultimate You longs to express life, and creating (and utilizing) a Self-Love To-Do List is the strategy and process that will keep you moving through your life in a kind and aligned way. It allows for growth and rest, compassion and ass-kicking accountability, when and in the way you need it the most.

Your Self-Love To-Do List can meet you wherever you are in life. Able-bodied or not. Youthful or older. In times of prosperity or stress. It exists to support you exactly as you are, and to help you to live as fully as you can. Create one. Use it. Live it. *Blossom.*

NEXT

I began this chapter claiming that this book has no end. Just as, after all that I have uncovered and all the ways I have unfurled in the past few years, I have not experienced an ending; I've progressed and moved through and moved forward. I've touched my Ultimate You and she is . . . stunning.

Sometime last year, I found myself automatically digging into the next layer of my Soul Archaeology. Having made peace with a whole level of personal discoveries, my heart started expanding into more without even trying. One day, I asked myself the question *What is the most self-loving thing I can do for myself right now?* and the answer became clear. I had to do the hard things that would improve my life—stuff that wasn't necessarily pretty or flashy and forced me to confront whole chunks of my life that felt scary to me. But it was all in service of myself, and so I started to embrace the feeling of "alignment" and what it would mean to live a life where I was truly aligned with myself.

From the outside looking in, this deep devotion to myself can appear achingly boring. It's not. It's graceful and powerful as fuck. What's come of this has been the single thing I've been the proudest of—how deeply I've committed to my mental health and physical health.

I learned, finally, that everything I'd ever done to lose weight in my past had been dieting. The relationship I'd had with my body had 100 percent been entirely shaped by diet culture. None if it was healthy for me—emotionally or physically—and none of it actually addressed one thing I realized was impacting both my body and my mind: the deeply dysfunctional relationship I'd had with food my entire life. This was something I couldn't see until I had cleared away the layers before me. My entire relationship with food has been changing. Now, I'm able to recognize when I've formed an attachment to specific foods, particularly those that cause a heightened emotional reaction. Lately, it's ice cream sandwiches, the kind you might remember from childhood, where the chocolate cookie part gets stuck to the paper as you peel it off. One day, while grocery shopping, I noticed a hyperreaction my body had as I passed by them in the frozen section. I felt like I needed to consume them as soon as I could. I used this as data to try to understand why I could feel calm around a pint of cookies-and-cream Häagen-Dazs, but a single off-brand ice cream sandwich could light my sensors up like a Lite-Brite toy. There's a reason why and a way for me to evolve my connection to ice cream sandwiches. A way for me to experience my life where the idea of ice cream sandwiches in my presence doesn't overstimulate my brain and send me into a tailspin. Where I don't demonize this food, nor do I elevate its status—where I can exist around it peacefully and help put it in its balanced place.

I care about my health, mentally and physically, and I'm invested in ways to honor and serve both without repeating toxic cycles. I am doing my best to move away from diet culture and find a highly nuanced space that allows for my weight loss but does so in a nonperformative way, in which I focus on the process of increasing my quality of life—like my strength and mobility—and not the loss of specific numbers on a scale. If I focus on a "goal weight" and I make it the main point of data, I'll give all my energy to some bullshit end result that elevates all the wrong things and leaves me in a place to chase my own tail for the rest of my life. Instead, I give my energy to the present and the process—the choices I can make and the way I can align my thoughts without any solid idea of what the result will be. To be honest? It feels fucking great. My health is better than it has been in ages, and I have never felt clearer and more at peace.

The intricacies of self-worth will always be in the cross section of my self-loving scrunchie. There is no doubt in my mind that this is "my thing" and it will always be "my thing." I don't expect to wake up one day and be solved or fixed, but what I do hope is that I get more graceful and agile and self-aware at addressing my self-worth challenges.

This isn't a book you read to help you learn how to get the guy or lose the weight. This book is meant for you to see what life looks like when you do deep personal growth work that changes how you see yourself and, therefore, changes how you show up and interact with others.

Doing all this work has helped me to get where I am in my life right now. This has included writing this book and working to heal my compulsive relationship with food while exploring ways to address my health and weight and staying mentally aligned and as self-loving as possible. It has brought me to this healthful place with both my parents, my relationship with my small but amazing group of friends, and, yes, my relationship with my romantic partner.

We don't do the work of our own Soul Archaeology so that we can find a magical happy ending that solves all our problems. We do it so that we can learn how to create joy and bring happiness into our lives at any time. We do it so that we can understand that problems are a part of life, and while many of them are simply out of our hands, we can get better at handling them when they come our way. We do the work on ourselves so that we can replace old patterns that didn't serve our Ultimate You with ones that will. We do the work so that we can learn who we are, on our terms, and we can let that messy-beautiful shine.

THIS IS IT

And now it's your turn. Remember, this book is all about YOU. It seems about me at times because I'm sharing a lot of personal stuff, but I'm sharing it because I hope it's stuff you can learn from. If people don't tell us what growth looks like by sharing their real experiences, how can we ever realize just how normal our messy-beautiful is?

If you made your way through the exercises as you read this book— you are a fucking badass. If you didn't, that's totally okay! I expected that you would read it, do lots of thinking, and then come back to the work when you felt ready. If you feel ready to jump in at this moment, I want to give you a few concrete steps you can do right now—yes, right now.

First, start with this one question and answer it as honestly as you can: Where does it hurt in your life right now? Asking this and answering the best you can may be the single most important way to show yourself the commitment and love that you deserve. If you can do that—if you can look at and listen to what your heart tells you and have the courage to acknowledge it...keep going.

Next, you can go back to the Dig Deeper sections peppered throughout the book, or go straight to chapter 6 and claim your feeling word so you can start creating your very own Self-Love To-Do List. Having this list will change how you prioritize your life—how you decide what to do, what not to do, and what to give your energy to. Hasten anon, my good lady! Seriously—it will change your life.

Third, if something in this book has cracked you open—get help from someone who knows a lot more than me. Take this book to a therapist or counselor and show them what it is that has touched your soul, and work on it together. There are big ideas that come up in this book, and you deserve all the support available to help you work through the big feelings that come with them!

As we end our time together (for now), I would love to come sit next to you for a minute. May I? Let's allow time to slow down and take a big, juicy, deep breath and exhale. (I feel like some tears are filling the corners of my eyes...) A few years ago, the reality that I probably wouldn't be having kids of my own started to creep into my life. For the most part, I was okay with it—it wasn't what I planned, but that's how life works. But what made me really sad was the idea that I might not get to nurture and love someone other than myself. (Selfish, I know. But true.) How could I leave the world better in any small way if I could not create an offspring of my own to spread the kind of love I saw this world needing? And really, giving love is all I have ever wanted to do—how could I give it if I had nobody to give it to? I'm going to allow myself to pretend that this book is my child, and in these pages is the love I want to spread out into this world; the words I would have shared with a daughter if I had one.

Please know, from the bottom of my heart, that you are not broken. You have never been broken—no matter how you have been hurt or hurt others in the past. No matter what shame weighs heavily on you today. No matter how conflicted and torn you feel about your body as it beautifully ages and as it has changed over the years. No matter how you felt at war with your body over the years. No matter how life has told you, again and again, that you are wrong and that you do not belong. *You do.* No matter how many times you have been shown you are not enough...you are. None of that matters. Not a single ounce of what has held you back in the past must define how you show up for your-self tomorrow. You will always have a home with me, and you can—and will—always have a home within yourself. And THAT is what matters the most. You can be at home within yourself.

Stop trying to fix yourself. Start trying to *become* yourself. I know change is scary, and to let go of what you've been holding on to for so long requires a huge amount of strength. I also know you have that strength.

If nobody has ever told you before, I will tell you now that you are treasured, exactly as you are.

The way I see it, right now you are on the verge of unfurling. Like a big sail, ready to catch wind, remember? You are sitting in a boat, undo-ing the knots and ties that hold your big, billowing main sail in place—it longs to be untethered and freed to catch the wind! You are ready for the wind. It catches your hair and kisses your skin. And when the knots release, that same wind catches the sail—once held in place, restricted and tied back—now getting more full and more powerful with every second.

You don't need to know your destination—destination unknown, baby. To guide yourself, you simply ask yourself time and time again, *What is the most self-loving thing I can do for myself right now?* And have the courage to listen to the answer. And the commitment to yourself to fol-low through on the things you see that need to be done. That is all you need to feel free.

EPILOGUE

Allow me, if you will, to make a full-circle moment. I've shared so much in the process of teaching you that I'd like you to understand how a few things have evolved for me because these are things that serve as testimony to my path of growth.

DAD

There came a time in my Soul Archaeology where I was able to see that a need to please others had robbed me of my ability to allow myself anger; I never wanted anyone to feel I was unhappy or upset with them as I was certain that would make them leave me. A conversation I'd had with a coach revealed this was part of the reason I felt so invisible in my own life, and part of the reason that I found myself in failing relationships with guys who wanted things from me but would fail to give things back in return: I had unresolved, unexpressed anger toward my parents, specifically my father, who I'd always seen as the ultimate perpetrator in my parents' divorce even though, in rational hindsight, I know this wasn't the case. The coach assured me that anger was normal and, as a child, I was entitled to feel the confusion and hurt that I did—I shouldn't have had to search for answers or fill in the blanks for myself.

I didn't plan to formally "confront" my father about the feelings I had growing up—about not having a bedroom at his houses and how I always felt like a guest in what should have felt like home for me—but there was a moment, totally organic and without fanfare, where the opportunity to discuss it presented itself. It was inevitable for my growth, so I seized the opportunity, no matter how my voice warbled or my throat gripped tight with nerves.

As I began to speak, I wasn't sure what I expected to happen during this fateful, much-anticipated exchange, but a secret part of me wished it would be something dramatic that involved the "1812 Overture" (with the real cannons, thank you) playing in the background while every member of my immediate family plus my reincarnated dead ex-boyfriend Jake and possibly my asshole college boyfriend would get together in one place to re-create the "Dance of the Sugar Plum Fairy" from the *Nutcracker* while I sat in front of them, calmly eating Wasa Crispbread crackers, feeling vindicated and validated, humming the chorus of Paul Simon's classic hit "You Can Call Me Al"... FINALLY.

None of this happened. What did happen was something much quieter, but impactful. I told my dad everything—about the coming and the going with my Gap duffel bag, the bedroom, how I counted the photos on the wall. I told him I'd spent my entire life trying to find a home with men because I never felt like I had a home with him. *And there it was. What had held me captive for thirty-two years was now out in the open.*

He paused and then said quietly, "Did it ever dawn on you that there was a reason why you never had a bedroom?" *Of course it did, duh. And the reason was because there wasn't room for me in your life, Dad, I know.* "Your mother didn't want you to have one, Sarah; you weren't supposed to spend the night. It's what she thought was best and would make things easiest for you."

I could feel my heart grip itself and I made a mental note (*Clearly, Mom and I are going to have to talk about that at some point because that was a shit call*). But now I could see why he made the decision he did years ago. He wanted things to be easy; nobody wanted to hurt me, and divorce hurts; why would you make a room for someone who was never going to use it? That would only make things worse, right? For a moment I wondered if what I'd been feeling all those years was wrong. No. He should have done it anyway or done something. Put my stuff in a plastic bag in the closet and then taken it out again for the three hours I was there. I should have known. I should have *always known* that I had a home that was safe and a position of love and value in whatever house he lived in. Because that was his job. I was the kid. It wasn't MY job to know the truth; it was just my job to receive the love. I wasn't supposed to have to figure out the answers—I was supposed to have been given the information that I needed to feel safe and loved by both my parents. "It doesn't matter, Dad. It shouldn't have happened," I said, softly but with firm resolution.

I could see that I was breaking his heart just a little bit, and I hated that. He was not the villain. Nobody was—certainly not the people who were flawed themselves and tried to love me the best they could and stumbled intentionally along the way. But, at the same time, if I was ever going to be free, I couldn't sit with this any longer.

"You're right," he said. "I'm the dad. I should have tried harder." And there it was. This false truth—that had twisted and distorted my sense of self and touched every single piece of my life—was now out in the open. I was no longer ashamed, no longer scared of it. It was no longer my responsibility.

We think that resolution comes with fanfare. Maybe for some people it does, but it has not for me. In the time since that conversation with my father, history has not been rewritten, but what has emerged is new information and a new level of honesty between us. An ease in saying "I love you" that had never been there before, and a clear outward appreciation. I've gotten better at speaking up for myself with him, learning that not only is it okay for me to say, "Hey, this doesn't work for me," but that I can say those things and still be loved if not as much, then even more for saying them.

My father visited me while I was writing parts of this book. During that time, we revisited the pains we both felt—this time even more calmly. As we talked, he looked at me with an expression that could only be construed as his wishing his daughter had chosen some normal occupation, any normal occupation, like beekeeping or exotic dancer/welder—anything other than turning into a writer whose deep call for self-analysis compelled her to share painful family lessons for all to read. But, at that point, he was taking it in stride. He knew that none of this was about him as much as it was about sharing the way I'd worked through feelings and patterns that emerged as a way to deal with the hard things that happened in life when complex people stepped all over one another accidentally while doing the best they could to navigate life.

It was when we were at the airport a few days later, and he was wrapping his arms around me to hug me goodbye, that I squeezed tightly, maybe a little tighter than a grown daughter should squeeze her father. And he hugged me for maybe a little longer than he ever had before. And with his chin resting on my head, I felt him stroke my hair and he said to me, "You know, Sarah, it's time to let all of that go. It's in the past. It's not true. You can let it go." And as he spoke, he released me, and gave me the permission I didn't know I even needed to move forward.

I cried. I tried to do it on the sly, but I know the shake in my voice and the wet stains on my cheeks gave me away. But I knew he was right. Of course he was right. It was time to let all of that go. It was in the past. My worst fear wasn't true. I could let it go. The only thing that mattered now, the only thing that really was true, was love in all its many shapes and forms.

NO LONGER SELF-ABANDONING FOR LOVE

"Jack," I whisper, summoning my inner Kate Winslet, playing Rose in *Titanic*. Except I'm fat. And we're not on a floating door in the middle of the frigid North Atlantic. "There's a boat, Jack..." I lean over Man Candy, who is half-asleep, dipping my fingers into a cup of water and flicking droplets into his face while the musical swell of "My Heart Will Go On" sweeps dramatically through the bedroom, breaking the silence. "There's a boat, Jack, wake up!" I see an initial wave of "WTF" pass over his body, and then, cloaked in the (now) damp darkness, I see his shoulders shudder with laughter...

"Only you, babe. Only you," he says, covering his face with his hands.

And yet, this is why he loves me. One of the reasons, at least. According to Man Candy, I have a special talent for making things weird. It's entertaining, bizarre, and also charming.

In my relationship with Man Candy I am fully myself. I am not worried about being palatable to some unattainable standard my fear created for me a long time ago. I don't feel like I must dampen myself in order to keep him happy. I've learned it's not my job to keep him happy in his own life; it's my job to be happy in mine and invite him to join me while learning how to be a good partner to him. Because of this, I am able to be things I've always been in my heart but I never felt safe enough to reveal. This is not by accident. This is very deliberate. And it began the minute we started talking, before our first date. I have cultivated my connection to myself since the day we met.

While dating, every chance I had to either do what felt aligned for me or do what I thought I "should" do, I chose to stay aligned with myself. Every time there was a fork in the road—where I could stay aligned or self-abandon in some way—I stayed true to myself. I viewed our dating as an opportunity for me to date myself. Getting to know him and love him has been a vehicle for me to know and love myself. The result has been a partner who understands why I take pleasure in organizing a set of 250 colored pencils by shade, and who shares in my joy when I bake a perfect loaf of challah bread from scratch—who will even roll up his sleeves to braid and plait the dough with me.

The hundred small ways I chose myself early in our relationship paved the way for bigger ways I would continue to choose myself to express my needs and establish boundaries. Whereas in prior dynamics, I felt achingly scared that expressing any disapproval or dissatisfaction would be a reason for a man to push me away, in this relationship I view potential challenges as bridges that can bring us closer if I communicate them properly.

Our relationship is full of sticky conversations, on purpose. Though nothing between us is perfect, I know we both are committed to ourselves and each other—and the rest will play itself out in time. This is the first time I've ever lived with a partner, and it's the first time he's been in a relationship that isn't tumultuously codependent. We aren't trying to save each other. Instead, we are together to experience life as a team, creating conditions that help us both to grow, laugh, and learn alongside the other. And that is a good thing no matter how you look at it.

NOTES

Introduction

1. Sharon Robertson, Matthew Davies, and Helen Winefield, "Why Weight for Happiness? Correlates of BMI and SWB in Australia," *Obesity Research & Clinical Practice* 9, no. 6 (2015): 609–12, https://doi.org/10.1016/j.orcp.2015.04.011.
2. Katie Hanson, "What Exactly Is Hope and How Can You Measure It?" *Positive Psychology*, April 8, 2017, http://positivepsychology.org.uk/hope-theory-snyder-adult-scale/.
3. Catherine W., "'Obese' Is a Bad Word—It's Got to Go," *Fit Is a Feminist Issue* (blog), November 2, 2015, https://fitisafeministissue.com/2015/11/01/obese-is-a-bad-word-its-got-to-go/.

Chapter 3

1. James R. Hagerty, "Entrepreneur Sold High Fashion in Plus Sizes at Forgotten Woman Stores," *Wall Street Journal*, January 7, 2021, https://www.wsj.com/articles/entrepreneur-sold-high-fashion-in-plus-sizes-at-forgotten-woman-stores-11610031600.
2. Kelly Wallace, "The Ripple Effects on Girls When Moms Struggle with Body Image," CNN, June 7, 2017, https://www.cnn.com/2017/06/07/health/body-image-moms-impact-daughters/index.html.
3. Mary Reese Boykin, "Who Influences Teens the Most?" *Los Angeles Times*, September 12, 1998, https://www.latimes.com/archives/la-xpm-1998-sep-12-me-22017-story.html.
4. Simon Kemp, "Reels Grew by 220M Users in Last 3 Months (and Other Jaw-Dropping Stats)," *Hootsuite* (blog), October 26, 2022, https://blog.hootsuite.com/simon-kemp-social-media/#Social_users_have_a_new_2nd_favorite.
5. S. Dixon, "Daily Time Spent on Social Networking by Internet Users Worldwide from 2012 to 2022," Statista, August 22, 2022, https://www.statista.com/statistics/433871/daily-social-media-usage-worldwide/.
6. Statista Research Department, "U.S. Internet Reach by Age Group 2019," Statista, July 26, 2022, https://www.statista.com/statistics/266587/percentage-of-internet-users-by-age-groups-in-the-us/.
7. Pew Research Center, "Social Media Fact Sheet," April 7, 2021, https://www.pewresearch.org/internet/fact-sheet/social-media/.
8. Werner Geyser, "What Is an Influencer?—Factors That Define a Social Media Influencer," Influencer Marketing Hub, March 24, 2023, https://influencermarketinghub.com/what-is-an-influencer/.

9. Statista Research Department, "Instagram Influencers by Age 2019 L Statistic," Statista, June 7, 2021, https://www.statista.com/statistics/893733/share-influencers-creating-sponsored-posts-by-age/.

10. Erin Duffin, "Resident Population of the United States by Sex and Age as of July 1, 2021," Statista, September 30, 2022, https://www.statista.com/statistics/241488/population-of-the-us-by-sex-and-age/.

11. Ani Petrosyan, "US Internet Penetration 2021, by Age Group," Statista February 23, 2023, https://www.statista.com/statistics/266587/percentage-of-internet-users-by-age-groups-in-the-us/.

12. Pew Research Center, social media fact sheet, April 7, 2021, https://www.pewresearch.org/internet/fact-sheet/social-media/.

13. Carolyn Coker Ross, "Why Do Women Hate Their Bodies?" PsychCentral, June 2, 2012, https://psychcentral.com/blog/why-do-women-hate-their-bodies#1.

14. Shaun Dreisbach, "Shocking Body-Image News: 97% of Women Will Be Cruel to Their Bodies Today," *Glamour*, February 3, 2011, https://www.glamour.com/story/shocking-body-image-news-97-percent-of-women-will-be-cruel-to-their-bodies-today.

15. Jes Baker, "Why I've Chosen Body Liberation over Body Love," *The Militant Baker* (blog), December 1, 2020, http://www.themilitantbaker.com/2018/06/why-ive-chosen-body-liberation-over.html.

Chapter 4

1. Catherine Choi, "New Year's Resolution Statistics," *Finder* (blog), December 18, 2019, https://www.finder.com/new-years-resolution-statistics.

2. Jason Henry, "The Curse of the Codependent," *Medium* (blog), March 18, 2019, https://alchemisjah.medium.com/the-curse-of-the-codependent-e9abdededa5b.

3. *APA Dictionary of Psychology*, American Psychological Association, s.v. "enmeshment," https://dictionary.apa.org/enmeshment.

4. Marcel Schwantes, "Studies Show 91 Percent of Us Won't Achieve Our New Year's Resolutions. How to Be the 9 Percent That Do," *Inc.*, January 8, 2022, https://www.inc.com/marcel-schwantes/studies-show-91-percent-of-us-wont-achieve-our-new-years-resolutions-how-to-be-9-percent-that-do.html.

5. Ashley Stahl, "This New Year's Set Goals, Not Resolutions," *Forbes*, https://www.forbes.com/sites/ashleystahl/2021/12/09/this-new-years-set-goals-not-resolutions/?sh=512a0e7d1ece.

6. Statista Research Department, "United States: New Year's Resolution for 2021," Statista, November 15, 2022, https://www.statista.com/statistics/378105/new-years-resolution/.

7. James Clear, *Atomic Habits: An Easy & Proven Way to Build Good Habits & Break Bad Ones* (Avery, 2018).

Chapter 5

1. Special love to my dear friend Robin, who dropped these bomb questions one day; my world has never been the same.

2. Jeremy Sutton, "Maladaptive Coping: 15 Examples & How to Break the Cycle," PositivePsychology.com, October 28, 2020, https://positivepsychology.com/maladaptive -coping/.

3. Sutton, "Maladaptive Coping."

4. "Next Time, What Say We Boil a Consultant," *Fast Company*, October 31, 1995, https://www.fastcompany.com/26455/next-time-what-say-we-boil-consultant.

5. Eliana Tossani, "The Concept of Mental Pain," *Psychotherapy and Psychosomatics* 82, no. 2 (2013): 67–73, https://doi.org/10.1159/000343003.

Chapter 7

1. Chuck Creager Jr., "Inductive Reasoning," March 21, 2010, https://www.youtube .com/watch?v=wzEOwleZNnA&t=6s.

2. Chuck Creager Jr., "Deductive Reasoning," March 31, 2010, https://www.youtube .com/watch?time_continue=43&v=oBnKgxcdSyM&feature=emb_title; Lumen, "Inductive and Deductive Reasoning | English Composition I." Kellogg Community College, n.d., https://www.kellogg.edu/upload/eng151text/chapter/text-inductive-reasoning /index.html.

3. Matt, "What Is Deductive Reasoning? Definition, Examples & How to Use It • Filmmaking Lifestyle," Filmmaking Lifestyle, November 26, 2021, https://filmlifestyle .com/what-is-deductive-reasoning/.

Chapter 8

1. Brianna Johnson, "Are You a Chronic Self-Abandoner?" *NAMI Blog*, April 30, 2018, https://www.nami.org/Blogs/NAMI-Blog/April-2018/Are-You-a-Chronic-Self -Abandoner.

2. Sharon Martin, "Why We Abandon Ourselves and How to Stop," PsychCentral, December 21, 2018, https://psychcentral.com/blog/imperfect/2018/12/why-we-abandon -ourselves-and-how-to-stop.

3. Courtney E. Ackerman, "Self-Fulfilling Prophecy in Psychology: 10 Examples and Definition (+PDF)," PositivePsychology.com, May 2018, https://positivepsychology .com/self-fulfilling-prophecy/.

4. Eva M. Krockow, "How Many Decisions Do We Make Each Day?" *Psychology Today*, September 27, 2018, https://www.psychologytoday.com/us/blog/stretching-theory /201809/how-many-decisions-do-we-make-each-day.

Chapter 10

1. Stephen Wolinsky, *The Way of the Human* (Quantum Institute, 1999).

2. Felicia Giouzelis, "Core Wounds: What They Are and Why It Matters," *Angelic Badass* (blog), April 22, 2019, https://www.feliciamarieg.com/blog/2019/4/22/core-wounds -what-they-are-and-why-it-matters.

3. Molly McElroy, "Children's Self-Esteem Already Established by Age 5, New Study Finds," UW News, November 2, 2015, https://www.washington.edu/news/2015 /11/02/childrens-self-esteem-already-established-by-age-5-new-study-finds/.

4. Sharon Martin, "Why Do We Repeat the Same Dysfunctional Relationship Patterns Over and Over?" PsychCentral, July 13, 2018, https://psychcentral.com /blog/imperfect/2018/07/why-do-we-repeat-the-same-dysfunctional-relationship -patterns#Breaking-old-patterns.

5. Martin, "Why Do We Repeat."

6. American Psychological Association, "Trauma," 2021, https://www.apa.org/topics /trauma.

7. Robby Berman, "New Study Suggests We Have 6,200 Thoughts Every Day," Big Think, July 16, 2020, https://bigthink.com/neuropsych/how-many-thoughts-per-day/.

8. Emma Young, "Lifting the Lid on the Unconscious." *New Scientist*, July 25, 2018, https://www.newscientist.com/article/mg23931880-400-lifting-the-lid-on-the -unconscious/.

9. Olga Blias, "Your Subconscious Mind Creates 95% of Your Life," Thrive Global, June 6, 2021, https://thriveglobal.com/stories/your-subconscious-mind-creates-95-of -your-life; Catherine Collautt, *Success v. Freedom—and How to Get Them Both*, 2012, https://s3.amazonaws.com/marieforleo.com/CatherineCollauttMarieTV.pdf.

10. Collautt, *Success v. Freedom.*

Chapter 11

1. Byron Katie, "Whose Business Are You In?" *The Work of Byron Katie*, September 7, 2006, https://thework.com/2006/09/whose-business-are-you-minding/.

2. Pema Chödrön, *Living Beautifully with Uncertainty and Change* (Shambhala, 2019).

3. Pema Chödrön, *When Things Fall Apart: Heart Advice for Difficult Times* (Shambhala, 2016).

Chapter 12

1. "The Amazing Power of Breathing," Yoga for Modern Life, September 11, 2016, https://www.yogaformodernlife.com/blog/powerofbreathing.

2. *Merriam-Webster*, s.v. "reactive," accessed January 8, 2023, https://www.merriam -webster.com/dictionary/reactive.

3. *Merriam-Webster*, s.v. "proactive," accessed January 8, 2023, https://www.merriam -webster.com/dictionary/proactive.

4. Pema Chödrön, "Turn Your Thinking Upside Down," Lions Roar, September 28, 2021, https://www.lionsroar.com/turn-your-thinking-upside-down/.

Chapter 13

1. Bessel van der Kolk, *The Body Keeps the Score: Brain, Mind, and Body in the Healing of Trauma* (Penguin Books, 2014).

2. Everett L. Worthington Jr., "The New Science of Forgiveness," *Greater Good*, September 1, 2004, https://greatergood.berkeley.edu/article/item/the_new_science_of _forgiveness.

3. Yoichi Chida and Andrew Steptoe, "The Association of Anger and Hostility with Future Coronary Heart Disease," *Journal of the American College of Cardiology* 53, no. 11 (March 2009): 936–46, https://doi.org/10.1016/j.jacc.2008.11.044.

4. Michelle J. Watson, Janet A. Lydecker, Rebecca L. Jobe, Robert D. Enright, Aubrey Gartner, Suzanne E. Mazzeo, and Everett L. Worthington Jr., "Self-Forgiveness in Anorexia Nervosa and Bulimia Nervosa," *Eating Disorders* 20, no. 1 (2012): 31–41, https://doi.org/10.1080/10640266.2012.635561; Neel Burton, "The Psychology of Embarrassment, Shame, and Guilt," *Psychology Today*, August 26, 2014, https://www.psychologytoday.com/us/blog/hide-and-seek/201408/the-psychology-embarrassment-shame-and-guilt.

5. Brené Brown, *Rising Strong: How the Ability to Reset Transforms the Way We Live, Love, Parent, and Lead* (Random House, 2017).

6. Brown, *Rising Strong*.

7. Burton, "Psychology of Embarrassment."

8. van der Kolk, *The Body Keeps the Score*.

9. E. Tory Higgins, *Beyond Pleasure and Pain: How Motivation Works* (Oxford University Press, 2012).

10. Linda M. Hartling, Wendy Rosen, Maureen Walker, and Judith V. Jordan, *Shame and Humiliation: From Isolation to Relational Transformation* (Wellesley College, 2000).

11. Marilyn A. Cornish and Nathaniel G. Wade, "A Therapeutic Model of Self-Forgiveness with Intervention Strategies for Counselors," *Journal of Counseling & Development* 93, no. 1 (2015): 96–104.

12. Kathryn Britton, "Curiosity, an Engine of Well-Being: An Interview with Todd Kashdan, Part I," *Positive Psychology News*, April 15, 2009, https://positivepsychologynews.com/news/kathryn-britton/200904151805.

13. Philip M. Sutton, "The Enright Process Model of Psychological Forgiveness," n.d., https://couragerc.org/wp-content/uploads/2018/02/Enright_Process_Forgiveness_1.pdf.

14. Kristin Neff, Self-Compassion (website), https://self-compassion.org/.

15. Sutton, "Enright Process Model."

Chapter 14

1. Michael Beckwith, *Life Visioning: A Transformative Process for Activating Your Unique Gifts and Highest Potential* (Sounds True, 2013).

2. Oprah Super Soul Sessions with Michael Beckwith, https://www.facebook.com/watch/live/?ref=watch_permalink&v=758972038175.

3. Pema Chödrön, *When Things Fall Apart: Heart Advice for Difficult Times* (Shambhala, 2016).

RESOURCES AND FURTHER READING

Throughout this book I've included a number of Dig Deeper opportunities for you to do your own soul work. Additionally, I've shared a number of sheets, graphs, and charts for you to fill out on your own. You can find all the blank pages referenced in this book on my website in a section of free goodies just for you! **In order to find all the resources listed below, and more, you can visit my website at SarahSapora.com/Soul.**

Suggested Reading, Thought Leaders, and Community Leaders

My journey has been influenced by many great teachers, writers, and thought leaders. The following is a (nonconclusive) list of books that have shaped my growth the last few years. Additionally, I am sharing another (also nonconclusive) selection of books that can help you explore some of the topics addressed in our Dig Deeper on body liberation.

On my website, you can find an organic, evolving resource list that includes social media accounts to follow by topic, as well as community and thought leaders, podcasts, and content creators who can assist in your Soul Archaeology. This list takes care to include thought leaders in marginalized bodies, those that are Black and other persons of color; it is imperative that we acknowledge the role people of color have played in fat liberation and that we acknowledge that fatness is also an issue of racial and social justice.

Personal growth books that have been deeply meaningful to me:
Pema Chödrön—*When Things Fall Apart: Heart Advice for Difficult Times*
Michael Beckwith—*Life Visioning: A Transformative Process for Activating Your Unique Gifts and Highest Potential*

Neil Strauss—*The Truth: An Uncomfortable Book About Relationships*
Geneen Roth—*Women Food and God: An Unexpected Path to Almost Everything*
Esther Perel—*Mating in Captivity: Unlocking Erotic Intelligence*
Gary Zukav—*The Seat of the Soul*

Books about fatness and social justice, fat activism, and body-inclusive fitness:

Sonya Renee Taylor—*The Body Is Not an Apology: The Power of Radical Self-Love*

Sabrina Strings—*Fearing the Black Body: The Racial Origins of Fat Phobia*

Roxane Gay—*Hunger: A Memoir of (My) Body*

Da'Shaun L. Harrison—*Belly of the Beast: The Politics of Anti-Fatness as Anti-Blackness*

Kate Harding and Marianne Kirby—*Lessons from the Fat-O-Sphere: Quit Dieting and Declare a Truce with Your Body*

Aubrey Gordon—*What We Don't Talk About When We Talk About Fat*

Jes Baker—*Things No One Will Tell Fat Girls: A Handbook for Unapologetic Living*

Stephanie Yeboah—*Fattily Ever After: A Black Fat Girl's Guide to Living Life Unapologetically*

Jessamyn Stanley—*Every Body Yoga: Let Go of Fear, Get on the Mat, Love Your Body* and *Yoke: My Yoga of Self-Acceptance*

Laura Burns—*Big & Bold: Yoga for the Plus-Size Woman*

Louise Green—*Big Fit Girl: Embrace the Body You Have*

Dianne Bondy—*Yoga for Everyone: 50 Poses for Every Type of Body*

Note: I do not endorse the work of Lindo Bacon, especially *Health at Every Size: The Surprising Truth About Your Weight.*

**Visit my website at SarahSapora.com/Soul
for resources, downloadable worksheets, and
exclusive bonus extras!**

ACKNOWLEDGMENTS

For my mom, who is everything and my reason. Who never gave herself the love she deserved or saw herself in the bright light that everyone else could so clearly see. This book will help others heal, help me to heal, and, hopefully, help her to heal as well.

For my father, my hero, who understood that other people would heal by hearing about our stuff, and who helped my heart that day at the airport when he said, "It's all in the past. You can let it go now."

This may be the one chance I have to really thank the people who helped me get here. I won't let it slip by.

To the people who have helped me become myself...My Man on the Ground, Kate. And to Mandi for always reminding me what's true when my head is up my ass.

To the people I love who have stood beside me. Carl, for being my best friend and partner, accepting when I burp like a velociraptor, and always making sure there is grilled chicken and fruit in the house. For Robin Cricket, who has always believed in me and, more importantly, *in all of us* reading this book. To Jarrett, for understanding the importance of being my catalyst, and for seeing that we could grow alongside each other together. To Jennifer Quinn, my "Jucies" Mel, and Lex. To Kelsey. And to Arlene and Joe, John and Lexi, and my stepmother, Carol.

To the people who changed the course of my life in deeply profound ways they can't even possibly know. Kjord Davis, who told me I was a teacher before I knew I was one. To Blake Elarbee, who took me seriously and introduced me to my own strength. To John and Cecilia, who brought music back into my life and unconditional love into my heart at a time when I felt I had none to give anyone, not even myself.

To the people who (quite literally) made this book possible. My agent, Stephanie Tade, who rejected me three times before saying, "Yup, this is the book" and then went to work showing publishing why the voice of a fat, middle-aged woman mattered. To Nana K. Twumasi, my editor and publisher, who came back for a second look because she felt, in her heart, that there was something here worth sharing. To Kristen McGuiness, for her guidance.

Last, my deepest thanks to those who have supported and believed in my work even when I did not believe in myself. To Heather and my original community members, who have been around for it all. To those who have sent me the DMs and commented on social media, and to those beautiful humans who felt safe and inspired enough to join me at my live events, and to my Lovers. To those who have given me grace and watched me try new things, fail at some, and grow. To those who found my words hit "too close to home" and had to step away, and then found themselves returning because they needed what I offered. To my community.

You have all helped me to grow into the woman I am today. Thank you. I love you.

INDEX

Page numbers in *italics* refer to illustrations.

ABOUT THE AUTHOR

Sarah Sapora loves cowboy boots, meditation, and straight-talking self-love. As a writer, inspirational speaker, social media community leader, and creator of size-inclusive live events and retreats, Sarah uses her voice to make personal growth accessible to "plus-size women old enough to remember life before the internet." Combining radical vulnerability with tenacity and (sometimes delightfully inappropriate) humor, she is known for creating relatable conversations that have helped hundreds of thousands of women learn to navigate the sticky place between self-acceptance and self-improvement.

Over the course of twenty years working in marketing, Sarah has accumulated lots of experiences that make for great stories—like her time working for Chippendales, or her years in plus-size fashion. She is a certified Kundalini yoga teacher and, as a thought leader in plus-size personal growth, has partnered with brands like Nike and Big Fig Mattress. She has written for or been featured in a variety of publications, including *Time*, *Women's Health*, *Health*, *Mantra Wellness*, and more.

When she's not working, you can find Sarah on a Pilates reformer, seeking out the Montana sky, strength training, or in the kitchen, cooking up a storm. She currently lives in Las Vegas with her boyfriend and her foster-fail American bulldog, Eliza.

You can learn more about Sarah and her work on her website, SarahSapora.com, and find her on Instagram at @SarahSapora and other social media properties.